MULTILINGUAL MATTERS 17

Language Acquisition of a Bilingual Child:
A Sociolinguistic Perspective (To Age Ten)

Alvino E. Fantini

MULTILINGUAL
MATTERS LTD

British Library Cataloguing in Publication Data

Fantini, Alvino E.
    Language acquisition of a bilingual child: a
    sociolinguistic perspective (to age ten). — (Multilingual matters; 17)
    1. Bilingualism   2. Children — Language
    I. Title
    404'.2'088054   P115

    ISBN 0-905028-40-6
    ISBN 0-905028-39-2 Pbk

Multilingual Matters Ltd,
Bank House, 8a Hill Road,
Clevedon, Avon BS21 7HH
England.

Typeset by Wayside Graphics, Clevedon, Avon
Cover designed by Julia Morland
Printed and bound in Great Britain by
Short Run Press Ltd, Exeter EX2 7LW.

A mis dos hijos,
de quienes tanto aprendí;
y a su mamá.

"¿Por qué yo nací como nene, mamá?
¿Por qué no nací como Dios . . . o como el sol,
como una bola de fuego?"

(Mama, why was I born a little boy?
Why was I not born like God . . . or like the sun,
like a ball of fire?)

Mario, Age 5;2

Multilingual Matters

Please contact us for the latest information on recent and forthcoming books in the series.

**Derrick Sharp, General Editor, Multilingual Matters,
Bank House, 8a Hill Road, Clevedon, Avon BS21 7HH, England.**

Language Acquisition of a Bilingual Child

Contents

Preface

Over a quarter of a century ago, Roman Jakobson (1968) advised linguists ". . . concerned with the fully developed structure of language, (that) its acquisition . . . cannot fail to provide much that is instructive." Today his viewpoint is widely shared among students of linguistics and the study of child language has increasingly attracted the attention and support of scholars. Observation of the child in process of development somehow seems to hold the key for understanding all that we are, or are to become. And no matter with what original perspective scholars observe the child — psychological, biological, linguistic, or sociological — one is invariably led to conclude that to understand any single aspect fully, consideration of all aspects is essential to a grasp of the total process of human development.

Dan Slobin (1973) wrote about cognitive prerequisites for language development; Eric Lenneberg (1967) emphasized the biological foundations; others underscored the psychological and linguistic bases. This study seeks to investigate still another dimension, *viz*, sociolinguistic aspects of language acquisition. Since language is rooted in the social context, it both reflects the roles and relationships of its speakers while at the same time it perpetuates them through those new to the system. These social bases are mirrored in speech almost from the onset of language and they are integral to an understanding of language and language use. Few developmental studies to date, however, have focused on sociolinguistic aspects of child language.

Observing child development is a fascinating endeavour. However, like the anthropologist, Castaneda, I have learned that the effective researcher is first and foremost an apprentice; my "Don Juan" in this case being a young child. And just as Castaneda continually strived to learn how best to set about to understand the world of the old Yaqui Indian, I too have recognized that the approach to the study of the child proceeds with patience and without pretension if one is to learn to "see" the world as the child "sees". Only in this way may it be possible to enter another speaker's world view, to grasp its coherence and to understand how all aspects form part of a systematic whole at every stage of development. It is my hope that this work will stimulate others to investigate language and language use in evolution by becoming apprentices to the child linguist-ethnographer.

The present study was begun 15 years ago and it will probably continue for many more years to come as it is my hope that this will become a truly longitudinal investigation. It is a developmental study of dual language acquisition by a single individual. And although the specifics of a single case study can never be directly generalized to other populations, what may be extrapolated is the interplay of variables which form the process of language development which we are attempting to understand more fully.

A report of the period from the child's birth to age five was presented originally in 1974 as a doctoral dissertation undertaken at the University of Texas. That work was subsequently translated to Spanish in 1975 and entered into an International Linguistic Competition sponsored by the Academia Mexicana de la Lengua in Mexico City where it was awarded second prize and honorable mention. In 1976, the English version was printed by The Experiment Press, Brattleboro, Vermont under its original title; and in 1982, the Spanish version was printed by Editorial Herder, Barcelona, Spain, under the title *La adquisición del lenguaje en un niño bilingüe*. Various aspects of the research have been updated and revised, appearing in a variety of professional journals. The present edition attempts to update the entire study by incorporating data from the second five year period, permitting a lengthier examination of the child's language development from his birth to his tenth birthday.

As with any work, the writer is indebted to numerous persons for their support and assistance. First of all, the various members of the Dissertation Committee who provided significant encouragement and suggestions are to be cited: Dr Joseph Michel, Dean of the College of Multidisciplinary Studies, University of Texas, San Antonio, who served as Chairman of the Committee. Other members at the University of Texas, Austin, deserving special mention were Dr Theodore Andersson, Professor of Spanish and Portuguese, and of Education; Dr David Hakes, Associate Professor of Psychology; and Dr Ben G. Blount and Dr Joel Sherzer, Assistant Professors of Anthropology. Their participation greatly enhanced the content and scope of the study by providing the writer with the benefits of their experiences and knowledge in a number of related disciplines: Language Education, Bilingual Education, Psycholinguistics, Cognitive Anthropology, and Socio-linguistics.

To various other persons who contributed assistance, the writer is also indebted: Dr John A. Wallace, former Director of the School for International Training of The Experiment in International Living, Brattleboro, Vermont, for his continued and unqualifed support; to the staff of the Southwest Educational Development Laboratory, Austin, Texas, and in particular to Dr Murray A. Newman, Coordinator of the Thinking and Reasoning Program, for his help in providing test instruments and in interpreting results; to Nell Cary Sather, Learning Disabilities Coordinator, Windham Southeast Supervisory Union, Brattleboro, Vermont, for her assistance in obtaining test data; to Mary Carnahan, Kindergarten Teacher, Dummerston School, West Dummerston, Vermont, for her time and comments in assessing the child; to Elizabeth Thompson, Kindergarten teacher, Ridetop Elementary School, Austin, Texas, for permission to observe classes and for reports on the child's language progress; and to Brenda Willis, Elementary School Teacher, Allison School, Austin, Texas, for her special interest in the child and her aid in administering English Proficiency Tests. My gratitude is extended in addition to all the teachers at both the West and East Dummerston Schools who so kindly shared observations of the child's language performance throughout his nine years in attendance at these institutions. Special appreciation is also conveyed to the National Endowment for the Humanities for financial support in the form of a stipend to attend a Summer Seminar for College Teachers on Bilingualism during the summer of 1977, guided by Dr Bernard Spolsky at the University of New Mexico, Albuquerque. This experience was extremely helpful in continuing and furthering the work begun in the original dissertation. To Alex Silverman, Director of the Master of Arts in Teaching Program at the School for International Training, I am grateful for his support through professional leave time to prepare this manuscript. And to Karin Wishner and Naomi Till Santos, both graduate students at this same institution, who lent their excellent typing skills and linguistic talents in the transcription of the diary data and the production of the final manuscript.

Finally, the writer is especially indebted to his wife, Beatriz Céspedes de Fantini, who provided him with the subject of this investigation, assisted him in all phases of its undertaking, and helped to bring this study to print in both its original form, its translated version, and now in this substantially expanded presentation. Gracias.

A.E.F.

1 Introduction

General comments

Child language acquisition has fascinated people for thousands of years. Sporadic accounts appear from the time of the Greeks and Egyptians throughout history. One of the earliest accounts was reported by Aristotle (see Richter, 1927); another was a psycholinguistic experiment reported by Herodotus, dating back to about 600 BC (see Dale, 1972, the same story is also briefly recounted by Ferguson & Slobin, 1973). Circa AD 400, St Augustine wrote about the process of native language acquisition by resorting to introspection and the memory of his own experience (see Slobin, 1971a). Centuries later, King James VI of Scotland ordered two babies to be put in the care of a deaf and dumb nursemaid as part of a linguistic experiment to determine the original language of humankind (see Deese, 1970).

Other accounts of the process of language acquisition were engendered by people's fascination with the bizarre and unusual. Stories of feral and wolf-children were reported as far back as pre-Roman days in the tales of Romulus and Remus. Other cases were those of the Hessian wolf-boy in 1349; the Lithuanian bear-boy in 1661; Wild Peter of Hanover in 1724 (see Brown, 1958); and Victor the Wild Boy from Aveyron in 1797 (see Lane, 1976). Even in the twentieth century such stories have been reported with the discoveries of Kamala and Amala in India in 1920, and two cases in the United States in the late thirties (see Singh & Zingg, 1966). One of the most startling cases and probably the best documented is that of Genie, already a young adolescent when discovered in 1970 in the United States. Genie had been deprived and isolated to an unprecedented degree and her case was carefully documented by psycholinguists (Curtiss, 1977). From these accounts it becomes clear that children acquire language only when born

1

into a linguistic community. Without language contact, there is little likeli-
hood that a child will ever be capable of developing language entirely alone.

Aside from these bizarre accounts, reports of child language were
usually incidental to the main purpose of studies done by educators, physi-
cians, and psychologists. Although more systematic language studies
appeared toward the end of the nineteenth century, it was not until the
beginning of the present century when Clara and William Stern (1929), both
psychologists, devoted their entire attention to the problem. Others followed their example, and in the past three decades, this newfound interest in
child language has culminated in vast and extensive studies, providing the
basis for a new understanding of language and language acquisition.

Linguists who studied the problem, however, concerned themselves
primarily and almost exclusively with linguistic data. Their goal was to set
down a linguistic description of the process, and depending upon their
specific linguistic interests they wrote about phonology, morphology and
syntax, more rarely about lexical and semantic aspects. Concurrently with
this newfound interest on the part of linguists, psychologists contributed
their approaches and methods to those already in use by linguists. Yet
something was still missing. If language emerges only when the human
infant is reared in a social context — that is, in a community with other
human beings — then the child's social environment must be considered
relevant in an account of linguistic development. The notion of a social *and*
linguistic description was finally advanced by Hymes, one of its most
prominent advocates. He termed this an "ethnography of speaking".
According to Hymes (1974: 341) ". . . with this change the process that
began with phonology and morphology will have come full circle — linguistic description will find its own development to require . . . considerations
from which at first it sought to be free."

A sociolinguistic approach to language was both timely and necessary,
especially since generative-transformational theory helped make such tremendous strides in the field of linguistics. Generative grammarians emphasized the distinction between language "competence" and language "performance" (i.e. between the knowledge of the abstract rules of language and
the social use of the medium). They chose to study competence ignoring
performative aspects almost entirely. However, the recent awareness that to
understand language fully, linguistics cannot ignore the "speech act" itself
(which involves the use of language in its social context) has encouraged a
field of sociolinguistics. Some generative grammarians have now begun to
take social aspects into account in writing their grammars, as increasing
sociolinguistic data become available. This trend has demanded a shift of

approach from one which studied language and society separately (a co-occurrence approach) to one which studies the interaction between language and its social and situational contexts (a co-variation approach).[1] The assumption is that much more can be learned about languages in this way than if language and society are treated independently. Hymes (1974: 342) sums up this development when he states:

> "Saussure is concerned with the word, Chomsky with the sentence, the ethnography of speaking with the act of speech. . . .
>
> The goal of the ethnography of speaking can be said to be to complete the discovery of the sphere of 'rule-governed creativity' with respect to language, and to characterize the abilities of persons in this regard. . . . In extending the scope of linguistic rules beyond sentences to speech acts, and in seeking to relate language meaningfully to situations, this approach, although compatible with Chomsky's goals, does critically recast certain of his concepts."

A team of scholars subsequently echoed this call for ethnographies of speaking when they prepared a manual for researchers, entitled *A Field Manual for Cross-Cultural Study of the Acquisition of Communicative Competence*, published in 1967. The writers list three aspects of child language in which data are most needed:

> "(1) We need information about the learning of languages which are structurally different from English . . . (in order to find) certain universals in terms of stages of development in children.
>
> (2) . . . language acquisition studies (should) be broadened to include not only the traditional formal core of language, but competence in the *use* of language. Not only do children learn the phonology, grammar and vocabulary which permit us to identify a language, but they learn when to speak, when to be quiet, when to use ritual language, when to use baby talk, when to use polite forms, and when to shift language in a multilingual community. We know nothing about the relation between these aspects of learning and the learning of the basic code. . . .
>
> (3) There has been considerable controversy over the role of the social milieu in language development. . . . The controversy turns on the degree to which a strong maturational component in language development may make linguistic competence relatively impervious to acceleration through changes in the milieu. The linguistic repertoire of the community clearly must influence

the content of the child's learning, but it is not clear whether the order of acquisition of grammatical or sociolinguistic rules might be altered either by their place in the adult system or by specific values and practices of the child's caretakers." (Slobin, 1967).

In all three areas, the direction is clearly toward the sociolinguistic and cross-cultural. This manual plus *Leopold's Bibliography of Child Language* (Slobin, 1972) also point to a need for research in languages other than English. In Spanish, (one of the languages examined in the present work), for example, the bibliography records only seven studies, four of which were listed as on-going research as of the date of printing, in March 1972. The *Field Manual* lists only one study of Spanish acquisition (Slobin, 1967: 127–28). A third work printed in Spain in 1972 compiles earlier studies by Samuel Gili Gaya, under the title *Estudios de lenguaje infantil*. And whereas Abrahamsen refers in the Preface to her 1977 book, *Child Language: An Interdisciplinary Guide to Theory and Research*, to an information explosion, stating that ". . . child language literature is spreading exponentially through hundreds of journals and dozens of publishers' book lists . . .", her extensive bibliographic work cites only three works which include Spanish as part of their content. One has to search primarily in the professional journals and anthologies to find articles about Spanish acquisition. Yet for the most part these are limited in scope, reporting on particularist features of development, or on children observed over relatively limited periods of time.

All in all, one is amazed by the paucity of works on the acquisition of Spanish, which is one of the major tongues of the world. Longitudinal studies are even rarer. English remains the language most commonly researched. However, as the phenomenon of bilingualism increasingly attracts attention — in the United States and worldwide — more scholars have devoted research efforts to examine and understand bilingual behaviour. And since Spanish is the language of the largest minority population in the United States, it, too, is receiving increasing attention through the examination of Spanish–English bilingual children. This is especially true in areas of the country where there are large numbers of bilingual or Spanish dominant schoolchildren for whom educational programmes are being designed, enlisting the attention and imagination of educators. A serious lack, however, has been a clear theoretical model of how children — both monolingual and bilingual, in English and Spanish — acquire their ability to communicate. Longitudinal studies can provide additional insights to those gleaned from particularist studies to serve as a basis on which to formulate sound educational programmes to foster — rather than hinder — the natural abilities of young children.

The present work has its roots in the developments and trends sketched above. As its title implies, this study is concerned not only with language acquisition, but also with incipient and continuing bilingualism, the development of English and Spanish, and the social milieu in which this unfolds — as witnessed through the experiences of one small child — Alvino Mario.

The study and its objectives

The present report is a general, descriptive case study of the dual language acquisition of one bilingual child. It is concerned primarily with developmental sociolinguistic aspects of the learning process, leaving detailed linguistic analyses to future study. The report is based on the lengthy observation of the author's son, from birth to present, a period covering more than fifteen years, although analysis is completed only till his tenth birthday. It is not a typically contrived and controlled experiment, but rather it grows out of the accumulation of data collected through participation in the daily life of the child. Analysis of these data served as the basis for this report.

The principal objectives inherent in the current treatment of the data were the following:

1. To contribute additional information to current knowledge concerning child language acquisition;
2. To examine how the process of acquiring two languages differs from or resembles the process of learning only one;
3. To provide specific information concerning the acquisition of Spanish, given the paucity of materials in this area and the absence of longitudinal case studies on children learning Spanish;
4. To determine how and when a child begins to differentiate languages so that he eventually realizes that he is, in fact, learning two different communication systems;
5. To ascertain what are some of the social factors which contribute to the child's growing awareness that he is bilingual;
6. To uncover some of the ways in which the socialization process affects language acquisition;
7. To determine what are some of the relevant social factors which affect the child's switching from one code to another;
8. To examine possible interference or transference across languages and any discernable causes;
9. To see to what extent the young child alters his speech, or adopts alternate styles in accordance with factors present in the social context;

10. To gain some measure of the child's relative proficiency in each of his two languages.

Some of these objectives address themselves to the desiderata expressed in the *Field Manual*. Others reflect many of the issues discussed by scholars at an international seminar at the University of Moncton in 1967, which dealt with the description and measurement of bilingualism.[2] Hopefully, the observation, description, and measurement of the bilingualism of one child will contribute to an understanding of the issues which were raised.

The following chapters deal first with the child — who he is, and who the people are with whom he has had the greatest interaction. Chapter 3 also examines the environments to which Mario has been exposed and the degree and frequency of contact with each language. Chapter 4, on sociolinguistic aspects of the acquisition process, represents the main body of this report, addressing itself to statements contained in the list of objectives. Chapter 5 provides a linguistic profile of the child, highlighting areas of linguistic interference and transference, and assessing his proficiency in Spanish and English. Since it is impossible to include the voluminous speech diary of the child, excerpts were selected for inclusion in the appendix (see Appendix 2). These were chosen as samples of Mario's speech at different stages of linguistic and sociolinguistic development during the ten year period under consideration. In some cases, they were also selected for their content, reflecting the child's thoughts as he learned increasingly about the world around him.

Method

Material for this study was collected from the child with considerable regularity from the child's birth until age 6, and thereafter less regularly, and mostly when significant developments occurred. The data were obtained essentially in two ways: through direct observation of the child and from occasional taped recordings of his speech. During the first year, greater reliance was placed on recorded sessions, and written notes were few. Through these earlier tapes, made at a minimum of one each month, one can trace various stages of Mario's pre-speech period until the articulation of his first speech sounds.

Once the child began to utter words, written notations based on observations were increasingly made in the diary. This began just after the child's first birthday. From that time on, attention was devoted primarily to vocabulary growth and phonological development during the single word phase which lasted until approximately 1;10. These words were compiled into a list which reflects the development of lexical items and their phonological evolution. The list also shows the chronological order of the appearance of words, the age at which specific words were first uttered, the types of words used (i.e. in accordance to their part of speech), and the dimensions of the child's lexicon.

When Mario began to join words to form longer utterances, notetaking became necessary on a daily basis. However, recording sessions were still held at least once each month. The material was randomly collected, on the one hand, since no specific type of data was sought, nor was a specific linguistic feature being studied. However, novel expressions or constructions were quite conspicuous when they appeared because of the investigator's familiarity with the child's speech. For example, the child's first use of the pronoun "yo" (I), or his first use of the past tense or a relative clause, were immediately noticeable when they made their debut.

The purpose of these efforts was to produce a sizeable corpus of data as the basis for later analysis. And although Hymes (1974: 345) warns that ". . . most linguists today scorn quantitative data . . ." he hastens to add that ". . . Labov has . . . shown that systematic study of quantitative variation discloses new kind of structure . . ."[3] (and knowledge of language we might add), thereby dramatizing the value of the collection of quantitative materials.

Throughout the collection, the writer's attention naturally focused on the prominent aspect of development at each stage. After the pre-speech period, phonology and the development of words were obviously the main concern. By 2;3 the child began to form two and three-word utterances and attention shifted to developing syntax. From 2;6 on, morphological detail began to form part of the child's speech patterns. And from 3;0 on, the reporter's interest focused increasingly on contextual aspects of the child's speech. Whole sequences of speech were transcribed, including notes concerning the setting, the participants, and interaction among the speakers — providing the basis for discourse analysis wherever desirable. Notes were made on both verbal and non-verbal aspects of communication, to whom the message was directed, other persons present, and the language used. It is this information — not simply the linguistic notations — which permits examinations into infant bilingualism, language differentiation, switching, interference and transference, and the effects of social factors on the child's developing styles and language use. Finally, occasional comments were also made in reference to the child's physical, mental, and cognitive progress. Notations appear concerning his curiosity in graphic stimuli (especially letters and numbers), colour recognition, and slowly emerging reading ability. All of these data form the basis of Mario's developmental language diary.

Data were collected by the author with some assistance from his wife. When there was doubt concerning a speech item, it was often checked with the author's wife for accuracy. The material collected to date has filled numerous note books, reel to reel as well as cassette tapes, and also some video-taped materials.

Early diary notations were made in phonetic transcription (refer to Appendix 1 for the symbols used). As the child's pronunciation approached adult language, entries were more commonly made in standard orthorgraphy. This is especially true for Spanish in which the standard spelling is close to the phonetic form. Appendix 2 has several excerpts modelled on the format of the *Field Manual*. Through the diary one can trace Mario's development primarily in Spanish and English, and to a lesser degree in Italian (to which he was also exposed).

The diary contains two gaps during brief periods of separation from the child during his earlier years. The first was from age 2;5 to 2;7, although some information was provided during this time by the child's mother as well as through occasional telephone "conversations" with the child. The second separation lasted six weeks and occurred when Mario was 5;4. Some anecdotal information was provided by his maternal grandparents whom he visited during that time. However, their information was primarily on behavioural and social aspects, rather than linguistic in nature.

The methodological strategies employed in this work may be summed up in this way:[4]

1. By and large, the diary reflects natural speech recorded in natural settings;
2. On a few occasions, it also contains natural speech recorded in contrived settings (these are so labelled);
3. In a few instances, there are notes of speech which was elicited specifically for the purpose of learning more about particular speech items (also labelled);
4. This investigation studies only one child through a period of time as opposed to the examination of one or several children at a specific stage of development;
5. It attempts to trace general language development rather than the emergence of particular items (e.g. the development of the negative or passive transformations); however, particular items may be sifted

out of the general data at any moment and their evolution examined;[5]

6. It examines the production and *use* of speech (rather than simply the production of linguistic elements).

Once methodological procedures were considered and implemented, and the diary produced, analysis of the corpus was the next concern. Although the corpus may serve as a source for many kinds of information, for the purpose of this study it was scrutinized primarily for details which illuminate the developing social use of the child's languages. Linguistic analysis in this examination is treated only as it serves to understand sociolinguistic developments.

Notes to Chapter 1

1. This approach has been advanced by researchers such as Susan Ervin-Tripp, Roger Brown, William Labov, John Gumperz, William Bright, Dell Hymes, Joshua Fishman, Joel Sherzer and Ben Blount, among others.
2. Consult seminar reports published in the text by Kelly, 1969.
3. It should be noted that several of William A. Labov's works are based on a quantitative approach to speech analysis; the best known is perhaps Labov, 1966.
4. See McNeill (1970: 6–14) for further discussion of methodological strategies.
5. Exemplified in works such as: Bloom, 1970, Chomsky, 1969; Anglin, 1970. These constitute only a few of numerous works which examine specific aspects of language acquisition or selected linguistic items.

2 Aspects of the problem

Related studies on developmental bilingualism

Werner Leopold (1939–1949) noted that although numerous studies have been done on the subject of child language acquisition, few, indeed, dealt with the learning of two languages simultaneously by small children. Others have also deplored the paucity of records dealing with child bilingualism, and called specifically for investigation in this area (see Leopold 1971: 12–13). Vildomec's book on *Multilingualism* (1963), cited only three important works on pre-school children who acquired two languages simultaneously from the beginning of their speech (pp. 25–28) — those by Ronjat (1913), Pavlovitch (1920), and Leopold (1939–1949). Slobin's *Field Manual* (1967), listed seven reports of bilingual children, of which only three were general longitudinal case studies — the same three referred to by Vildomec. And although approximately 50 studies were mentioned in Slobin's updated publication of *Leopold's Bibliography of Child Language* (1972), closer inspection reveals that the same three works stood out as the only full case reports; the others, by and large, were particularist descriptions of specific aspects, or reports of acquisition at a specific stage of development (pp. 168–69).

The first of the three general descriptions — that by Ronjat (1913) — dealt with a case of complete bilingualism up to age 4;10. Ronjat's method was basically — "one person–one language", or, as later characterized by Penfield & Roberts, 1959: 253–54), as "one environment–one language". Ronjat's son, Louis, learned German from his mother and French from his father while they lived in France. His pronunciation from the beginning was that of a unilingual child in each of his two languages. His borrowings from one language remained isolated, and according to Ronjat, there was parallel development of phonetics, morphology, and syntax in both languages. The

10

child soon became aware of his bilingualism and translated messages from one language into the other; he also acquired the abstract idea of language. Later, the use of each of his languages became specialized but he continued to be able to use both languages with equal facility in ordinary conversation.

Pavlovitch (1920) likewise recorded the simultaneous speech development of his son, Douchan, in both Serbian and French. However, since his records only went up to the child's second year, they were considerably less useful in discerning much about the child's awareness of his bilingualism or the possible specialization of language use.

Geissler, who lived among Germans in Yugoslavia, also reported on infant bilingualism. Geissler published his study on the bilingual development of German children in Belgrade in 1938 (see Leopold, 1971: 12). His is the only book aside from Ronjat's work which treated the linguistic development of children from the point of view of bilingualism. However, Geissler was not a linguist and his work was criticized by Leopold (1971: 12) for poor recording and too many vague generalizations.

Among these early studies, Leopold's work, *Speech Development of A Bilingual Child*, published in four volumes between 1939 and 1949, remains today one of the classic studies in this area. It was definitely the most thorough study of the speech of an individual bilingual child, and probably of any child. Leopold recorded his first daughter's speech from her birth to age 15;7 with emphasis on the first two years. The child, Hildegard, learned German and English; however, her ability with both languages was not nearly as complete as that of Ronjat's son. Her German remained considerably less developed than her English. Furthermore, although her bilingualism was important in her first two years mainly in vocabulary, there were only a few traces of the influence of bilingualism later. Soon after her second birthday, she started to distinguish two separate systems which she used in accordance to her interlocutor. Leopold notes that there was some influence of one language on the other in lexicon, idiomatic phrases, and syntax; less in sounds, morphology, and word formation.

A review of the literature on early developmental bilingualism, completed by Redlinger in 1979, revealed a new trend in bilingual studies. Redlinger reviewed a total of 51 publications on the topic, classifying these into four categories: (1) descriptive studies of infant bilingualism which concentrate on the early stages of acquiring two or more languages; (2) works on child bilingualism which investigate various aspects of bilingualism in its later developmental stages during the preschool years; (3) works which focus on the sociolinguistic factors influencing bilingual acquisition and development; and (4) works which discuss the preschool biliteracy movement aimed at fostering balanced bilingualism in a monolingual society (see Redlinger, 1979: 11).

Among the first two categories on infant bilingualism and later bilingualism still in the preschool years (covering the period from birth to five), Redlinger cited 38 publications (including the early studies already cited above). Of those in the first category, few covered more than 2–3 years with the notable exception of Leopold's work. The same is true of those dealing with child bilingualism. The most relevant studies to the present work, aside from those already cited, are those addressing Spanish–English bilingualism. These include: (1) a descriptive analysis of the language of a bilingual Spanish–English child done by Mazeika (1971, 1973) in which he reports the results of analysis of taped materials collected during a period of four months beginning when the child was 26 months of age (Redlinger, 1979: 14); (2) a report describing the speech development of three Spanish–English bilingual children in California done by Padilla & Liebman (1975) based on data collected from children ranging in ages from 1;5 to 2;2, observed over periods ranging from three to six months (p. 16); (3) a study by Bergman (1976) reporting on her daughter's simultaneous acquisition of Spanish and English over a period of about three years; (4) an investigation by Padilla & Lindholm (1976a and b), who worked with 19 bilingual Mexican–American children aged two to six (p. 18); (5) a report by Carrow (1971) on a developmental study of English and Spanish comprehension by 99 preschool Mexican–American children in Houston, Texas, aged three to six (p. 19); (6) research by Keller (1976) investigating the acquisition of active and passive voice among 70 Spanish–English bilingual children between the ages of three and six; and (7) a work by Cornejo (1973) which studied the language development of bilingual Mexican–American children in Texas by analysing the speech of 24 five-year-olds (p. 20).

Whereas all of these works comment on bilingual aspects of children's acquisition, most fail to explore the interrelationships of speech and the children's environments. The *use* of language — especially by bilingual children — remained a relatively unexplored area. In her report, Redlinger (1979: 22–24) listed only 7 works which discuss bilingual acquisition from a sociolinguistic perspective, beginning in 1974 with works by the present writer and another by Eddie Chen-Yu Kuo who investigated the bilingual socialization of 47 Chinese preschool children in the Minnesota Twin Cities area (p. 22). Other researchers interested in a sociolinguistic perspective investigated basic language strategies of a bilingual family (Schmidt-Mackey, 1977); bilingual socialization in a Mexican–American community of Tucson, Arizona (Redlinger, 1979); the nature of parental speech to

children and various dimensions of language interaction in Spanish-speaking
and English-speaking families in Austin, Texas (Blount, 1977); the onto-
geny of bilingual child language among Mexican-Americans in the El
Paso–Ciudad Juárez–Las Cruces triangle area, considering language
varieties and strategies (Ornstein, Valdés-Fallis & Dubois, 1976); and factors affecting child language acquisition in plurilingual environments
(Khubchandani, 1976). A recent study by the Australian author, George
Saunders (1983), reports on the bilingual development in German and
English of his two sons over an eight year period. Although not presented
primarily as a longitudinal study, but as an examination of factors affecting
the establishment of bilingualism in a family, Saunders takes on a particularly sociolinguistic view of the phenomenon which makes his work of
special interest to researchers in this area. This work, then, seeks to provide
an extensive investigation into the developmental sociolinguistics of bilingualism by spanning a period of ten years.

On the nature of bilingualism

In reviewing the case studies dealing with infant bilingualism, it becomes
patently clear that the type and degree of bilingualism referred to is not
always the same. Since Pavlovitch's work only went as far as the child's
second year, there could not have been substantial speech in either language. Even Leopold's daughter who was initially bilingual became increasingly monolingual as her German fell into disuse. Only Ronjat's study
spoke of complete bilingualism during the period observed. Yet all of the
children in these studies were termed "bilingual" (not equilingual or ambilingual)[1] by their reporters, even though their abilities were not at all the
same. The problem was that "bilingual" was imprecisely defined. How to
define bilingualism is, in fact, such an elusive thing that a seminar held in
Canada in 1967 was dedicated entirely to the description and measurement
of bilingualism (see Kelly, 1969). In his introductory comments, Mackey
pointed out that bilingualism has been described and measured in essentially
three ways, by category, dichotomy, and scale. But in spite of the many
attempts to describe bilingualism, Andersson & Boyer (1970: 12) concluded
that

> ". . . the only agreement among its various users is that it refers
> to the knowledge and use of two languages by the same person.
> Some writers emphasize the use of the languages, e.g.,
> Weinreich . . . who defined bilingualism as 'the practice of alter-
> nately using two languages' . . . Since it is quite possible to be
> bilingual without using one of the two languages one knows,

others have emphasized the knowledge or competence of the speakers, e.g., Haugen, . . . who defined a bilingual as 'one who knows two languages,' . . . Another difference in the use of the term is that some scholars extend it to include the mastery of more than two languages . . . which is more precisely referred to as multilingualism. . . .

"Within this framework, however, the major problem is that bilinguals differ widely both in their knowledge and in their use of the two languages they master. . . .

"The usual definition has been a rather narrow one, summed up in Bloomfield's use of the term 'native-like control'. A German writer, Maximilian Braun, demanded 'active, completely equal mastery of two or more languages'. Such bilinguals are rare, if they exist at all, and most students prefer a wider definition."

From this summary we can see that the definition of bilingualism ranges all the way from the extreme of "equal mastery" to the opposite pole in which individuals have at least some knowledge (even if only receptive) in at least one skill (even if only reading) in a second language. Baetens-Beardsmore (1982: 36) reinforces this concept when he contrasts the ". . . minimalist standpoint which defines the onset of bilinguals, different degrees and types of bilingual ability . . . (and) the maximalist position . . . whereby bilingualism is equated with equal native-like mastery of two or more languages." The concept of bilingualism, therefore, is a relative one; it constitutes a continuum rather than an absolute phenomenon and persons may have varying degrees of skills or abilities in the two or more languages involved.

Since bilingualism is a relative concept, we are naturally forced to face the question of degree; that is, how well does the individual know the languages in question? To determine this, of course, involves tests and measurements which also formed part of the Canadian seminar on bilingualism (see Kelly, 1969). Measuring relative proficiency requires separate measurement of each of the languages used by the bilingual person. This is no easier than measuring the proficiency of the language used by a monolingual speaker. And those involved in the field of foreign language teaching are well acquainted with the difficulties of measuring *oral* language proficiency . . . another relative concept.

Besides the imprecision of definition and the difficulty of measuring bilingualism, most scholars have studied it primarily from their own bias — within a linguistic, sociological, or psychological framework. Linguistics, for example, has examined linguistic interference; sociology has looked at languages in contact and their effects upon each other; psychology has been concerned with such things as the relationship between bilingualism and intelligence, etc. Yet all of these are interrelated. For example, it is commonly recognized that the age and manner of acquisition as well as the environment or environments in which the individual becomes bilingual have definite psychological and linguistic consequences. Hence, the acknowledgement of the social milieu on the type of bilingual produced.

According to Fishman (1966: 128), two major types of bilingual speakers are generally identified by linguists and psycholinguists:

> "One type of bilingual thinks only in one of his two languages, usually in that which is his mother tongue . . . based upon a neurological organization fused so that one language depends substantially on the same neurological component as the other. . . ."

This type is the compound bilingual. The other type is:

> ". . . the individual (who) keeps each of his languages quite separate. He thinks in X when producing messages (to himself or to others) in X, and in Y when producing messages in Y."

This type is the co-ordinate bilingual. Fishman, goes even further in describing the bilingual speaker, and says:

> "Not only does the bilingual master two different codes, but he masters two different selves, two different modes of relating to reality, two different orders of sensitivity to the wonders of the world." (pp. 130–31)

Implicit in these types is the impact of social conditions (how, when, and where the languages are acquired) upon the psychological and neurological organization of the speaker as well as his resultant ability with the languages concerned. The degree of switching and interference inherent in his speech is apparently related to all of these factors as well as to the context of the speech event.

Mackey (1970: 554) indeed places the emphasis on the social domain as the starting point of the phenomenon:

> "*Bilingualism* is not a phenomenon of language; it is a characteristic of its use. It is not a feature of the code but of the message. It does not belong to the domain of 'langue' but of 'parole'.
>
> "If language is the property of the group, bilingualism is the property of the individual. An individual's use of two languages

supposes the existence of two different language communities; it does not suppose the existence of a bilingual community."

Several years before, scholars attending an International Seminar on Bilingualism held in Wales (1960), had already recognized the need to include various components in a full bilingual description — type, degree, function, alternation, and interaction (interference) (see Andersson & Boyer, 1970: 10):

1. *Number* — the number of languages used by the individual;
2. *Type* — the linguistic relationship between the languages;
3. *Function* — the conditions of learning and use of the two languages;
4. *Degree* — the proficiency in each language;
5. *Alternation* — switching from one language to another;
6. *Interaction* — the way in which the languages affect each other linguistically.

Mackey (1970: 583) echoes the need for inclusion of these items in a theoretical framework for the description of bilingualism. In this way he hopes to avoid the narrower definitions of the past, and points the way for a new direction:

> "Bilingualism cannot be described within the science of linguistics; we must go beyond. Linguistics has been interested in bilingualism only in so far as it could be used as an explanation for changes in a language, since language, not the individual, is the proper concern of this science. Psychology has regarded bilingualism as an influence on mental processes. Sociology has treated bilingualism as an element in culture conflict. Pedagogy has been concerned with bilingualism in connection with school organization and media of instruction. For each of these disciplines bilingualism is incidental, it is treated as a special case or as an exception to the norm. Each discipline, pursuing its own particular interests in its own special way. . . . But it seems to add little to our understanding of bilingualism as such, with its complex psychological, linguistic, and social interrelationships.
>
> "What is needed, to begin with, is a perspective in which these interrelationships may be considered."

Considering the need to understand bilingualism from many approaches, and recognizing that it is an individual rather than a group phenomenon, Mackey calls for ". . . description(s) of a variety of cases of individual bilingualism." This report is one such case, for no matter what definition is applied to the subject of this study, Mario is clearly operationally bilingual in Spanish and English, as well as receptively bilingual in Italian.

Language and the social context

Since the present work deals with child language and bilingual acquisition from a *sociolinguistic* perspective, we shall now review some general background work which has been produced thus far concerning language and the social context.

Hymes (1974: 354) commented on the relevance and importance of contextual information to linguistic studies:

"Discovery of structure in linguistics has proceeded mostly as if the function of language is reference alone. The common account of language as mediating merely between (vocal) sound and meaning manifests this assumption. It pictures language as structure between the two continua of possible meanings and possible sounds. The image of man implied is of an abstract, isolated individual, related only to a world of objects to be named and described. Ethnography of speaking proceeds on the hypothesis that an equally primary function of speech is 'address'. Speech . . . mediates between persons and their situations. . . . One must begin from speech as a mode of action, not from language as an unmotivated mechanism."

Language is never used in a social vacuum, and only a sociolinguistic approach brings out the extra-linguistic influences on the acquisition of language and verbal behaviour. Yet heretofore it is primarily the linguistic system which has been described, ignoring the social context in which it is used. There is no sociolinguistic theory yet so explicit as the present theory of language. Linguists have studied the sentence, but what is needed, according to Hymes, is

". . . the extension of analysis beyond the sentence to sequences in discourse; beyond the single language to 'choices' among forms of speech; and beyond the referential function to functions that may be loosely grouped together as stylistic. Each of these can be seen as involving kinds of knowledge and ability (i.e., competence) on the part of members of a community." (p. 347)

Hence, both language and language use are structured and every utterance has both social and referential meaning. Furthermore, there is a direct relationship between linguistic and social facts. A sociolinguistic approach attempts to delineate both the social structure and linguistic structure inherent in the utterance, and to correlate the two. This is possible because linguistic choices are available to each speaker, and the choices he makes reflect the social factors present at the time of speech. Hence, linguistic alternates always convey social information, fairly well known to all members of a speech community. This encoded social information reflected in speech is not done randomly but in accordance with prescribed norms. Also as Gumperz (see Slobin, 1967: 130) points out, these ". . . social markers occur in clusters such that the selection of one of a particular set of alternates in one part of an utterance restricts the freedom of selection among subsequent sets." That is, the style (on register) adopted in a particular circumstance is consistent. If one is delivering a lecture to an audience, a set style of speech is maintained consistent in phonology, morphology, syntax, and choice of lexicon. The lecturer does not normally shift styles midway in his presentation to use a type of speech he might use a few hours later at home with his children.

What affects the speaker's choice of styles in the above example are factors in the setting. Some of the social factors which commonly affect linguistic choices are:[2]

1. *the setting* — that is, the situation in which the speech event is occurring, in terms of time and place;
2. *the topic of discourse*; i.e. the content or referent of speech;
3. *the form of communication* (instrumentality) — whether oral or written, spoken or sung, etc.;
4. *tone or mood of the act*;
5. *the function or norm of the interaction*; i.e. whether its purpose is to ingratiate, insult, oblige, convince, explain, etc.;
6. *the participants* — which includes consideration of the status, sex, age, and occupation of the speakers as well as their roles in relationship to each other and in relation to the social situation at hand.

Not only the identification of social variables relevant to each speech act concerns the sociolinguist, but also the correlation of these variables in terms of their impact on the speaker's adoption of one lingistic style or another. In fact, some sociolinguists, notably Ervin-Tripp, suggest that the social factors are arranged hierarchically as stages in the communicative process. Certain social factors are primarily considerations assuming more underlying importance in terms of their effects on the speaker's choice, than others. Among these, social relationships seem to be the major determinants of verbal behaviour. According to Gumperz (1967: 132),

"Communication is seen as a single process in which the speaker
modifies stimuli from the outside environment in accordance with

his cultural background and thus derives the communicative norms that apply to the situation at hand. These norms, in turn, determine his selection of verbal signs."

There can no longer be a division of linguistic and social categories if one accepts this premise.

As social factors present in the setting vary, so does the speaker's choice of style. No person speaks in exactly the same manner at all times in all places to all people. This holds true for everyone, whether monolingual or bilingual. However, whereas the speaker of only one language shifts styles within a single language system, the bilingual has even greater options — he can also shift from one language to another. Such code switching[3] is also replete with social significance. This has been described by scholars such as Gumperz, Ferguson and Rubin. Gumperz (1970: 468), for example, distinguishes between vernacular speech (that used in the home and with peers) and other varieties which are learned after childhood and are used only in certain more socially definable communication situations. Ferguson (1959) identifies special types of high and low varieties of language which he dubbed diglossia. And Rubin (1970: 512–30) speaks more precisely of full code switching from one language to another in her work on the Spanish–Guaraní speakers of Paraguay. Hence, the bilingual shifts codes to mark contrasts in the same way as the monolingual shifts styles within a single language.

In the following chapters we shall identify some of the social factors which affect Mario's choice of a particular language, or language style; the degree to which code switching occurs; and in what order, and when, the child becomes aware of social factors which influence selection among linguistic options. For the child acquires not only the phonology and grammar of his language, but also a tremendous amount of information about the community in which he lives if he is ultimately to *use* language appropriately. The child's language is judged for its grammaticality as well as for its appropriateness. The child is both linguist and enthnographer — and he is incredibly expert as both.

Notes to Chapter 2

1. Hugo Baetens-Beardsmore, in his book *Bilingualism: Basic Principles* (1982: 7–9), distinguishes between an "equilingual" who ". . . may have a fairly balanced knowledge of two languages but is clearly discernible from two monoglot speakers, respectively, through possible traces of interference in both", and an "ambilingual" who is ". . . capable of functioning equally well in either of his

languages in all domains of activity and without any traces of the one language in his use of the other."
2. The reader is referred to three works which discuss social variables affecting speech: Susan Ervin-Tripp, 1970: 192–211; Hymes, 1974: 352–53; and also Mitchell (see Slobin, 1967: 160).
3. It should be noted that the terms "code" and "style" are not always used consistently in the literature. In this work, "code" is synonymous with language, whereas "style" refers to the modification of a specific set of linguistic features within the same code. Merrill Swain (1971), in a paper entitled "Bilingualism, Monolingualism and Code Acquisition" questioned "the utility of the bilingual/ monolingual distinction in the development of a psychological theory of code-switching." The implication is that all speakers perform code-switching of some sort, whether they switch languages, dialects, or sub-varieties of dialects, and in fact, code-switching is a part of all linguistic activity.

3 The child and his environment

Parents and other caretakers

In this study we are concerned with both the linguistic and cultural inputs which affect acquisition. In the case of the child, input is usually quite limited, but it increases and diversifies as the child matures and begins to interact with varied groups of people. For most children, their primary sources immediately after birth are their parents. The child's mother and father serve as the first models and information resources for the young ethnographer-linguist. In Mario's case this was also true, except that, in addition to his parents, he also had prolonged and intensive contact during the early years with others who resided with the family and who therefore were significant to his developing communication behaviour.

Mario's mother was born in Rome, of Bolivian parents. She lived the first three years of her life in Italy where she learned Italian and Spanish simultaneously. However, by three, her family returned to South America and she lost whatever proficiency she had in Italian. She spent the next years until age 12 in Argentina, Bolivia and Peru, five of which were spent in La Paz. Spanish continued throughout as her dominant tongue although she understood Italian, which was still spoken at times by her parents. In fact, she never entirely lost ability to comprehend Italian even though she had almost no active proficiency until she studied it years later.

Between 12 and 15 she lived in Peru, and later in Venezuela, where she stayed until age 20. Her stays in these countries produced only slight effects on her native idiolect which was a fairly standard variety of Spanish. She was educated entirely in Spanish, and had also formally studied French and English, although she had not learned to speak either very well at school.

21

She continued her education in the United States, after receiving a B.A. degree in Maracaibo. Her earlier study of English probably accounted for her rapid acquisition of English once abroad. After another year in Caracas, she returned to the United States. She married in 1966, and has lived primarily in Vermont since that time, with occasional stays in Texas. She obtained a M.A.T. degree from a Vermont institution in 1977.

At the time of Mario's birth, his mother spoke not only her native Spanish but also English at a level of FSI 4 (on a relative scale of 0 — no language ability, to 5 — native proficiency).[1] She controlled English grammar fairly well, making only occasional errors, but she retained a marked Spanish accent in pronunciation. She also spoke Italian and Portuguese at about a FSI 2 level, although her comprehension was much greater in both; she also knew a fair degree of French. She liked Italian and enjoyed speaking it with her husband, in contrast to her feeling about English.

Mario's mother had definite linguistic preferences. She firmly insisted on Spanish in the home and for use with her Spanish–English bilingual friends. She claimed not to like the sound of English in particular, finding it harsh and unpleasant. In her own language, she was well versed in literature, poetry, music, folklore, and knew many riddles and proverbs. She also spoke two versions of a type of "Pig" Spanish which she used with considerable fluency as a teenager. Finally, she was a writer and journalist, which reinforced her feelings for the richness of her own language.

The child's father was born in Philadelphia, of Italian parents, who had immigrated to the United States. Both English and Italian (two dialects from the provinces of Molise and the Abruzzi) were spoken in his home during his childhood. The use of Italian, however, diminished in later years when the family moved from an Italian neighbourhood, and after the death of his Italian-speaking grandmother who had lived in the same home. Italian survived mostly as an intimate language which was spoken with older relatives and special friends, especially on holidays when they visited in the home. Italian represented an aspect of the family's ethnicity and, for that reason, it was alternately treasured and at times rejected when it became an undesirable social stigma. Rejection was heightened during his adolescence which was spent in a suburban neighbourhood and high school. Knowledge of Italian, however, was never completely "lost" although his ability to converse decreased temporarily.

After two years' study of Spanish in high school, the child's father spent his first summer in Mexico. He acquired proficiency in Spanish quite easily, building on his Italian foundations. Furthermore, this experience stimulated such an interest in Hispanic language and culture, that it sparked, in turn, a desire to recover his earlier proficiency in Italian, which he did eventually through formal study.

The author was educated in English with the exception of two semesters spent in Mexico, and a third in Colombia. Besides Spanish and Italian, he also studied Portuguese, French, Esperanto and Aymara. When he completed the B.A. and M.A. degrees, he travelled extensively and frequent trips to Italy, Spain, and Latin America expanded his knowledge and proficiency in Italian, Spanish and Portuguese. He settled in Vermont just before marriage, where he directed language programmes for an international exchange organization. He completed a Ph.D. programme in Applied Linguistics in 1974.

At the time of Mario's birth, his father spoke his native English and was proficient in Italian at a FSI 4 level. He also spoke a standard variety of Spanish at a FSI 4 level, with distinct influence from Mexican colloquial speech. He experienced only occasional lexical or syntactic borrowing from English or Italian. In addition, he spoke Portuguese quite well, Esperanto to a functional degree, and he had some ability with French and modern Greek.

Mario's father was more inclined toward code switching than was the child's mother, possibly because they lived in an area where English, his native tongue, was the idiom, and also because he used it daily outside the home at work. He preferred English when discussing work and technical matters, but preferred Spanish at home with his family and Latin friends. Spanish served as the language substitute for Italian which served friendly and intimate conversation even more so than his native English. He also felt more comfortable, more expansive, and more prone to joke and use witticisms in Spanish.

Both of Mario's parents valued Latin culture as well as their Italian heritage, and, of course, both were bilingual and bicultural. They travelled considerably and maintained international outreach through their work with the Vermont-based exchange organization. Not only were they favourably disposed toward biculturalism and bilingualism, but so were most of their associates. Hence, their environment supported these attitudes, a situation which differed radically from the father's experiences as a child.

Spanish was the language they used with each other from their first acquaintance, and which they continued to use throughout courtship and after marriage. Although some switching to English occurred between parents, it was sufficiently checked by the mother's strong insistence on Spanish only. Italian was more likely a switch serving specific functions (one of which initially was to exclude the child, until he began to comprehend more and more). When his parents switched, however, they were normally consistent throughout an entire segment of discourse, or they switched with a change of topic. It was less common to switch either at the sentence level, or mid-sentence. In spite of this, neither parent addressed Mario in English, finding this quite unnatural since Spanish was established with the child from the time of his birth. This pattern, however, began to change as the child grew older, so that increasing amounts of English were interspersed in their conversations with him as he neared his tenth year.

Mario had other caretakers besides his parents. These persons were essentially nursemaids who lived with the family for a period of about eight of the ten years of the child's life. All of these individuals were monolingual Spanish-speakers (four Bolivians and three Mexicans), three of whom acquired limited English while living with the family in Vermont. They all spoke fairly standard Spanish with only limited traces of Bolivian or Mexican regionalisms which often were mirrored in Mario's own speech during their corresponding periods of contact. Each young woman stayed with the family for a period ranging from two months to a year and a half. And in most cases, Mario had more contact hours on a daily basis with the nursemaids than he did with his parents.

Besides these persons, Mario spent periods of one to three months visiting grandparents (both maternal and paternal), and his aunt and uncle. These relatives were all bilingual in either Spanish–English, or Italian–English. In most cases, then, the child during his pre-school years was surrounded by persons who themselves had been raised in bicultural settings and who commanded more than one language. These were the primary individuals from whom Mario acquired his early speech patterns and attitudes.

Attendance at public schools introduced a strong socializing influence of a quite different nature from that which the family and home had provided up to age five. Public education in the United States (in the schools Mario attended in both Texas and Vermont) was conducted entirely in English. This great amount of English exposure through the educational system was to have tremendous impact on the child's developing communication skills from ages five to ten (and beyond) as English became the dominant language of his environment outside the home, except for summer vacations usually spent in Mexico and a semester spent in a Bolivian private school during his tenth year (fifth grade). Furthermore, most of the child's peers at schools were monolinguals who had not travelled outside the area. The child's teachers and his peers during these school years provided significantly different input from that which persisted in the home. This one language–one environment provided the child with daily experiences in two distinct cultural and linguistic milieu. In such a case, an opportunity exists for the child either to develop further his bilingualism–biculturalism, or for the systems to compete with each other. What results is largely affected by the attitudes of the people surrounding the child. Positive attitudes can encourage or at least permit bilingual development to continue; on the other hand, negative attitudes and experiences can inhibit or thwart it. Once again, it is clear that developmental bilingualism is not exclusively a linguistic phenomenon, but one whose existence is rooted in the social environments of the child. The experiences of the child under study will be discussed in the chapters which follow.

The child

Alvino Mario was the name chosen for the child born in Vermont on July 27, 1968. Since it was known that he would eventually have contact with three cultures and three languages, "Mario" seemed a good choice in that it required no translation into any of the languages concerned. Mario's first months were spent in relative seclusion with his family in the woods of Vermont. At 0;6, however, he made his first trip to Bolivia to meet his mother's family; and from then on, his world expanded rapidly with many trips to nearby cities, a few more distant trips to Miami and Hawaii, and several lengthy stays in Mexico and Bolivia.

Mario was brought up in a home where he was shown a lot of affection and love. He was also brought up in a fairly permissive environment, at least until about age three, when he was given increasing direction, and increasing demands were made upon him. Although his parents were indulgent, there were also clear boundaries established for behaviour. As he matured, he was increasingly expected to conduct himself in "appropriate" manners and punitive action was taken when he misbehaved.

The child received considerable individual attention, not only because he was the first and only child for a time, but also because he had a nursemaid who was entirely dedicated to him. He had a very close and special relationship with each of the women who came to live with the family, and in turn each exerted considerable influence on his behaviour and language.

With so much attention and care, Mario was not encouraged to be independent. It was quite to the contrary. His mother and his nursemaid enjoyed, and fully expected — in the Bolivian manner — to treat the child as a "child". Their attitude was quite different from the prevailing American trend to encourage early independence. This is not to say, however, that he was not capable of doing many things for himself, but simply that it was not his role. His stays in Mexico and Bolivia, where servants were present, reinforced this situation. In any case, when he began school he adjusted rapidly, demonstrating his ability to perform without abundant assistance. By five years old, he was a fairly self-reliant and individualistic young boy.

The parents often had differing attitudes concerning many areas of the child's socialization, stemming in part from their own childhood. The father, with his Italian upbringing, was inclined to allow wider latitudes for behaviour, and to include the child (like all other members of the family unit) in all activities. The mother, however, was accustomed to a certain degree of separation between adults and children, especially during certain activities. This meant that Mario often had his meals separately, he was taken to another room when visitors were present, and his play was confined to certain areas. When he misbehaved, he was often entrusted to the nurse-maid.

Most significant, however, were their divergent attitudes toward verbal behaviour since each parent felt differently about when and how a young child should participate in adult conversation. Whereas his mother felt that children have their time and place to speak in the presence of adults, his father was accustomed to a home in which the purely expressive aspects of speech were often as important as its message. Persons of all ages talked together — often simultaneously. His mother expected a moderate tone and volume control; his father was undisturbed by loud speaking. However, since childraising was primarily a female-dominated activity, the mother's attitudes (and those of the caretakers) normally prevailed.

An important event in Mario's life was the birth of his sister, Carla, when he was 4;4. Her presence, however, did not alter his behaviour significantly. The fact that he continued to receive much attention and care from his nursemaid helped Carla's arrival into the family so that he did not see it as an intrusion at all. He developed a rather protective, caring attitude toward her, and in the absence of the nursemaid, he was sometimes observed taking on aspects of that role. He spoke to his sister in his usual manner without a distinct style shift, except when displaying affection in which case he invoked a style of Spanish he had heard adults use when speaking to children.[2]

Mario's extensive travels were a somewhat unusual aspect of his childhood. His trips were significant because they were not simply geographical moves, but they also provided contrasting cultural experiences and linguistic immersion from an early age. Mario showed no deleterious effects as a result of changing environments. On the contrary, he entered each new situation with a surprisingly high degree of self-confidence. In fact, he usually made the physical adjustments (extreme cold to extreme heat, sea level to 13,000 feet above, rural to city life, etc.); cultural adjustments (different foods, different eating schedules, different roles and relationships with people, contact and interaction with Bolivian "cholos" and Indians); and linguistic adjustments (switches from English to Spanish) with an ease uncommon for many adults.

Another result of his cross-cultural experiences was that Mario seemed to know and accept the fact that people behaved differently in different places. And so did he. Although he was accustomed to servants and service, he was equally comfortable without either. Although he was allowed certain behaviour in La Paz, he also knew that the same behaviour was not permitted elsewhere. Although he spoke Spanish in public places in La Paz during his various trips there, he spoke English in public places in the United States (with everyone other than his parents). There were many observable instances of his cross-cultural adeptness.

Knowledge of the variable behaviour of people and their differing attitudes provided him with considerable self-assurance in his own behaviour rather than the contrary. One illustration of this was his persistent use of the "mamadera" or "mamila" (baby bottle). Although he was teased and chided by others because he enjoyed the bottle even at age 5;6 (and occasionally beyond), he did not yield to their pressure. Neither did he attempt to conceal this habit by drinking in seclusion. Rather he took his bottle confidently — almost defiantly — and holding it high like a trumpet, he called teasingly to those who laughed at him: "Look, I drink!" He knew that in other places at least (Bolivia and Mexico), drinking from the "mamadera" was perfectly acceptable behaviour — even for children this age.

One other activity uncommon for many pre-school children deserves comment. When Mario showed curiosity in the printed word, his parents responded with techniques for teaching early reading along the lines suggested by Doman.[3] Although his exposure to reading at age 3;4 was done altogether casually, Mario made considerable progress in word recognition. Within a few months he was able to recognize (or read) a fairly large number of words which were later placed in running context. This exposure, although sporadic, stimulated his curiosity in all graphic material — numbers, letters, symbols — as well as in colour, shapes, and form. He was acutely aware of the fact that there was often meaning in graphic representations.[4]

Four months before kindergarten (age 4;9), Mario took a series of tests, to include the Peabody Picture Vocabulary Test. The results indicated that he was "normal for his age" in speech, he "appears normal for his age" in vocabulary, and adequate for school readiness in perception.[5] These evaluations, of course, were done in English, the weaker of his two languages at that time.

At age 5;4, after two months of kindergarten, he temporarily left school for a visit to La Paz. At that time his teacher described him as:

". . . extremely sociable. He gets along fine with all the children, and enjoys school. He is quite vocal. He does not seem at all conscious of his speech. His slight accent has had no effect on his relations with the others. Whenever I ask the class a question, he is always one of the ones with his hand up.

"His greatest problem seems to be in the give and take of conversation. Since he always has something to say, he often finds it difficult to wait his turn when others are talking. When he talks, there are moments when you can see his little mind thinking through language — for he sometimes has to stop to recall a certain word in English which he might not have at his finger tips.

"He seems exceptionally talented with anything visual or graphic. He does puzzles and other visual problems with amazing speed. In fact, he sometimes puts a puzzle together and when he finishes, turns it on its other side and he does the puzzle face down. He is the only child I have seen during my several years of teaching to have ventured to work on a specific graphic puzzle which is designed to test color and coordination. Most other children his age don't even attempt it, and those who do, usually give up. Mario was intrigued with it and worked the problem out to its completion. He seems to know colors, shapes, and numbers quite well, and also recognizes letters."[6]

In addition to his teacher's comments, it was also observed that he had vivid auditory recall. He seemed to learn songs and rhymes easily. He frequently came home singing songs in English which he had learned that day. Often he returned from school with the sound of a specific word he had heard which he had not understood. Even without meaning, he was capable of retaining the sound of the word — or a close approximation of that sound — for a period of several hours.

At 5;8 Mario transferred to kindergarten in Austin, after an interlude of three months without English. After three days his new teacher gave her impressions:

"There is no need to be concerned about his English; he speaks amazingly well for his age. I am also surprised by the naturalness with which he came into our class and became part of the group. Often new children take some time to adjust, but he came in as though he had always been there."[7]

In summary, it can be said that by age five, Mario was bilingual and bicultural with full awareness of these facts. Behaviourally, he was well-adjusted, with positive feelings about his own identity in spite of many environmental changes. He had received much attention and affection, and he was himself overtly affectionate. He was curious and interested in many things. He was also fairly obedient and respectful, normal in his aggressive feelings, and capable of being self-reliant and independent when the situation demanded this.

Linguistically, Mario was Spanish dominant upon entering kindergarten. Although fluent in English at this point, his speech deviated slightly from the norm of other monolingual English peers. The most obvious deviation was in pronunciation, although not enough that it affected his relations with friends. It did, however, attract the attention of a zealous "special ed" teacher, new to the school system, who cited Mario along with several other children for speech therapy. Unaware that Mario's deviations were of the "foreign accent" sort, rather than pathological or physiological in origin, she prescribed individualized instruction to remedy the problem. Needless to say, his parents opposed therapy, first on the assumption that his pronunciation would take care of itself quite naturally over time; and secondly, because they wished to avoid drawing undue attention to his "differentness" at this sensitive age. Mario's accent did in fact disappear. Only two years later, his third grade teacher was surprised when he learned that Mario spoke another language at home, testimony to the child's success as a native English-speaker. Mario's ability in both Spanish and English continued without interruption through his tenth year such that speakers of Spanish or English never perceived the child as anything but a native-speaker of each respectively. If they offered any comment at all, his teachers often cited his unusually clear enunciation, whereas Spanish-speakers remarked that his speech bore no clear regional trace. However, never did anyone perceive the child as not native to the language in use. By ten, then, Mario was fully bilingual (or "ambilingual" in Baetens-Beardsmore terms (1982: 7)) in two languages with increasing knowledge of a third. What was becoming increasingly obvious, however, despite his command of Spanish was the ever-deepening lexical command of English aided by the intellectual pursuits of school. Although his tenacity to Spanish at home was quite remarkable, vocabulary and stylistic options began to fall behind similar developments in English. Both will be discussed in detail in the sections which follow.

Language contact and exposure patterns

There is no set formula for producing a bilingual individual. Bilingual speakers may acquire their second or third tongue through a variety of means, at various ages, and under quite dissimilar circumstances. Yet, although most studies on child language have recorded what the child has emitted, few have recorded as faithfully the social circumstances in which the child acquired his languages. Such factors are specially significant in a bilingual study since they determine not only the type of bilingual — whether co-ordinate or compound — but they also influence his degree of control, fluency, interference and switching.

Mario was clearly a co-ordinate bilingual since he acquired each of his languages from separate speakers and under quite separate circumstances. Weinreich (1968: 72–74) stressed the importance of separateness of contact and exposure when he said ". . . the greater the differentiation in the topical and environmental domains in which the two languages are used, the less interference in association; only a functionally undifferentiated use of two languages induces 'inorganic' bilingualism that is subject to interferences of associations." Furthermore, ". . . the imbedding of a language in a definite and constant situation facilitates its learning in unmixed form." To understand Mario's linguistic abilities and the underlying factors affecting their *use*, then, it is imperative that the patterns of contact and exposure to English and Spanish be examined.

Mario's language contact is expressed graphically through a chart which represents the times, places and degrees of exposure (see Figures 1, 2 and 3). Assuming the child's normal waking day to consist of roughly 12 hours to age 3;0, and about 14 hours thereafter, the percentage of time which Mario spent in contact with each language is indicated by means of the graph bar. To review the basic situation, the home language was predominantly Spanish, also the sole language addressed to the child. The parents did some code switching to English but normally only with each other. Mario had limited contact with English initially because of the isolated location of his home in the woods of Vermont. This basic exposure pattern prevailed until the child entered school, and varied only when there were visitors in the home, when the child was taken to public places, or when the family spent occasional sojourns in other areas.

The drastic changes in environment are clearly reflected in the chart. For example, at age 0;1 English increased in the home when Mario's paternal grandmother spent six weeks with the family. His first exposure to Italian occurred at that time since his grandmother was inclined to speak to infants in Italian. At 0;4 and 0;5 he made his first visit to English-speaking relatives in Philadelphia; and at age 0;6 he spent one month in Bolivia in a totally Spanish-speaking environment. At 0;7, his first nursemaid (a monolingual Bolivian girl) joined the family; her presence reinforced the use of Spanish in his immediate surroundings. By age 1;0 and again at age 1;4 Mario spent several weeks in Philadelphia and New Jersey, where again he had increased contact with English. A second trip to Bolivia at 1;6 produced total Spanish contact for another one month period. At age 1;11 he made his first trip to Mexico where he stayed for three months, again receiving total exposure to Spanish. However, upon his return to Vermont at age 2;1, he attended a nursery for the first time with English-speaking children, where he continued almost until 2;5. This was the first complete switch for the child in terms of language contact; not only did he have more daily exposure to English than Spanish, but for the first time he was left alone without any support from a Spanish-speaking caretaker.

Other factors continued to alternate this exposure pattern, providing greater or lesser contact with English between age 2;6 and 2;8, owing to several more trips to Philadelphia and New York, and the arrival of a new caretaker (also a monolingual Spanish-speaker). At age 2;8 the family moved to Texas where Mario attended a day care centre and where again he had increased exposure to English through other children his age. This lasted only a few months, for at age 2;10 he travelled once again with his family, first to Bolivia, and later to Mexico, where he celebrated his third birthday. By age 3;1, he returned to Texas and to the nursery which provided English contact as before. With the exception of two brief trips, one to Philadelphia at 3;6, and another to Hawaii at 3;8, this pattern prevailed for a substantially long time. At 3;10 he returned to Mexico for the summer where he celebrated his fourth birthday. At 4;1 he returned home to Vermont and at 4;4 his third Bolivian caretaker arrived just prior to the birth of his sister, Carla. The pattern of exposure again remained fairly stable with predominant Spanish contact until the age of 4;11, with the exception of two interludes at 4;6 and 4;7 with brief trips to Philadelphia and Miami. At 4;11 Mario spent his fourth summer in Mexico.

Now fully five years old, he returned to Vermont and within a few weeks he began kindergarten, which provided the most significant English contact to date. However, after attending school only two months (from age 5;2 to 5;4), he left to return to Bolivia — this time alone — for a lengthy stay with his maternal grandparents.

FIGURE 1 *Exposure patterns (Birth to 3;0)*

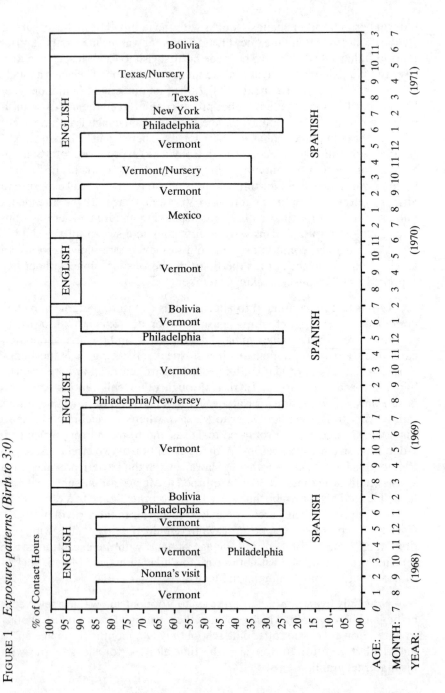

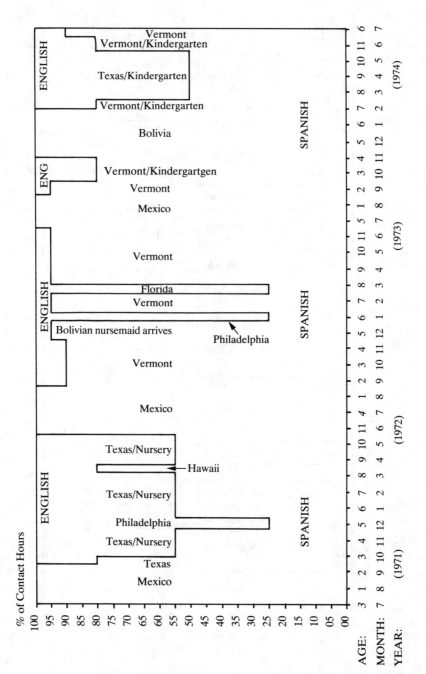

FIGURE 2   *Exposure patterns (3;0 to 6;0)*

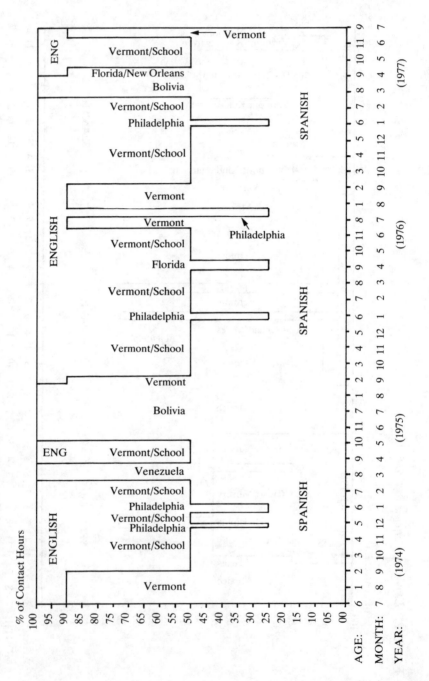

FIGURE 3   *Exposure patterns (6;0 to 10;0)*

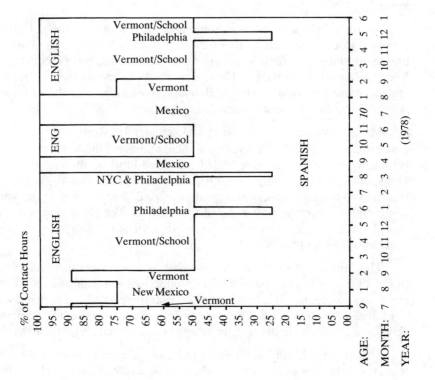

FIGURE 3   (continued)

He stayed in La Paz (and was later joined by his parents) until age 5;7. Then he returned to Vermont again, attended his former kindergarten for only one week, and by age 5;8, he was back in Texas where he entered a new kindergarten, returning to Vermont almost at the end of the school year to complete this grade where he had begun. The Texas kindergarten provided full day sessions, giving him almost equal exposure to English and Spanish — about 7 hours at school and another 7 at home. In Vermont, however, kindergarten lasted only half days, or about 3–4 hours, thereby reducing daily exposure to English in school and increasing contact with Spanish at home.

Summer 1974 was spent at home in Vermont, and in the fall Mario returned to the same school to attend first grade. The year passed almost uninterrupted except for brief vacations in Philadelphia, and a month trip to Venezuela during the winter. However, about one month before the year ended, Mario left again on a trip to Bolivia where he travelled alone to spend several more months with maternal grandparents.

Mario returned to Vermont in late summer 1975 and entered second grade in the fall of 1975. This year was spent entirely at the Vermont school. Again, with brief vacations in Philadelphia and Florida. Summer 1976 was also spent in Vermont with a brief trip to Philadelphia and in the fall Mario returned to the same school system although a different school in the same community, where he now entered third grade. The third year was also completed entirely in Vermont with brief vacations to Philadelphia, Bolivia, Florida and New Orleans.

The summer of 1977 was spent partially in Vermont and New Mexico. In fall 1977 Mario returned to the Vermont school where he entered fourth grade. As before, he completed the entire year there with brief periods away in Philadelphia, New York City and Mexico. Mario then spent the summer of 1978 in Mexico with his parents, where he celebrated his tenth birthday.

This pattern hardly paralleled the language contact described in the Ronjat, Pavlovitch and Leopold studies, owing to the frequently alternating changes of environment and the corresponding shifts of emphasis from one language to another. But in spite of this, there was usually consistency of language in each environment and with each interlocutor. Hence, a given environment normally provided one and only one language — e.g. Spanish in the home, in Mexico and in Bolivia; whereas English was the sole medium of the nursery, in Florida, Philadelphia, Texas and at school. Most inter-locutors, too, were consistent in the language they spoke to the child. Hence, his parents, caretakers and maternal grandparents used Spanish with him; his young friends at the nursery, classmates and teachers at school and paternal grandparents used English. Visitors to the home, of course, used either English or Spanish in accordance with their own ability. Even bilingual persons with whom Mario had contact normally used a single language with him. This was certainly true in the earlier years when people usually stayed in the language in which they had first come to know the child. For the most part, there was little or no intermixing of two systems and there was a fairly unvaried pattern of "one environment–one language", a situation which presumably fosters co-ordinate systems. As Mario matured and displayed adeptness in using either language or both toward the second half of his ten years, however, it became increasingly obvious that bilingual Spanish–English speakers were more prone to mix languages in their conversations with the child. This action evoked corresponding mixing from the child, a phenomenon to be examined more fully later in an examination of language styles.

Mario also experienced fairly consistent exposure to "standard" Spanish, barring slight regionalisms in a few cases. Conversely, he was exposed to many more varieties of American English, having had prolonged contact with both native and foreign-born speakers, and people from the northeast and southwest of the United States.

Besides those in his immediate family, many of the people he had contact with were, like himself, capable of switching from one language to another. He had many opportunities to observe individuals switch from English to German, others from English to Italian, still others from Spanish to Aymara. Having heard many languages, he knew that people speak and behave in a variety of ways. With those frequent observations, Mario was aware of many different types of communication behaviour. For him, language was not an abstract concept but a clearly observed phenomenon through his own direct experiences.

To summarize, we might apply some of the descriptive terms used to characterize the behaviour of a bilingual speaker. In this case, Mario might be described as one whose mother tongue is Spanish, but whose initial contact with English was only slightly delayed, providing fairly simultaneous exposure thereafter, hence a "simultaneous" bilingual; also as one who although an "incipient" bilingual at age two, later developed into a "complete" bilingual; as one who is "pluri-" or "multilingual" in that he has "passive" or "receptive" knowledge of a third language, Italian; as an "alternating" bilingual in that he switches from one language to the other as required; as "active" bilingual in that he continually uses both languages; as a "co-ordinate" bilingual in that he learned each language from different people in different circumstances; as an "ascendent" bilingual in that he is progressively developing in both languages, and therefore also as a "stable" bilingual in that both languages are being maintained; and finally, as an "equilingual" in that he has a fairly balanced knowledge of two languages, while movement toward increased "ambilingualism" remains to be seen. This will greatly depend on the amount of continuing exposure to both languages and some educational input in Spanish (Mario did enter a Bolivian school in his eleventh year) so critical to his becoming an "educated" bilingual speaker. Quantitative statements of his ability at various stages are the topic of a later section of this report.

Notes to Chapter 3

1. The FSI Oral Proficiency Rating was developed by the Foreign Service Institute, Washington, D.C., to characterize the oral proficiency of students of a second language. The scale range from 0 (no ability) to 5 (native proficiency) with intermediate steps between each category expressed by a plus (+). The criteria considered include vocabulary, pronunciation, grammatical control, comprehension, and fluency. This system was recently adopted by the Educational Testing Services, Princeton, New Jersey. It was retitled ETS Oral Proficiency Testing, and is now being widely disseminated throughout the Foreign Language Departments of many of the public schools in the United States.
2. Style Shifts are discussed in detail in a later section of this report. The reader is also referred to an article by Jean Berko Gleason (1973) on this same topic.
3. The reader is referred to a fascinating book on the techniques for teaching early reading by Glenn Doman (1964).
4. Separate data were kept concerning the child's reading progress and its effects upon language learning. However, this material is beyond the scope of the present report. Other researchers have made similar observations; see Söderbergh (1971). Christian (1971: 4–5) also makes several comments in this respect. See also *A Guide to Family Reading in Two Languages: The Preschool Years* (Andersson, 1977).
5. From a report distributed by Burton F. Eldridge, Assistant Superintendent, Windham Southeast Supervisory Union, Kindergarten Registration Program, Brattleboro, Vermont, Spring 1973.
6. Paraphrased from a verbal report made by Mario's teacher, Mrs Mary Carnahan, Kindergarten Teacher, East Dummerston School, Dummerston, Vermont, November 10, 1973.
7. Paraphrased from a verbal report made by Ms Elizabeth Thompson, Ridgetop Elementary School, Austin, Texas, March 9, 1974.

4 Sociolinguistic aspects of language acquisition

General comments

This study is based largely on empirical observation, the collection of information (in the form of the speech diary), and finally on an interpretation of data. Through this approach we are attempting a sociolinguistic examination of language development. Since this is a study of only one child, and since sociological factors vary with each individual, it cannot be implied that the findings are true in the same way for all children. However, although circumstances vary as well as the age at which different children mature, an individual case study can shed some light on the relationship of speech acquisition and the social context.

Basically, the questions of concern are:

1. How and when does the process of language differentiation occur?
2. How and when does Mario begin to "behave" as a bilingual individual?
3. What are some of the observable social factors which affect his choice of language?
4. How and when does Mario begin to perceive these factors?
5. Are some social factors more important than others in determining language choice?
6. In addition to code switching, what are some of the "styles" of language evident in the speech of a five-year-old child?
7. What factors trigger differing styles of speech?
8. How has the socialization process affected Mario's linguistic abilities and language use?
9. What linguistic interference and/or transference is noted in Mario's speech?

10. What effect do various social factors have upon the occurrence and type of interference and transference in the child's speech?
11. What is the child's proficiency in Spanish by school age? In English? How does his ability compare with monolingual speakers of the same age?
12. What social and psychological factors encourage or constrain the child's developing bilingualism?
13. What is the effect of monolingual education upon a bilingual child's development?
14. What is the child's proficiency by age ten in each language? Again, how does this compare with monoglot speakers?
15. What predictions can be made at this point for the child's continued bilingual development?

Language differentiation and bilinguality

Sitting by the side of a pool, Mario (5;6) was speaking to his father in Spanish. A four-year-old child overhearing them, turned to her mother and asked:

Child: Mommie, why does Mario speak that way?
Mother: He's speaking another language.
Child: I want to speak a langage (*sic*) too.
Mother: But you do speak a language. Everybody speaks a language!
Child: No, I want to speak like Mario!

Most children never think about their own ability to speak. And the first time they hear someone speak in a different way it is often a surprising, if not disconcerting, experience. Their reactions vary — they stare or they giggle; often they are intrigued. On the other hand, a child exposed to two or more languages is probably more sophisticated in this respect. He has observed people speak and behave in different ways. And if he has had sufficient exposure, chances are that he has himself acquired the ability to speak in one or more ways.

At what precise point a child becomes bilingual, and how he becomes aware of his own bilinguality, is the subject of this section. Jones (1969: 12), speaking at the Moncton Seminar, raised similar questions:

> "The question of time — When does a child become bilingual? — is certainly no easier to answer than the other time question — When does a child become monolingual? . . .

"The child inevitably enters language with an act of recognition (or decoding), which contains the whole primary organisation of any linguistic act, apart from the mechanism of utterance.

"He may be bilingual in this sense before the end of his first year, as was Leopold's child; a preferable way of describing it would be, however, to say he entered each of his languages at such and such an age, and from then on he possessed such and such a degree of bilingual attainment, reaching one key point of development when the whole of his phonology was in place and another when he had acquired all his basic grammatical machinery."

We are concerned, then, with the child's recognition of language as a system and the ability to differentiate one from another. These are prerequisites for an awareness of his own bilinguality. Although we cannot state with precision the moment in which Mario first noted that people with whom he had contact behaved in linguistically different ways, some indications are provided through his questions, his reactions to what he heard, and his own behaviour.

Developmental studies show that the infant begins to interact with his environment almost at once — to distinguish the familiar from the unfamiliar, the known from the unknown, and the similar from the different (see Lidz, 1968: 93–158). Similarly, when Mario was only a few months old, he showed that he distinguished his parents from others by crying when other people picked him up. This discriminating ability occurs auditorially as well as visually.

The discrimination and recognition of sounds

There are numerous entries in the child's diary which illustrate early recognition and differentiation of sounds. In the first few months, he already showed signs of recognizing his parents' voices and also that of his nursemaid; by 0;4, he began to respond to differing intonations of voice. If the voice was cheerful, he laughed; if soothing and gentle, he cooed; if harsh, he cried. By 0;11, he began to recognize specific utterances. For example, when the dog's name, Bimba, was said, it drew his attention or often caused him to stop crying. By 1;0, he produced sounds which, although meaningless in themselves, followed such familiar intonational patterns that they often sounded like real speech. He had apparently discerned, and he was able to produce — if not the sounds he heard — at least their intonational contours. By 1;4 Mario was capable of producing both intonation and a few words.

Between 1;8 and 1;10 several incidents occurred which demonstrated Mario's incipient ability to discriminate languages based on acoustic impressions alone. For example, on one occasion while his father read Spanish aloud from a journal, Mario, who was playing nearby, began to parrot his father. He did this easily but obviously without any comprehension. Noticing this, his father switched suddenly to reading aloud in English. Mario ceased to mimic. His father switched a third time to Japanese (acoustically similar to Spanish) and again Mario copied the sounds. When his father changed to other unfamiliar languages, or English, the child invariably became silent.

On another occasion, during this same pre-speech period, Mario's mother was in the process of correcting the results of some eighty taped Spanish exams which she played on a tape recorder. Since the questions were the same on each test, and the responses fairly similar, Mario became acquainted with the recordings after hearing just a few. Subsequently, each time a tape was played, he repeated the sounds he heard but did not understand. Sometimes he anticipated what came next on the tape, producing reasonably accurate sounds even before they came from the recorder. He enjoyed parroting, but he parroted only those sounds familiar to him, ignoring those that were strange.

This familiarity and discrimination of specific phones also began to affect Mario's interaction with other people as he began to distinguish people by the sounds they made. By age 1;10, at a party where both Spanish and English-speakers were present — all unknown to the child — he invariably responded enthusiastically to guests who addressed him in Spanish, ignoring those who tried to attract his attention in English. The consistency with which this occurred was striking. Mario sorted people in accordance to the language they spoke. Recognition and differentiation had clearly begun before the child ws capable of speaking himself, and language differences were already a factor which affected his relations with others.[1]

These incidents support Jones' comment that the child enters language with an act of recognition; beyond this point, it is a question of the degree and type of binguality he will attain. However, it appears that differentiation is affected by the way in which the two languages are used. That is, if the child moves in an environment where the languages are quite separate and there is little mixing, differentiation is facilitated. Hence, language differentiation is rooted in the social context. If the social milieu requires separateness (each language used within a specific context), then linguistic separation is encouraged; otherwise children may use inputs from dual systems without an awareness of their own binguality. Mackey (1970: 554) points this out when he says: "Bilingualism is not a phenomenon of language, it is a characteristic of its use."

Mario experienced quite separate exposure to English and Spanish which forced him to distinguish between the two systems at an early age. His first active use of Spanish occurred by age 1;4; however, it was not until 2;6 that he uttered his first words in English owing to minimal contact initially with this language. In the interim, nevertheless, incidents like those cited above point to the fact that he had begun to sort the sounds of Spanish from those of other languages — erring, perhaps, only when other languages were phonetically similar, as with Japanese. As his knowledge of Spanish increased — lexically, morphologically, and syntactically — increasing cues guided him in differentiating Spanish from other tongues, rather than relying upon sound alone.

Language mixing and language separation

When English first appeared, Mario mixed both languages within the same utterance. At this time he was in a period of rapid lexical growth. Since words developed in accordance with needs within a specific environment — often the nursery or the home — Mario initially had no counterparts for many of the words he acquired in one of the languages. This was quite noticeable during a visit to Philadelphia at 2;6. There, within a few days, Mario rapidly learned many new words for new things which were not necessarily synonyms of words he already knew in Spanish. In subsequent situations he used these signs whenever he needed to speak about the objects they signified; consequently he said "dessert, apple, gum", etc., without alternation. As equivalent signs were eventually learned in Spanish, a brief period followed in which he alternately used either the English or Spanish forms. He continued to use Spanish or English words inconsistently during his visit until he discerned that some interlocutors used only one set of words. Furthermore, when he made the wrong choice of words, he was often met with no response, with confusion, or sometimes with laughter or amusement. The sorting of lexical items with appropriate persons occurred at first on a trial and error basis. Later he paid more attention to the source of the language he heard. If he learned "orange" from his grandmother (pronounced [sósanj]), then he used that word with her (and with those who spoke like her). By the end of his visit, he had already become quite consistent in using "milk, gum", etc. with his grandparents, and "leche, chicle" (milk, chewing gum), etc. with his parents and nursemaid.

The onset of English was probably hastened by the child's sudden immersion in a nursery with English-speaking children. This experience accelerated productive use of the language with which he had already had occasional contact. Mixing of the two languages continued for approximately another two months, between 2;7 and 2;8. However, as he continued in the nursery, and as he progressed linguistically in both languages, mixing diminished and he improved in his ability to maintain the two systems separate.

Complete separation of languages occurred when Mario was 2;8 (his sister at 2;5). Once, while shopping, Mario met a small girl of about the same age. He tried to attract her attention by amusing her with facial expressions and motions as well as by speaking to her. Since his English was so limited he was able to say only: "Hey! Look! Watch! Here! Come!" and "Water!" (pointing to a nearby fountain). He judiciously avoided Spanish, which he could have used with so much more facility. This is significant in that it marks his first complete separation of languages by limiting himself to only those linguistic items which were approriate for use with the little girl.

His awareness of different verbal behaviours was witnessed not only in his conduct at this age, but also in comments he made concerning the way people speak. For example, at 2;8, recalling a recent aeroplane trip, he said: "gente 'hello' en l'ayón" (La gente dice "hello" en el avión or people say "hello" on the aeroplane). In other words, by calling attention to the fact that people on the aeroplane said "hello", he observed that they spoke differently from himself. Other examples of differentiated language use were witnessed at 3;0 and again at 3;4. In the first case he was travelling to Acapulco with his parents and an English-speaking aunt. In the midst of a conversation in Spanish with his parents, he turned to his aunt ("Zia" in Italian) and said: "Look, Zia, here!" showing her a mosquito bite on his arm. He then turned back to his parents and resumed his chatter in Spanish. He continued to switch from one language to the other appropriately and consistently throughout the trip. The second case occurred in Austin when Mario approached several children playing on a fire engine. Wishing to manoeuver himself into the driver's seat, he uttered several commands such as "move over, let me up, gimme (give me)", etc. Once in position, he yelled to his parents in Spanish: "¿Qué es eso? ¿Y eso? ¿Manguera? ¿Campanita? ¿Luz?" (What's that? And that? A hose? A little bell? A light?) When he addressed the children he switched back to English.

From this point on, all entries in the speech diary show that Mario clearly sorted the two languages and used them appropriately. With the linguistic systems separated, the process which ensued was one of determining which circumstances required the use of one or the other language.

Mario knew that most other people spoke differently from the way he and his parents spoke. Sometimes, in fun, he made renditions of his acoustic impression of English, or he imitated English-speaking people when he heard them speaking so rapidly that he could not understand; for example:

Age 3;2 Hello, blaka, blaka, blak . . . good bye! Ko pisko pisha.
Age 3;4 Wafe, wesi, wefíte.
Age 3;5 Yo hablo "avishótele" (presumably an onomatopoetic expression for English).
Age 3;7 Wa fa fa ta.
Age 3;8 O wae ho wác fae.
Age 3;9 Af shi fo suf.
Age 3;10 Dob i we fi ses.

As he grew older, rather than use nonsense words to convey his impression of English, he often used actual samples from speech; for example: "Hello . . . how are you . . . good-bye!"

Marked and unmarked uses of language

Mario became so accustomed to the use of one or the other language in a given situation, that he was surprised when he heard the opposite language used. This is evident from the following incidents:

Age 3;4 Watching a horse race on television, the broadcaster announced the horses: Red Sands, Amigo, etc. . . . Mario exclaimed with astonishment to his parents: "¡(El) dice amigo!" (*He says "amigo" (friend)!*)

Age 3;7 Watching television, a chef advertised a sauce with the words: magnifico superbiuo, fantastico. Although this was Italian, Mario took it for Spanish and exclaimed: "¡(El) habla español!" (*He speaks Spanish!*)

Age 3;8 Catching a glimpse of a Spanish-speaking movie on TV as he switched channels, he exclaimed, "¡Hablan español!" (*They speak Spanish!*)

On another occasion in church, Mario heard a woman use Spanish to reprimand her son: ¡Quieto, quieto! (*Quiet, Quiet!*) Mario turned to his parents and remarked with surprise: "¡La señora dice 'quieto'!" (*That woman says "quieto" (quiet)!*)

Age 5;6 In a Mexican restaurant in Austin, the waiter took the order in Spanish. This surprised Mario who asked: "Papá, ¿por qué hablan como yo . . . español?" (*Papa, why do they speak like me . . . in Spanish?*)

Age 5;7 In a shopping centre in Austin, Mario heard a child speaking Spanish with his mother. Greatly excited, he called across the parking lot to his father: "Ven a ver, papá, como hablan . . . ¡español! ¡Como nosotros hablamos! (*Papá, come here. Look how they speak . . . Spanish! Like we speak!*))

Age 6;6 On a flight to Caracas, Venezuela, he heard a lot of Spanish, and he commented with surprise: "¡Ah, todos hablan español aquí!" (*Hey, everybody speaks Spanish here!*)

In all these cases Mario was struck by the fact that, given his assessment of each situation, the language used was not the normal one to be expected (in anthropological terms, "marked" language use in opposition to "unmarked" use). Consequently both his surprise and comments on these unexpected events were justified. As he gained increasing experiences of these sorts beyond his seventh year, however, the now more sophisticated child became less prone to reveal surprise with such abandon. Subsequent comments were often reduced to non-verbal actions such as raising eyebrows or making eye contact with his parents to be sure they also registered the "marked" uses of either Spanish or English.

Interest in other codes

Of course these were not the only languages Mario heard. He had also had contact with speakers of several other languages and, of course, he heard considerable Italian in the home. When he was younger, Italian served primarily to exclude him from adult conversation. He recognized Italian whenever it was spoken and he knew it was different from Spanish and English. His awareness of its specialized use as a code to exchange secrets between his parents only increased his curiosity in it. He often imitated his parents when they spoke Italian by making humorous impersonations — some were noted at 3;4; or by laughing at its sounds — recorded at age 3;7. However, he eventually passed the initial phase of recognition and began to understand many cognate words. Although slightly different from Spanish, many words were easily understood.

Once at age 3;7, when his parents were speaking a mixture of Spanish and Italian, Mario's ears perked up when he understood they were speaking about him. In an effort to understand more of the conversation, he reminded his mother: "Mamá, no se mezcla", (*Mamá, don't mix*) accompanied by a gesture in which he crossed two fingers over each other several times to indicate mixing. Less than a month later (3;8), he used the Italian phrase — "Ti voglio bene" (*I love you*) appropriately to conclude a telephone conversation with his grandfather. A year later, by 4;9, his comprehension of

Italian increased so much that his father decided to use Italian for telling him stories, thereby assisting his developing ability even further.

Mario began to identify with Italian. He was proud to make his familiarity with the language known whenever an occasion arose, despite his limited knowledge. At 6;0, when an Italian visited the home he was quick to cite this ability.

Mario's father introduces the visitor, adding that he is Italian, to which the child replies:

Mario: ¿Italiano? Yo hablo italiano. (*Italian? I speak Italian*).
Papá (surprised): ¿Sí? ¿Qué sabes decir? (*Really? What do you know how to say?*)
Mario (hesitatingly): Mangia . . . lascia il naso . . . mangia tutto . . . (*Eat . . . leave your nose alone . . . eat everything*).
(He then continues with the following improvisations, using Spanish words with Italian sounds, and occasionally translating meanings.)
No ǧ i habla. Eso es 'no hables.'
Ǧi avioncito . . . e ǧi avionzote.
Pičístola es 'pistola' . . . ¿es así?
J̌acula es 'dracula'
Ǧigante
Ǧi sposa
Fagiolini
Špina es 'espina' . . .

Despite his fascination with Italian, the child's knowledge remained mostly receptive so that when he found himself in the presence of an Italian family at 9;5 he was at a loss to respond. The eight-year-old Niccola expressed surprise at first to find others who spoke Italian and said to his mother: Chi sono? Parlano come noi (*Who are they? They speak like us*). Mario understood but was unable to express himself and, instead, said as an aside to his mother: "Mamá, me vas a enseñar italiano para hablar con el nene, ¿ok?" (*Mamá, teach me Italian so I can speak with the little boy, ok?*). Yet even this limited ability was to serve as a basis for rapid development in productive Italian when Mario was to make his first trip to Italy just a few years later.

Mario was quite receptive to trying to say things he had not previously experienced. At 3;7, he heard the expression "aloha" upon arrival in Hawaii, and he immediately adopted its use. He was also curious about sounds he heard. Overhearing some children speaking Japanese on the beach a few days later, he ran over to his parents and asked: "¿Qué hablan 'í-á-ó, í-á-ó'?" (*What are they speaking 'í-á-ó, í-á-ó'?*), giving his rendition of the sounds of Japanese. He also imitated French which was spoken once at the breakfast table during the visit of a young woman from France: "Bla-la-la-la". He was intrigued by the sounds of Portuguese which he heard his father speak to a friend, especially since it was similar enough to comprehend, but somehow "sounded" strange. Taking his father aside, he whispered secretly: "¿Por qué habla así chistoso, papá? ¿Es payaso? Parece payaso." (*Why does he speak funny like that, papá? Is he a clown? He seems like a clown*).

On a variety of occasions over the next years, Mario exhibited interest in still other languages. Having no notion that many of the languages with which he had contact are often considered "exotic" or "esoteric" by many adults, he approached all with a singularly positive attitude, assuming that any and all were within his grasp. These included languages like Japanese, German, Twi, Greek, Aymara and Quechua.

Age 6;7 On an aeroplane returning from Venezuela he sits across from two Japanese children and is intrigued by their speech and by the comic book on monsters which they are reading. Mario comments: Quiero ir al Japón, papá. La señora (japonesa) dice que en japonés se empieza el libro de acá, ¿verdad? (*I want to go to Japan, papá. The Japanese woman says that in Japan they begin a book from the rear, right?*)

Age 7;9 Mario is intrigued by a German-speaking couple visiting the home. He asks the woman how to say various things and he repeats eagerly.

Age 8;0 He is very interested in various forms of writing. He tries to learn the Greek alphabet from a book and to use it by writing English phonetically in Greek script as a sort of secret code.

Age 9;6 Mario meets an instructor of Twi, from Ghana, and strikes up a friendship. He asks many questions about the language and is fascinated by the number system which he eventually figures out.

Age 10;8 While in La Paz, Mario asks the maids to teach him Aymara; later in Potosí, he attempts to exchange English lessons for Quechua with the cook.

Throughout the diary a trend is clear. Mario showed increasing interest in the way people speak, in other ways to say things, and in other forms of language. He especially enjoyed linguistic play; for example, his mother was quite fluent in two forms of "Pig Spanish". Mario tried several times himself: "Lipi, lopo, opo, sipli", and "pili, lopo, lopo, lopo. . . ." (3;6). He also enjoyed the custom of saying "good night" in five different ways:

"Good night, buenas noches, buona notte, boa noite, kali nicta," pointing to each of his fingers as he said each one. Mario also knew that spelling and writing were other forms of communicating. As Mario's knowledge of Italian increased, his parents resorted to spelling to conceal meaning from the child. He had often heard "b-e-d" and "c-a-n-d-y" spelled aloud and he guessed at their meanings. Mario was exposed to reading and writing by age 3;4 and, although his exposure was limited and sporadic, he developed considerable talent for reading within one year (see Chapter 3, notes 3 & 4). In any case, his experience was sufficient to arouse his interest in graphic representations of speech as another manifestation of language.

Naming and labelling language systems

Since Mario did not yet know the names of different languages, he usually referred to languages he heard by reproducing what struck him as the prominent sound characteristics (as illustrated above). To refer to his own language he usually said something to the effect: "Como estoy hablando ahora" (*Like I'm speaking right now*). In fact it was not until 3;6 that he first used the term "español" (*Spanish*) to label the language which he and his family spoke. This occurred in response to his mother who asked him which channel he wanted as she turned the TV dial. Hearing Spanish suddenly as she changed stations, he shouted: "¡Ese! ¡En español!" (*That one! In Spanish!*). Prior to this time he never seemed to understand what the term Spanish or English meant. And although he now used the term "Spanish" to refer to his own code, he still did not grasp what English referred to. "Español" was Mario's tongue; everyone else simply spoke differently. At 3;7 his mother told him to say "buenas noches" in English but he did not know which language she meant. However, spontaneous use of the label for Spanish became more frequent in his speech; witness the following conversation at 3;9 with his mother:

Playing with a teddy bear on the floor, Mario said to his mother:
Mario: Yo lo (*sic*) hablo al oso "español" . . . digo "mamá 'stá enfema (enferma)." (*I speak to the bear in "Spanish" . . . and I tell him "mamá is sick."*)
Later, overhearing his mother speaking in the kitchen, he asked — with peculiar influence from Italian:
Mario: ¿Mamá, qué PARLAS (hablas)? (*Mamá, what are you speaking?*)
Mamá: Español, amor. (*Spanish, dear.*).

When he finally incorporated the term "English" into his lexicon, he showed signs of confusion as to which label referred to which language. At 3;9 he erroneously told his father "habla español" when he really meant that his father should translate something for him into English. However, the following day during the visit of a Chilean woman who spoke English and Spanish mixed in the same conversation, he instructed everyone: "No inglés . . . ¡español!" (*No English . . . Spanish!*). But for the most part, Mario still used no label to designate the English language. By 4;2 he continued the device of referring to languages by their users, saying: ". . . como hablan los nenes," or ". . . como hablo yo," (. . . *the language the children speak, . . . the language I speak.*) Once, when his father read to him in Italian from a magazine, Mario interrupted:

Mario: Papá, habla como yo. (*Papá, speak like me*).
Papá: ¿Cómo? (*How?*) (trying to elicit the label).
Mario: Como hablabas . . . (*Like you were talking . . .*).

However, a few months later, by 4;6, he apparently clarified the association between labels and languages and now used "inglés" steadily for English and "español" for Spanish:

Mario: Papá, ¿cómo se dice . . . en inglés? (*Papá, how do you say . . . in English?*)

Using language to learn language

The technique of asking for translations became an effective tool for expanding his linguistic knowledge. For example, at 4;1, he asked his father: "Papá, ¿cómo se dice: yo tilé (tiré) mi chicle en el basulelo (basurero)?" (*Papá, how do you say: I threw my gum in the trash basket?*). Also at the same age he asked for translations of words he heard in English: "¿Cómo se dice 'play' en español?" (*How do you say 'play' in Spanish?*). Again, a few days later when an English-speaking visitor was in the home:

Visitor (to Mario): No, they're going to study.
Mario (turns to Mother): Mamá, ¿qué es 'estudy?' (*Mamá, what is 'study'?*).
Mother: Estudiar.
Mario (to visitor): O.K. Let's go study.

In the years which follow, the diary is replete with references to the use of translations both across languages as well as requests to clarify meanings within the same language.

Bilinguality and plurilingualism

As the child's language systems diverged in form, function and label, he became increasingly aware of his own bilinguality and that of others. At age 4;2 he contrasted his own ability with his cousin's:

Mario: Papá, yo hablo dos (holding up 2 fingers). Lisa (his cousin) sólo habla uno (holding up one finger). (*Papá, I speak two languages. Lisa only speaks one.*)

A few days later (a period when Italian was increasingly spoken), he said while listening to an Italian conversation at the table:

Mario: Mira, yo hablo así (holding up 2 fingers). Cuando yo sea grande, voy a avlar (hablar) así, (holding up 3 fingers). (*Look, I speak this many languages. When I grow up, I'm going to speak this many.*)

He showed interest in knowing what languages various persons spoke and, when he could not deduce this himself, he asked, as in this case just before Halloween at 4;3:

Mario: Papá, papá . . . ¿las brujas hablan así? ¿Como yo, así? (pointing a finger to his mouth). (*Papá, papá . . . do witches speak like this? Like me, like this?*)

He also commented on language differences, evidenced in the following example at age 4;4 when speaking of his cousin of the same age:

Mario: Ah, pero yo le digo "¿cómo?" . . . y él dice "please, please." (*Oh, but I say "cómo" to him . . . and he says "please, please".*) El no habla como yo. (*He doesn't speak like me.*)

The next example at 4;4 also reflects his interest in the differing verbal capability of people:

Nursemaid: ¿Cuántos idiomas habla Lisa (a cousin)? (*How many languages does Lisa speak?*)
Mario: Uno.
Nursemaid: ¿Y tú? (*And you?*)
Mario: Dos. (*Two.*)
Nursemaid: ¡Tú eres bilingüe! (*You're bilingual!*)
Mario: ¿¿Sí?? ¿Cómo hablan los bilingues? ¿Cómo? (*Really? How do bilinguals speak? How?*)
¡Díme! Se me olbidó (olvidó). (*Tell me! I forgot.*)
Nursemaid: Bueno, hablan dos idiomas como inglés y español. (*Well, they speak two languages like English and Spanish.*)
Mario: ¿Por qué (Lisa) habla uno? ¿Por qué sólo dice "Come on . . . "? (*How come Lisa speaks one? How come she can only say "Come on . . ."?*)

And at age 5;5, he commented on his own multilinguality. On a boat crossing Lake Titicaca, he was asked by a German–Spanish speaking woman

what languages he spoke, to which he replied: "español, inglés, italiano."
He also remarked on the plurilinguality of others during the same trip. For
example, he met a Brazilian child on the boat who spoke Portuguese, and
also English, which they both had in common. Mario commented on this to
his mother:

> **Mario**: Es como yo . . . habla dos cosas. (*He's like me . . . he speaks two
> things.*)
> Yo hablo español e inglés, y él habla inglés y . . . ? (forgetting the
> name of the other language) (*I speak Spanish and English, and he
> speaks English and . . . ?*)
> **Mamá**: ¡Portugués! (*Portuguese!*)

Increasing contact with other languages helped Mario to formulate an
abstract concept of language. He seemed to understand that there were
many types of verbal activities which characterize human beings, each with
its own name. The following conversation which transpired on a train to the
Peruvian port of Puno shortly after Mario met the Portuguese-speaking boy
reflects this:

> **Mario**: Papá, ¿qué hablan? ¿Por qué hablan así? (*Papá, what are they
> speaking? Why do they speak like that?*)
> **Papá**: Hablan portugués. (*They're speaking Portuguese.*)
> **Mario**: ¿Por qué la gente habla diferente? (*How come people speak
> differently?*)
> **Papá**: Porque hay muchos idiomas. (*Because there's a lot of languages.*)
> **Mario**: ¿Qué son idiomas? (*What are languages?*)
> **Papá**: Tú sabes . . . tú hablas español e inglés; los alemanes hablan
> alemán, como Georg; los franceses hablan francés; los indios
> aymara. (*You know . . . you speak Spanish and English; Germans
> speak German, like Georg; French people speak French; the
> Indians, Aymara.*)
> **Mario**: ¿Qué es francés? (*What's French?*)
> **Papá**: Así: Comment allez vous? Je suis bien, etc. (*Like this: Comment
> allez vous? Je suis bien, etc.*)
> **Mario**: Ah . . . ¿y aymara? (*Oh . . . and Aymara?*)
> **Papá**: Como habla Basilio, así: Kamisaki, rákta . . . chachanáka,
> warmináka, llocaya . . . (*Like Basilio speaks, like this: Kamisaki,
> rákta . . . chachanáka, warmináka, llocaya . . .*)
> **Mario**: Ah. (*Oh.*)

Compare this awareness of multiple behaviours at age 5;5 with that of a
monolingual child of about nine whom Mario met in Albuquerque when he
was also that age:

Mario and his sister are playing by the swimming pool and talking to each other in Spanish. A new boy, Rodney, arrives with his mother. Hearing Mario and Carla speaking, he is surprised and asks:

Rodney (to everyone): Hey! What's wrong with you guys? Whatcha speaking?

Mario (to Rodney): Spanish.

Rodney (to his mother): Why do they speak to her (to Mario's mother) like that?

Mother (to Rodney): Well, 'cause the mother speaks Spanish.

Rodney: How come I can't speak like that?

Mario (to Rodney): I can teach you for an hour. Will that be all right?

Rodney: Yeh.

Summary

In summary, language differentiation evolved as part of an on-going process which began in the pre-speech period. Language sounds were only some of the many types of stimuli which surrounded the infant. The infant learned to differentiate those sounds which had meaning from those which did not. However, speech sounds were not employed indiscriminately; they occurred in sets, each belonging to a different language. The use of each set in separate circumstances assisted the child in relating each language to its appropriate context. The more separate the environments in which each language was used, the more rapidly and the more easily he learned to differentiate linguistic systems. Sufficient exposure to a set of alternates, and the need, enabled Mario to attain productive skills in two languages. Since he was also in contact with alternate codes, he learned that people also communicate in a variety of other ways. Mario was well aware that things were called in one of several possible ways, that the same story could be retold in another language (he was capable of doing this himself), and he knew that thoughts were convertible or translatable through other forms of expression. He was aware of a variety of codes, not only of Spanish, English and Italian, but also of others like Aymara, French, German, Twi, Japanese and Quechua. He knew that a code could be varied so as to make it sound funny or to render its messages less transparent such as in Pig Spanish. He knew too that communication was also transmitted through written symbols or oral spelling and he learned both as he advanced through school. Having mastered these codes he sought for still other codes (like Greek script) which were less extensively used and thereby afforded some secrecy or privacy. Furthermore he learned how to use language to find out more about language itself (metalanguage), by asking: "¿Cómo se dice?" and "¿Qué significa?" (*How do you say? What does it mean?*). He became increasingly analytical about the medium which so many take for granted as their sole form of expression. He demonstrated interest, for example, in the multiple meaning of some words ("'right' means three things"); and in peculiar usages ("Why do you call the car 'she'?"); as well as intuitions about the origins of words "'soufflé' sounds French").

Mario was conscious of, and commented on, his own bilinguality and the bilinguality of others. He was intrigued by the fact that some persons can speak several languages and wondered what it was like to speak only one. He learned to label each code he came across, showing he grasped language as an abstraction as well as speech. Mario behaved like a bilingual individual through his differentiated use of at least two systems, and he was fairly tenacious about the circumstances for using each. What remains to be seen is how he discerned which system to use and when.

TABLE 1 *Stages in language recognition, differentiation and bilingual development*

Age	Event	Observation
0;11	Recognition (Spanish)	First signs of recognition of some words.
1;4	First words (Spanish)	First active use of a few words.
1;8	Sound reproduction (Spanish)	Recognition of Spanish sounds with attempts to reproduce them.
1;10	Differentiation (Spanish)	Differentiation of Spanish from English and other languages present in the environment.
2;6	First words (English)	First active use of a few words.
2;7	Mixing	Considerable mixing of both languages.
2;8	Separation	Separation of the two systems in speech; comments on the English behaviour of others.
3;0	Two systems	Clear and consistent separation of Spanish and English, bilingual behaviour.
3;4	Recognition (Italian)	Recognition of Italian, the third "distinct" code.
3;4	Other forms	Demonstrates curiosity and interest in other forms of language (channels) such as reading, writing, spelling.
3;4– 3;8	Code/Context	Demonstrates established expectations concerning the *use* of Spanish and English in specific contexts.
3;6	Other codes	Shows curiosity in other languages and language play (Pig Spanish); imitates the "sound" of unfamiliar languages.
3;6	Spanish label	First spontaneous use of the label "Spanish" to identify his own language.
3;7	Awareness of other languages	Recognizes people speak other languages beyond Spanish and English; occasionally tries to imitate, rendering acoustic impressions.

Age	Event	Observation
3;8	First words (Italian)	First active use of an Italian phrase in appropriate context.
3;9	English label	First use of a label to describe the English language.
4;1	Metalanguage	First use of metalanguage to explore and expand his linguistic knowledge (asks for translations, Spanish–English).
4;2	Observes bilingualism	Comments on bilingual behaviour; shows interest in the languages people speak.
4;2	Acknowledges own bilingualism	Comments on his own bilingualism ("Yo hablo dos"/*I speak two*).
4;3	Curiosity in others' language(s)	Asks what language others speak when he can not deduce this for himself.
4;6	Use of labels	Fairly consistent use of labels to refer to Spanish and English.
4;9	Receptive use of Italian	Italian used as the language for storytelling; child demonstrates comprehension.
5;5	Comments on own multilingualism	Child comments on his own multilingualism — the knowledge of 3 languages — for the first time.
5;8	Linguistic analysis	Asks questions about specific aspects and use of linguistic forms.
5;8	Recognizes "foreign accents"	Aware of "foreign accents" and can identify when speaker is non-native of Spanish or English.
6;0	Semantic insights	Aware of non-equivalence of words across languages and multiple meanings of some words.
6;0	Intensified interest in other languages	Interest in other forms of communication intensified, and persists (Italian, 6;0; Japanese, 6;7; German, 7;9; Twi and Greek, 9;6; Aymara and Quechua, 10;8).
7;3	Identifies source of "foreign accents"	Aside from his awareness of accents foreign to Spanish and English, the child can identify when the accent in English is attributable to a Spanish-speaker, and vice-versa.
7;5	Judges proficiency of non-native speakers	Judges and comments on the relative proficiency level of non-native speakers of English or Spanish.
7;6	Curiosity in monolinguals	Shows curiosity in monolinguals and their perceptions of bilinguals.
7;11	Recognizes regional accents in English	Sensitive to regional language variations of English-speakers.
8;1	Recognizes regional accents in Spanish	Sensitive to regional language variations of Spanish-speakers.
8;2	Linguistic judgements sharpened	Increasingly capable of making judgements about the proficiency of non-native speakers (both English and Spanish).
9;0	Distinguishes some Spanish dialects	Develops ability not only to recognize language variations of Spanish-speakers, but also notes their specific characteristics.

Age	Event	Observation
9;1	Language intuition	Shows ability to make guesses as to origins of foreign words used in English.
10;6	Acquires Bolivian regionalisms	Incorporates Bolivian regionalisms into his own Spanish speech.

Language choice and the social variables

All speakers alter their language in various ways in relation to the particular social circumstances at the moment of the speech act. How these factors affect linguistic items is of central interest to sociolinguists; one prominent work in this area is a study by William Labov (1969, 1966). Others, like Joan Rubin (1970: 152–53) and Susan Ervin-Tripp (1970: 192–211), have concentrated more specifically on code switching among bilingual speakers.

The bilingual speaker presents an especially interesting opportunity for study in both areas. Not only does he command several "styles" of speech like everyone else, but he also has another option — that of switching from one entire language system to another. He can change from code to code in addition to modifying styles within the same code. These changes in language are not arbitrary or erratic behaviour, but rather are related to indentifiable social factors.

To be able to switch codes at all, active use of at least two languages is obviously required. The second requirement is an awareness of the basic social conditions which call for the use of one code or the other. Mario began active use of Spanish at 1;4, and English at 2;6. From the onset of his second tongue, he was immediately faced with the task of sorting appropriate linguistic sets for each situation. In other words, to communicate, he had to make an appropriate language choice — with the right persons, at the right time, and place. Although this seems an inordinate task for such a young child, mixing of Spanish and English — limited as they were — occurred for only a brief period of time.

Early signs of switching occurred within a few days of Mario's first production of English utterances. At this time he was visiting relatives in Philadelphia with his parents and nursemaid. This visit was previously described wherein Mario acquired many new lexical items and almost immediately began to sort them into sets — one for use with his parents and caretaker, the other with his grandparents and other relatives. The circumstances were quite clear — of the ten to 12 people with whom the child interacted, some used one code, others used another. Appropriate code choice depended entirely upon the interlocutor.

During the next two months, Mario's world consisted primarily of home and nursery. At home, Spanish, was the medium; at the nursery, it was English. Again the division of language use was clear, marked this time by place (or setting) *in addition to* interlocutors. Since this was a time of rapid acquisition, some mixing of codes occurred. However, transference occurred in only one direction — from English to Spanish. At home, Mario was prone to use the new words and expressions learned at the nursery; but on the other hand he was never reported to have used Spanish at the nursery. The utterances which Mario carried into the home were primarily commands, salutations, a demonstrative, and various expressive interjections common to children this age, such as "unhuh, yuk", and "ouch". For example:

> *Age 2;7* Hi! Oh boy! So long! Bye Bye! O.K. Thank you. Here it is! Yeh!
> *Age 2;8* Move! Watch! See that!
> *Age 2;9* O.K. Bye Bye! Open!

During this period of limited language, Mario apparently drew upon all of the linguistic resources available to him, knowing his parents understood both languages. However, when necessary, he also demonstrated ability to use only one language without borrowings. This was illustrated in the earlier account of his conduct with a little girl he met at a shopping centre in Austin, Texas. On this occasion at age 2;9, he spoke only English. The account is also important because it was the first time in which two variables (inter-locutor *and* setting) were relevant to his choice of code, by contrast with the incident in Philadelphia where only interlocutor was a factor to consider, the setting being constant. This development may be pictured as follows:

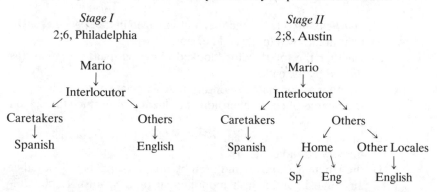

Stage I	*Stage II*
2;6, Philadelphia	2;8, Austin

In stage II, a public setting reinforced the choice of English as the language required, although some doubt was still possible within the home when interlocutors were not Mario's caretakers. From 3;0, Mario maintained clear and consistent separation of the two codes.

As Mario's world expanded, and also his interaction with people under still different circumstances, other factors complicated the picture. Other sociolinguistic studies suggest numerous factors which affect code switching in adults; some of these were cited earlier: the participants, setting, topic of discourse, the form of communication, and the function or norm of the interaction. Presumably these factors will eventually all come to bear on Mario's behaviour and language choice as he moves toward adulthood. But by 5;0, those factors affecting choice were still rather few. Interlocutor and setting were obviously the main determinants; however, most of the attributes of the participants (e.g. age, sex, and occupation) still had no effect upon the child's language choice. Two other aspects of interlocutor, however, did affect language choice — the physical characteristics of that person and his or her degree of proficiency in the language being used. Both will be discussed below. By age ten the same scheme generally prevailed. It is worth noting that one of the variables — topic — affecting code-switching in adult bilinguals had no effect on the child's language selection until nearly his tenth year. As his language use became increasingly specialized (and most significantly, through education), topical switches became more and more frequent.

A review of speech acts in Mario's diary reveals the following variables as most significant to language choice: speaker, setting, function, and the form of the act itself. Furthermore, it appears that this order also reflects their degree of importance to the child.[2] Let us consider each variable plus its relevant aspects:

1. *The participant(s)* (i.e. other persons engaged in the speech event):
   a) whether known to the child or not;
   b) whether the interlocutor "looked" Spanish-speaking or not (as judged by the child);
   c) whether an intimate or non-intimate associate of the child;
   d) the degree of comprehension and fluency with which the person used the code;
   e) his or her role, if relevant to the child (e.g. caretaker, babysitter, nursery attendant);
   f) the languages known and used by the participants (i.e. whether an English or Spanish monolingual or a Spanish–English bilingual);
   g) the verbal behaviour of the interlocutor (whether he or she

       maintained use of one code or engaged in frequent mixing or
switching behaviour);

  h) the accent and nativeness or non-nativeness of the speaker; and

  i) audience (i.e. other persons present).

2. *The setting:*
   a) whether the event took place in a predominantly Spanish-speaking locale (e.g. Bolivia, Mexico), or not;
   b) if an English-speaking setting, whether the event occurred in the home or in a public location; and
   c) whether a gathering of obvious Spanish-speakers (regardless of locale).

3. *Function* (i.e. the purpose and/or intended outcome of the speech event):
   a) whether the purpose of the speech act was "normal" communication and exchange of information (i.e. unmarked verbal behaviour); or
   b) to shock, amuse, or surprise the participants; or
   c) to underscore, replicate, or emphasize a previous statement;
   d) a translation or explanation of a previous comment (metalinguistic); or
   e) self-expression or private speech (the child to himself); or
   f) to exclude or include others; or
   g) to convey insistence, severity, or a command.

4. *Form* (i.e. the message couched in a special form as distinct from that used in normal conversation), such as:
   a) play;
   b) quoting, or citing a quotation;
   c) roleplay;
   d) story-telling;
   e) songs;
   f) jokes.

5. *Topic* (i.e. the content or subject of the conversation), such as:
   a) experiences had primarily through a particular language; and
   b) often technical or specialized areas of discussion.

Arranged hierarchically, the interlocutor or other participant in the speech event consistently emerged as the primary determinant. If the participant and the language he or she spoke were both known to the child, the code choice was obvious. Examples abound in the diary in which there was unequivocal use of the appropriate code. In mixed company which included speakers of both languages, Mario rapidly and naturally switched, as he alternately addressed each individual in the proper code. This was seen in previously cited anecdotes occurring at 3;0 and 3;4. Another example also at 3;4 was a visit to a New York apartment where monlingual speakers of Spanish and of English were both present. Mario invariably made appropriate language choices with each of the persons present. Many more examples were noted throughout the diary from that age on, often involving fairly complex social situations (see Appendix 2).

Complete switching was performed not only at the sentence level but even at the phonological level where single word cognates were involved, for example:

A little boy was speaking to Mario when his father interrupted:
Boy (to Mario): What's your name?
Mario (to Boy): Mario (pronounced /mǽrio/).
Father (to Mario): ¿Cómo le dijiste?
Mario (to Father): Mario (pronounced /mário/).

Or the following:

Mario and his father are watching television. The grandfather enters. Mario points to the man on the screen and identifies him:
Mario (to Grandfather): Look, doctor (/dáktor/).
Father (to Mario): ¿Quién es?
Mario (to Father): Doctor (/doktóř/).
Grandfather (to Mario): Who?
Mario (to Grandfather): Doctor (/dáktor/).

At another time:

Mario is calling his dog when his English-speaking cousin approaches:
Mario (calling the dog): Pepito, Pepito (/pepíto/).
Lisa (to Mario): What do you call him?
Mario (to Lisa): His name, Pepito (/pʰepʰítow/).

Attributes of interlocutors

Known/Unknown. In cases where the interlocutor was unknown to the child and there were doubts as to the language he or she spoke, Mario faced an arbitrary choice between Spanish and English. There was normally no question when this occurred in a Spanish-speaking environment; the resultant code was obviously Spanish. When the event occurred in an English-speaking environment (whether in the home or in a public place) English was the normal choice, unless Mario judged the interlocutor to be a Spanish-speaker based on certain physical characteristics.

Physical Characteristics of the Speaker. The child was accustomed to meeting some people in English-speaking environments who did in fact speak Spanish so that he was forced to consider other attributes. Their physical characteristics therefore became mediating considerations. If the speaker was clearly a Latin type (in Mario's perception), this fact normally overruled the choice which might have been determined by the setting.

By age 2;8 Mario had obviously begun classifying people on the basis of their looks. Time and again he identified racial types as he perceived them. On the street he singled out an Oriental-looking girl as 'japonesita''; he did the same with a playmate at his nursery (who turned out to be Chinese). In magazines and also on a wall poster he identified all Oriental types with the label "japoneses". His attention was attracted to several Black children on television and also on wall posters for whom he improvised the term /nigo/, i.e. "negro", simply by association with the colour black ("negro", in Spanish). "Latin" types he classified with the label "mexicanos", their most distinguishing characteristics being dark skin, eyes and hair, and sometimes moustaches and big hats (according to pictures he had seen). Within these broad categories which he created — each with a label — he included other races or nationalities, as best they fit; e.g. an Afghan friend was also called "mexicano", and was therefore addressed initially in Spanish until no response was obtained.

An excellent example of the child's attention to physical types is evident in the following anecdote, recorded at age 6;6. Mario had flown from New York to Caracas with his parents to spend a vacation with relatives. The elapsed time from departure to arrival at his aunt's apartment in Caracas was only a matter of hours. Mario was received at the door by the maid whom he greeted spontaneously in English. Everyone was amused and puzzled over his assumption that the maid spoke English (rather than Spanish). In this case, however, the maid was Black and up to that point the child's experiences led him to believe that all Negroes spoke English. He now found this not to be true. Moments later, Mario went into the kitchen to ask for something and again, without thinking, addressed the maid in English. This time, however, he realized his error and immediately switched to Spanish.

Intimate/Non-Intimate. When the interlocutor was not a native Spanish-speaker, but had an especially intimate relationship with the child, Mario used English but with an interesting inclination — almost an expressed desire — to switch intermittently to Spanish. This occurred at various times with two persons in particular. The first was a close family friend who was especially gentle and showed considerable interest in Mario. The other was an elementary school teacher who liked small children and who had also shown interest and affection. Mario knew they spoke only English, yet he slipped back and forth into Spanish. He did this with no one else.

Because Spanish was the language of his home, and a language associated with persons of intimacy, it conveyed a degree of unity and affection not yet attributed to English. Mario's frequent interjections in Spanish seemed an attempt to convey this to his two special friends. This is plausible since there were no persistent attempts to interject English when speaking with Spanish-speaking interlocutors (also intimately related to the child).

Degree of Comprehension and Fluency. The degree of proficiency with which people spoke was another factor affecting language choice. This implies judgements concerning the fluency, accuracy and oftentimes the pronunciation of his interlocutors. The child's ability in this respect was manifested in numerous cases, recorded from about his fourth year on. For example, between his fourth and fifth years, Mario met several individuals who, having studied Spanish, achieved varying degrees of oral ability. Some of these persons tried enthusiastically to speak with him in Spanish, but often not convincingly enough. When he sensed that others spoke in an "artificial" manner, he normally switched back to English, often despite their attempts to maintain the conversation in Spanish. The reverse was noted in Mexico and Bolivia when people tried English with him. Mario responded in English only when the interlocutor's speech was fluent and natural.

At 5;0 while in kindergarten in Texas, Mario was confounded by Mexican American children who constantly mixed codes. Consider the following incident:

> Mario's father met him one day after classes at school. Mario was observed playing with several Mexican–American classmates and despite their frequent switching between English and Spanish, all of Mario's comments to them were in English. His father asked about this:
>
> **Papá**: Mario, ¿por qué no hablas en español con esos nenes? (*Mario, how come you don't speak Spanish with those children?*)
> **Mario**: Ah, esos nenes no hablan muy bien. (*Oh, those kids don't speak very well.*)

The interpretation drawn was that Mario's judgement about their linguistic ability stemmed from the fact that he himself was unaccustomed (and probably unable) to switch within the same discourse to the extent that his friends did.

However, Mario eventually showed increasing acceptance of this form of behaviour among some people. For example, on one occasion a year later, a family friend who was a graduate student of Spanish stopped by to visit for a few days before leaving for Spain. During the first moments, the student spoke Spanish, but his limited fluency began to give way to English as the conversation continued, with only occasional reversion to Spanish. Mario likewise spoke Spanish to him initially but used increasing English in response to increasing English used by the guest. English continued except when the visitor addressed Mario in Spanish, in which case Mario responded accordingly. Nonetheless, most switches were made, if not at the discourse level, certainly at the sentence level. Switching within the same utterance was still a rarity except for occasional lexical borrowings.

A second example was noted in the diary at age 7;1 during the visit of a Filipino friend. Although her Spanish was also limited in some areas of vocabulary, her pronunciation and fluency were close to that of a native. Nonetheless, she also mixed Spanish and English throughout her conversations. Mario did likewise when speaking to her, accommodating his speaking pattern to hers. In general he appeared to take the cue from his interlocutors. It was noted also that even though English was the language in use, Mario took the liberty of switching to Spanish at certain critical moments. When he recalled something experienced in Spanish, or when excited, he sometimes reverted to Spanish. A bilingual interlocutor who did considerable codeswitching, like this Filipino friend, cued Mario to utilize both codes in a manner not normally observed with his parents or with monolingual English-speakers.

Attempts to prime the child to speak a given language normally failed; the child clearly made his own selections. For example, when Mario was 7;5, a Bolivian meal was prepared for several students of Spanish who were invited to the home. The intent, in part, was to have them practise Spanish throughout the evening. Mario was coached and instructed to speak only Spanish when the guests came. However, when the first individual arrived, Mario looked him up and down (he was a tall fair individual) and immediately interrogated the guest:

> **Mario** (to Student): Do you speak Spanish? (in disbelief)
> **Student** (to Mario): Well . . . not very well.
> **Mamá** (from the kitchen): Háblale en español, Mario. (*Speak to him in Spanish, Mario.*)
> **Mario** (to Mamá): ¡Tú me mentiste, mamá! (*You lied to me, mamá.*)

Besides deducing Mario's ability to judge linguistic performance through observation of his behaviour, several of his own commentaries confirmed this. At age 7;2 Mario observed an actor on television extolling the virtues of the Cordova auto (Ricardo Montalbán, a Mexican movie star). Mario was quick to comment on Montalbán's speech:

> **Mario**: Ese señor habla español, pero poco inglés, ¿verdad?, papá. (*That man speaks Spanish, but only a little English. Right, papá?*)
> **Papá**: Sí, es cierto. (*Yes, that's right.*)

The following day Mario witnessed the same advertisement and added:

> **Mario**: Aquí está otra vez el señor que habla español . . . Habla *mucho* español y poco inglés, ¿verdad? (*Here's that man again who speaks Spanish . . . He speaks a lot of Spanish and a little English. Right?*)

At a later date (age 8;2), Mario returned home from school one day and reported the following:

> **Mario** (to Parents): Un señor de mi escuela habla poquito español. (*A man in my school speaks some Spanish.*)
> **Papá**: ¿Cómo sabes? (*How do you know?*)
> **Mario**: ¡Me habló! (*He spoke to me!*)
> **Papá**: ¿Y tú, le hablaste en español? (*And did you speak to him in Spanish?*)
> **Mario**: No . . .
> **Papá**: ¿Por qué? (*How come?*)
> **Mario**: No habla bien. (*He doesn't speak well.*)

Role. Thus far the role of the interlocutor has had no effect on code choice with but one exception — the babysitter. Mario demonstrated a propensity to speak Spanish with the girls who came to babysit. He often did this in spite of his knowledge that they spoke English. This tendency probably resulted form his previous linguistic relationship with all other persons in a caretaker role. For over five years, Mario had nursemaids from Latin America with whom he used only Spanish. For this reason, it is understandable that he felt inclined to use Spanish with his babysitters as well, given their particular role and relationshp to him. It was somewhat unnatural and artificial to use English with an individual in a caretaker role.

More on setting

If a speech event occurred in a predominantly Spanish-speaking setting such as Mexico or Bolivia, the choice of code was obvious. In English-speaking environments such as Texas, Florida, Philadelphia, New York and Vermont, however, English was the usual language choice outside the home, after considering any obviating aspects related to the speaker.

Mario developed a fairly good concept of "place" or setting. Frequent trips to the same locations helped to establish the notion meant when one said "Vermont" or "La Paz". Naturally he did not understand these with a sense of distance, time, directionality, but each term did evoke appropriate sets of words related to the place in question. For example, some of the responses elicited at age 2;10 to each of the following places named were:

Vermont: nieve (snow), skiis, tractor rojo (red tractor), Bimba (his dog), el kilto (the swing), Marina, Georg, snowsuit.

Philadelphia: grandmom or nonna, grandpop or nonno, Billy chiquito (his cousin), Robertino, Zia, juguetes (toys).

New York: Isabel, Tía Pochi-Pochi, Enrique, su bigote (his moustache).

La Paz: abuelita (grandmother), abuelito (grandfather), Basilio, Tinky (the dog), indios (Indians), nenes (children).

Oaxtepec: Blanca, piscina (swimming pool), la torre (the tower), los carritos que van al cielo (the cars that go to the sky; i.e. funicular cars).

Acapulco: pirata (pirate), barco (boat), piscina (swimming pool), Pedrito.

Texas: Sharon, el parque (the park), la bicicleta (the bicycle), Taco Bell, bichos (bugs), the bunny rabbit.

All these word associations were correctly related to their proper setting.

In a similar manner, Mario had notions about what language was to be expected on an airplane, especially if that plane was boarded from a setting in which English was spoken. For example, on his flight to Caracas, referred to earlier, Mario heard Spanish spoken and commented with obvious surprise:

Mario (to Parents): ¡Todos hablan español aquí! (*Everybody speaks Spanish here!*)

The plane was obviously considered an extension of the English-speaking setting. Yet when different passengers later addressed him in Spanish or English, he responded appropriately in each case. One gentleman also asked Mario his name in Italian:

Passenger: Come ti chiami? (*What's your name?*)
Mario: Mario.

But when the gentleman continued his conversation in Italian, Mario responded in English which suggests again that the plane was considered a setting where English was appropriate.

Various "channels" might also be considered as extensions of their setting. For example, it was normal for the child to expect that in an English-speaking milieu the television, radio and telephone were all devices through which English was heard and used. The same held true for these media in a Spanish-speaking environment. When occasional Spanish was heard on the radio or television in Vermont, the child inevitably commented or showed surprise. Also, when Mario answered the telephone in Vermont his first comments were always in English, even though it was fairly common for the person at the other end of the line to be his mother or father, calling from work.

Aspects of function

If the purpose of a speech act was the exchange of information, or when its primary intent was of a purely referential nature, Spanish or English was used in accordance with considerations stipulated above. However, when Mario had another purpose in mind (such as to surprise, amuse or shock his interlocutors) then the language choice was often "marked" by being the reverse of what might be considered normal for the situation. For example, when Mario wished to amuse his parents, he jokingly spoke English; to tease his grandparents, he sometimes rattled words off in Spanish; to exclude his aunt, he defiantly persisted speaking Spanish in her presence in spite of her protests.

Abundant evidence of marked behaviour is found in the diary. For example, the following events both occurred on the same day at age 8;1, and illustrate the use of language both to include and exclude various individuals.

Mario was in the car with his parents on his way to the General Store. Crossing a covered bridge, Mario sees some bathers in the river below and yells out the window in Spanish:

Mario (to bathers): ¡Cállense ustedes! (*Keep quiet!*)
Mamá (to Mario) (Surprised): ¡Alvino Mario! ¡No se dice así a la gente! (*Don't speak to people that way!*)
Mario: Ah, pero no entienden. No saben español . . . (*But they don't understand. They don't know Spanish.*)

Thinking about that for a while, he then adds:

Mario: Mamá, así puedo hablarte mucho. Si veo un señor, puedo decir: ¡Mamá, mira un señor gordo! (*Mamá, I can say a lot to you like this. If I see a man, I can say: Mamá, look at that fat man!*)
Mamá: Ah, y en Bolivia puedes hablar inglés. (*And in Bolivia you can speak English.*)

Mario: No, en Bolivia mucha gente sabe inglés. (*No, in Bolivia too many people know English.*)

Later, the same day, Mario was in the kitchen where his grandmother who was visiting was preparing a meal. His mother was also present. Mario began to speak English to his mother who immediately corrected him, telling him to speak Spanish. Mario protested by saying that he wanted Grandmom to hear.

Finally, another interesting example of code switching to permit privacy in public places was recorded several years later at age 10;8. In this case, Mario and his father were in La Paz, Bolivia, walking down the main thoroughfare:

Mario spots some individuals who are obviously foreign, and assumes they are American. Since they are at a distance, he switches to English so that other Bolivians nearby will not understand.

Mario (Lowering his voice): They look like Americans.
Papá: Why?
Mario: 'Cause they look like hippies.
Papá: Oh, are all hippies here American?
Mario: Well, most.

When Mario was unconcerned with the effects of his speech upon others, but spoke primarily as a form of self-expression, the language chosen varied with his mood, his thoughts, or his feelings at the moment. However, in most cases of private speech (or thinking aloud), Mario used Spanish. Consider the following notation recorded at age 6;1:

An English-speaking friend was visiting, Mario was showing her his book of drawings and pointing out various details:

Mario: Here it is (pointing to a specific page). The one that you didn't saw (*sic*). His name is Shazam? (Then thinking out loud to himself, he says): Algo 'ta mal. (*Something's wrong.*) (Turns again to the friend)
Mario (to Friend): Wait a minute.
Friend: That's O.K.
Mario: No, we saw dis one (confused). Oh, have ta start all over again. (Then shouting to mother in the kitchen): Mamá, pregúntale a Dios si vimos a esta parte. (*Mamá, ask God if we already saw this part.*)
Mamá: Dice que sí. (*He says "yes."*)
Mario (to Friend): I was going . . . turning da page daet (*that*) way.
Friend: No this way.

In other cases of private speech, Spanish was also the language heard when the child spoke aloud while sleeping or dreaming. An exception to this occurred at age 10;0 a few days after he returned from a summer camp. While asleep that night, and obviously dreaming, he shouted out in English: "Wait, Wait! I want to show you something." However, this was a rather untypical example.

A rather common function of code switching was to emphasize, underscore or replicate something just said in the first language. Examples are scattered throughout the diary:

> **Mario** (to Mamá): Mira . . . look, look!
> **Mario** (to Papá): Ven, ven, papá; come!
> **Mario** (to Mamá): Batís (Beatriz), ven aquí; come on!
> **Mario** (to Witch): Get auta (out of) here . . . fuera, fuera, fuera!

This technique was commonly noted and generally revealed the severity, urgency, or persistence of the child's requests or commands. Although this type of code switch did not always obtain the desired results from the child's caretakers, at the very least it usually guaranteed their attention. The marked use of English invariably brought a reaction, if only to remark in response, "¡Habla español!" (*Speak Spanish!*)

Finally, code switching provided a convenient metalinguistic device. It allowed the child to step out of one language system and to consider it from the vantage point of a second system. In this way, it permitted him to analyse and explain the system by going outside of itself.

> At age 9;6, Mario and his papá are having a conversation:
> **Papá**: ¿Cómo sabes todo eso? (*How do you know that?*)
> **Mario**: Porque sí . . . soy astuto. (*Just because . . . I'm astute*).
> **Papá** (surprised by the word used): ¿Qué es eso? (*What's that?*)
> **Mario**: "Astute" (he says in English).
> **Papá**: Sí, ¿pero que significa? (*Yes, but what does it mean?*)
> **Mario**: Bright, smart . . . and sneeky!

Explanations about the meaning of words, or other aspects of language, were commonly sought for in this way, or provided by others in the other language.

Aspects of form

Another consideration which invariably affected language choice was the "form" of the communicative act. When the speech act was in the form of a normal dialogue, then all the usual considerations affecting language choice prevailed. When the act assumed some special form, however, such as when Mario was engaged in a roleplay, quoting someone, using play language, singing or telling a joke, then language choice was often affected by considerations related to the specific form of the act. Mario sometimes recounted an experience, for example, in the language in which the experience occurred, especially if the interlocutors were his parents. Obviously if the interlocutors were monolinguals he narrated the experience in the only language they understood. Storytelling, likewise, was sometimes done in the same language in which Mario had originally heard the narration; or, if he translated the story, he often preserved key phrases and expressions in the original. For example, in retelling the story of Jack and the Beanstalk to his younger sister, Mario used Spanish, but preserved key items in Italian (age 5;3):

> Había una vez, Giacomo era muy pobre. Tenía tres FAGIOLINIS mágicos (/májikos/). Y crecieron y crecieron al cielo. Giacomo (/jíakomo/) subió y vino un gigante (/jigante/).
> (*Once upon a time, Jack was very poor. He had three magic beans. And they grew and they grew up to the sky. Jack climbed up and a giant came along.*)

Or, when recounting the story of The Three Little Pigs, he enjoyed uttering the key phrases in either Spanish or English, since he had heard this story in both languages:

> **Mario**: I'll huff and I'll puff and I'll blow your house in.
> Or:
> **Mario**: Soplaré y soplaré y tu casa derrumbaré.

Quotations were normally spoken in the language of the original utterance, provided the audience understood that language:

> *Age 3;5* — Recounting a show seen on television which pictured Lucille Ball in a hijacked aeroplane, Mario referred to her as 'la loca' (*'the crazy woman'*).
> **Mario** (to Papá): Tú viste la loca que va en l'ayón (avión) y dice: 'Sticki.'
> (*Did you see the crazy woman who goes on the airplane and says: 'Stick 'em up.'*)
> Y tenía un chaleco para que no se caigue (caiga) l'ayón. (*And she had a lifevest in case the plane fell.*
> Y un policía . . . um . . . "wha happin?" (*And a policeman asked: 'what happened'?*)
> Y va con Zipi Mooney. Palece (parece) un ayón gande (grande).
> (*And he goes with Mister Mooney. It looks like a big aeroplane.*)

Age 3;6 — Quoting a playmate.
Mario (to Papá): Cory (a friend) dice (says): "Come play my toys!"

Age 3;6 — Quoting his teacher at the nursery.
Mario (to Papá): "Come here, you no do dat no more! Mario, what you do? You don't no more! . . . bam, bam (spanking)."

Age 8;10 — Mario meets a woman and discovers that her husband was a substitute teacher one day in his class. He tells his parents, quoting something the teacher said (and replicating at the same time):
Mario: . . . que en esa clase había un muchachito que era "something else" . . . muy especial. (. . . *that there was a little boy in that class who was "something else" . . . very special.*)

Age 9;3 — Conversing with his sister, they recall a TV show they have seen about a giant:
Mario: Después viene un gigante. (*And then a giant came.*)
Carla: Sí, otro gigante más chico. (*Yes, another smaller giant.*)
Mario: Lo mordió. Sí el penúltimo trata de saltar a su pantalón. "The Three Sillys" se llamaban. (*He bit him. Yes, the next to the last one tries to jump on his pants. They are called "The Three Sillys."*)
Carla: Sí, y una cosa allí que decían . . . "they're gonna kill us." (*Yes, and something they said there . . . "they're gonna kill us."*)

Age 10;5 — Mario is recounting the news he has just witnessed on TV:
Mario: Mamá, en vez de cantar "death" al Shah, están cantando "death" a "Jimmy Carter." (*Mamá, instead of singing "death to the Shah," they're singing "death to Jimmy Carter."*)
Carla: (Playing behind the sofa with her dolls) ¿Por qué dijeron "death?" . . . A mí, me gusta Jimmy Carter. (*Why did they say "death" . . . I like Jimmy Carter.*)

Roleplaying was usually performed in the language of the persons being portrayed:

Age 3;7 — Mario instructed his father to pretend he was David; Mario assumed the role of Jerry. Both were friends from the nursery:
Mario (to Papá): I'm Jerry. You David.
Papá: Oh, do you want to play?
Mario: Unhuh.
Papá: What do you have?
Mario: Motorcycle, boat.
Papá: Where are the toys?
Mario: In der (there) (pointing to other room). Les (let's) go play. David, for you, David (handing over a toy).
Mother calls from kitchen to announce that breakfast is ready.

Mario (to Papá): Les go, David!
Mario (to Mamá): Waita minute.
Entering kitchen, he forgot the game.
Mario (to Mamá): Mamá cheyo (quiero) ese ceyál (cereal). (*Mamá, I want that cereal.*)

The choice of the language used for play was usually determined by the children playing with Mario, and in this sense, followed the usual pattern in which interlocutor was the primary consideration affecting code. However, when he played alone or with his sister, there was a high degree of code-switching to English presumably as they addressed comments to imaginary playmates, also English-speakers, or when they themselves assumed roles such as cowboys. Yet note that Spanish was always used when comments were expressions of his own thoughts said aloud:

An imaginary dialogue with a playmate which became a monologue, followed by a question to his mother:

Age 3;5
Mario: Yo tengo un juguete. (*I have a toy.*)
　　　Oh yes?
　　　Mi mamá . . . o wha happen? Mayo (Mario) está domido (dormido). (*Mario's asleep*) At' boy, come on. I call a doctor.
Mario (to Mamá): Mamá, ¿dónde está mi "doctor oídos"? (*Mamá, where's my "doctor ears"*; i.e. stethoscope.)

Age 3;6 — Dialogue with imaginary friend:
Mario: You bad boy.
　　　Nofing (nothing) da toys.
　　　No toys for you.
　　　No, you no play toys . . . you baby. (No, you don't play with the toys . . . you are a baby).
　　　I no baby, I love you.

Age 6;0 — Playing alone and speaking aloud to an imaginary person:
Mario: Now you look what [ču] (you) done . . . an' you look out for dat (that) monster.

Age 8;11 — Mario and Carla are playing cowboys in a large closet and converse entirely in English, attempting to speak like cowboys do. However, whenever they step out of these roles and give instructions on the side, or protests, they revert to Spanish.

Songs were naturally sung in the language in which learned:

Age 7;2 — Mario sitting on the floor, playing and singing:
Mario: I'M been workin' on the railroad . . . etc. (Father interrupts and corrects)
Papá (to Mario): I'VE been . . .
Mario (resumes singing): I've been workin' on the railroad . . . etc.

Jokes were also preserved in the original, if the interlocutors were capable of understanding in the language in which expressed:

Age 7;4
Mario (to Parents): What did the bird say when his cage got broken? Cheap, cheap.

However, several incidents were noted when Mario's interlocuters were monolinguals with no knowledge of the language of the joke. In such cases, Mario attempted to translate the joke in order to share it with the other participants:

Mario (to Caretaker): ¿Qué dijo el pájaro cuando se le rompió la jaula? . . . Barato, barato. (???)

Despite valiant attempts to convey the joke through direct translation, Mario was confounded by its lack of humour and the lack of response from his caretaker. He was aware that something was not quite right but was unable to convey the point of the joke. Several more years were required for him to grasp that the humour revolved around a play on words which could not be replicated in the other language.

Another example at age 9;9 shows clear code switching with his parents, from his initial announcement in Spanish that he was going to tell a joke, and the telling of the joke itself in English:

Mario (to Parents): Les voy a contar un chiste. (*I'm going to tell you a joke.*) Um . . . there was a boy so dumb . . . (he interjects) Esto saqué de BOY'S LIFE . . .) (*I got this out of* BOY'S LIFE . . .) . . . that when he looked in the mirror, he often wondered where he had seen himself before.

This incident clearly shows how although a joke was a form which elicited the language of its original telling (in this case English), the basic interaction was maintained in the unmarked language. Hence, both the prefatory remarks and the child's interjections evoked switches to Spanish which is normal for use with his parents.

Code switching by topic

Topical code switching was almost unknown to the child until nearly his tenth year. Up to this point, no topic was apparently so complex or so technical that it required a switch of codes in order to express himself on the item. What was obvious, however, was that some topics related to experiences in English, often produced increased lexical borrowing or interference although not a complete code switch. As the child progressed through the educational system, in English, moreover, his tendency to switch codes intensified when discussing homework and other school subjects. These tendencies were often thwarted by the parents' insistence that he maintain their conversation in Spanish. However by about fifth grade (age ten), he had entered into realms of experience for which he had no counterpart in Spanish. A clear example was an attempt to prepare for a fifth grade test on the topic of "The Industrial Revolution in England and France". It soon became clear that it was an impossibility to try to constrain the child to review materials read and discussed at school — in English — through Spanish. With this incident, topical switching became a fairly well established procedure when discussing other school topics, including science, mathematics and the like.

At age 10;1, an incident was recorded, demonstrating again topical switching. In this case, Mario was at a lake with family friends. Although the conversation about swimming was in Spanish, when he attempted to explain how to do a crawl stroke, he simply did not have the Spanish words easily accessible. Technical discussion of the stroke caused him to switch codes. It became obvious that both academic topics and technically complex ones began to play a significant part in his code switching behaviour.

Analysis of significant variables

An analysis done of the social variables which affected Mario's choice of code at age 5;0 is expressed in chart form (Figure 4). It is important to note that the chart incorporates only the two initial dimensions, namely, interlocutor and setting, and limited characteristics of each. In a sense, the chart is a predictive scheme reflecting the child's expectations governing language use given certain combinations of social variables which he perceived as relevant at that stage. The chart does not include instances of "marked" speech associated with a form of verbal behaviour not normal for a situation (such as the examples cited involving surprise, shock, amusement, etc.); nor is the scheme complicated by including instances of "retrieved" speech such as when the child articulated a past linguistic experience (such as a song, joke or quotation) which were preserved in the original language. Hence,

FIGURE 4 *Interplay of social variables and code choices in normal dialogue*

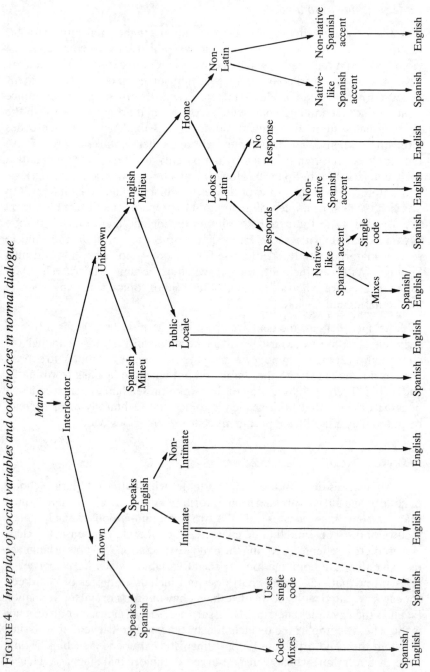

considerations of form and function are not included as part of the predictive chart. By age ten the scheme remained substantially unchanged except for additional refinements which reflected increasing awareness of other attributes of both interlocutors and setting.

Presumably the interplay between social factors and linguistic form will become increasingly complex, or else revised, as the child has additional experiences and acquires increasing knowledge of his social and linguistic environment. His own changing social status and perceptions will most certainly affect future language use. Nonetheless the chart depicts Mario's *modus operandi* to the present by showing those factors which he considered in determining which language to speak. The accuracy of this framework was supported by the fact that Mario normally reacted in some demonstrable way when the language used in a given situation was other than what he perceived as normal for the circumstances. Numerous behavioural responses demonstrated this; often he made explicit comments about his observations (some of these were cited in the previous section). Another such incident was the following at age 4;9:

> A friend whom Mario had met initially in Mexico was visiting the home. The visitor, although Greek, "looked" Latin. Mario was coming down the stairs and was surprised by his mother's conversation with the friend in English rather than Spanish. He eventually interrupted with the puzzled question:
> ¿Por qué hablas así mamá? No hables así; no "blaka bla". Así como yo estoy hablando ahola (ahora). (*Why do you speak like that, mamá? Don't speak like that; no "blaka bla". Like this, like I'm speaking right now.*)

The child's surprise was caused by the fact that the language used was obviously inappropriate or unanticipated for the circumstances.

Mario adhered so strictly to the scheme described, that he further became the guardian of the Spanish language, reminding his parents (and especially his father) when either spoke in English rather than Spanish. Mario's adherence caused him to react even to the use of single words in English. For example, one day his father returned to his place of employment to pick up the family which waited for him there. As he approached, he saw the children and rolled down the car window to yell out "Hi!" Mario's immediate retort was "¡Habla español!" Although said in jest, it nonetheless demonstrated that any switch to English seldom failed to escape the child's attention. On another occasion, Mario's father entered from the garden, exclaiming: "Phew. It's hot outside!" to which the child immediately retorted: "No se me habla así." (*You shouldn't speak to me like that*).

On still another occasion, while at the breakfast table, Mario (10;1) and his younger sister, both noticed that their father was speaking English to their mother. Both children commented:

Carla (to Papá): ¡No hables en inglés a mamá! (*Don't speak English to mamá!*)
Papá: ¿Por qué? (*Why?*)
Carla: Porque mamá no le gusta hablar en . . . ep . . . (*Because mamá doesn't like to speak Sp . . .*) (Looks to Mario for support)
Mario (to everyone): ¡Español! A mamá le gusta hablar en español. (*Spanish! Mamá likes to speak in Spanish.*)
Carla (to Mamá): Papá está hablando en inglés a tí . . . (*Papá is speaking English to you . . .*) then she adds, jokingly ¡Y yo le pego para que hable en español! (*And I'll spank him so that he'll speak Spanish!*)

Conversely, Mario (7;6) was exhilarated on another occasion when he noticed his younger sister interject a word of English in her speech:

Mario was upstairs getting ready for bed. He suddenly called downstairs to his mother.
Mario: Mamá, díle a papá que escriba en su libro de Carlina que ella dijo "monkey". (*Mamá, tell papá to write in Carlina's book that she said "monkey".*)

Having become accustomed to the fact that his father often noted interesting things either child said, Mario wanted to assist by reporting this unusual aspect of his sister's speech.

The late code-switching development associated with a particular topic of speech is indeed surprising, especially since this is so commonly reported by other sociolinguists studying the speech of adult bilinguals. However, there was only recent evidence in the data to show that Mario chose either English or Spanish in relation to a specific topic of conversation. That is not to say that topic had no effects upon the child's speech in at least some respect even earlier. For example, in an analysis of the child's interference (to be discussed later) topic was indeed a relevant factor. An increase in interference and linguistic borrowings was clearly associated with specific topical areas. However, because the child's parents were aware of the effects of education on language development, and given the fact that no bilingual programme was available in the area where the child resides, some attempts were made to offset Mario's monolingual education by providing him with textbooks in Spanish used in Bolivian schools. The result has been that Mario is almost as capable of dealing with mathematics, reading and other content areas in Spanish as he is in English. It is likely, however, that English will eventually become more fully developed as the child's education continues in this language.

Summary

To summarize, some of the salient factors both present — and absent — which may have contributed to the child's distinctive use of codes were: (1) clear and consistently differentiated use of codes by his parents; (2) insistence by his mother on the exclusive use of Spanish; (3) distinctive environments in which each code was used; (4) the fact that the child (and his family) were among few Spanish-speakers in an English-speaking milieu, again reinforcing their distinctiveness; and (5) the fact that Spanish had become so closely associated with the family image and the child's identity. Mario mused about his destiny when he asked at age 8;1: "Papá, ¿Por qué yo nací español?" (*Papá, why was I born a Spanish-speaker?*)

Absent from the child's experience thus far was any incident reflecting negative social attitudes or prejudices. At no time was Mario noted experiencing a difficult or embarrassing situation because he spoke one language or the other, nor did he ever report such incidents. If anything, many of the persons with whom he associated valued his ability to speak two languages and their comments consistently reflected this. Unfortunately this is not always the case for so many other bilingual children. Mario's self-confidence, in fact — in either language — was so great that he spoke spontaneously and naturally in Spanish to his parents even when they visited him at school, this often being the acid test. The only effect produced when he spoke was amazement in his classmates who seldom — if ever — heard other languages. Eventually, of course, most of his classmates became aware of this other side of Mario. One instance (age 7;7) brought this clearly to view when Mario's parents gave a presentation on Bolivia to the second grade class. After showing movies, several objects were passed around and their uses explained to the class. To provide the children with the experience of hearing another language, Mario's parents spoke in Spanish and Mario translated to English. His willingness and naturalness in doing so was possible only because he was so completely uninhibited about the use of either language.

Code-switching was quite an early development, beginning only a few days after the introduction of English words into the child's active speech. In only a brief period the child was able to sort linguistic sets. The initial sorting was done wholly in response to specific persons present within a limited social situation. As the child's language developed, and also as his world enlarged, other social factors influenced language differentiation. The next major factor was the setting of the speech event. Initially there were two clear-cut divisions — the home, and the world outside the home. The child formulated a clear notion of place or setting. Characteristics of place formed the second broad category serving as a determinant of language choice. This simple dichotomy give way to further refinements as the child had other experiences which forced him to consider additional factors in making language choices.

Aside from interlocutors, either known or unknown to the child, Mario began early to differentiate and categorize people based on their physical appearance. Other aspects of interlocutors also weighed on his choice of language; degree of intimacy, degree of the interlocutor's comprehension and fluency, certain roles, switching patterns, the presence of audience, etc. These cues assisted him in electing the code to use.

Increasing social and linguistic sophistication permitted the child to make judgements about the speech of other persons. He also decided whether their use of a specific code met his terms of appropriateness for a particular circumstance. The "wrong" language, or insufficient facility with a language, provoked comment or visible reactions.

Because of a high degree of consistency in the patterns of language behaviour displayed by the child in each situation, it was possible to establish a scheme which reflected the relationship between various social conditions and language choice. This framework tended to serve as a predictive guide for establishing expectations about the appropriate language for a given set of conditions. Furthermore the framework predicted language choice only when the child was engaged in normal dialogue. The scheme was validated by the child's own reactions when these expectations were not fulfilled.

The form and function of the speech act sometimes took precedence over other variables (interlocutors and setting) as when the child desired to produce special effects upon his listeners or when he "retrieved" a linguistic experience from the past. In such cases, other than the normal language choice resulted. The outcome was often a "marked" use of the alternate code. And topical code-switching appeared as a late development fostered by increasing socialization (primarily education) through only one of the child's languages.

Hence, code-switching — the beginning of bilingual behaviour — began as early as 2;6 despite the delayed onset of English. By 2;8 it was fairly well established and well executed. By the third year, the child was capable of making appropriate language choices — he switched rapidly and naturally. By age five he behaved like a normal child (as perceived by others) — in either of two languages — with the appropriate people, and in the right time and place. His sensitivity to appropriate language use with varying persons was remarkably evident in the following incident at 6;3:

> Mario is writing a letter in Spanish to his grandparents in Bolivia, spelling phonetically, and unassisted for the most part. He then asks:
> **Mario** (to Papá): ¿A Bolivia se va en avión? (*Will it go to Bolivia by plane?*)
> **Papa**: Sí, ¿por qué? (*Yes, why?*)
> **Mario**: Nada. (*Nothing.*)
> He then selects an airmail stamp to place on the envelope. Papá notices that the child is sounding out English phonetically and writes "B-O-L-I-F-Y-A" on the envelope, and asks:
> **Papá**: ¿Pero por qué escribes en inglés? (*But, why are you writing in English?*)
> **Mario**: Sí, pero el cartero no sabe español! (*Yes, but the mailman doesn't know Spanish!*)

By ten, Mario displayed rather sophisticated code switching behaviour which now took into account a great variety of social factors of increasing importance to the child.

Language and socialization

In most cases, the child's caretakers are primarily responsible for his socialization during the pre-school years, serving as models of behaviour, giving direction, and providing input. Much of this is accomplished through language as well as through example. The language adults use with the child often varies with his age. The infant, who has not yet acquired language, is obviously not addressed in the same manner as the two- or five-year-old. The way in which adults talk to children often reveals a variety of things: it embodies their beliefs and expectations concerning youngsters of varying ages, and it reflects their attempts to socialize the child in ways appropriate to their world view. Since adult language varies with the age of the child, it is clearly differentiated speech. Consequently their language serves as the first source of differing speech styles and usage which the child will eventually acquire. Hence, before examining styles in Mario's speech, discussion of adult usage and adult attempts at socialization through language is needed.[3]

Early language input

One of the main purposes of using language with the newborn infant appeared to be to establish contact. The initial style was often some form of baby-talk composed of monophonemic or biphonemic sounds: "a-bú-bú-bú-bú-bú", or "jí-gi-jí-gi-jík". These vocalizations were usually made to elicit some reaction from the infant in acknowledgement or recognition of the adults around him. In a sense, the parents reached out for their first contact with their new son. They sometimes interspersed these sounds with real speech, but the purpose was basically the same. By the seventh week, Mario began to react to sounds with smiles and laughter and clear signs of recognition were noticed by 0;4. By this age, the child reacted readily by smiling, cooing or gurgling in response to the sounds his parents made. Mario also displayed recognition of the dog by making sounds upon sight of the animal. Language was now also used for several other purposes: to calm the child when crying, to entertain or distract him, as well as to elicit visible or audible responses. Already varying voice modulation produced differing reactions. The child responded differently to whispering, normal voice volume or shouting.

As the child matured to the point where he was physically able to begin exploring his environment, from about nine to 11 months, adult language was used with a new purpose. Caretakers began to circumscribe boundaries for the child's movement by telling him to return to a certain area when he wandered off too far or by physically returning him. They also gave directions with words like "no, no . . . no se toca", and even "don't touch". Hence they used language to express approval or disapproval, to establish boundaries to the child's movements, and to steer and direct him. They also pointed out dangers through expressions like "bú-bu" (Italian), "chi-chíu" (Bolivian baby-talk meaning something like "you'll get hurt"), "caliente" (hot), or "se cae" (you'll fall).

It is no wonder that many of these same expressions form the beginning of the child's own lexicon. Mario's first words were those which verbally confirmed his recognition of months earlier: "papá, mamá" at 1;4 and "Bimba" at 1;10. By 1;10 he added the expressions "chi-chíu" and "no, no". He showed that he had learned what things were off-limits by touching the objects in question, saying, "no, no", and shaking his head at the same time.

Language and social norms

Once Mario began saying his first words, his parents used language now to point out and name the things surrounding him. Mario began to learn new words at a rapid pace, adding also two important utterances which helped to find out about things: "¿Dónde está?" (*Where is it?*) and the response, "Aquí está". (*Here it is.*) This was also a period of increasing commands directed at the child, controlling his behaviour and interaction with others: "Di 'bye bye'", "Di 'ciao-ciao'", "Díle gracias a Marta", "Mándale besitos", or "Díle 'Te quiero' a grandpop". (*Say "bye bye", say "ciao-ciao", say "Thank you" to Martha, Throw her kisses, or say "I love you" to grandpop*). From 1;10 to 2;7, the child's own speech reflected this area of socialization:

1;10	/táw-táw/	ciao-ciao	(*ciao-ciao*)
2;2	/áš:yas/	gracias	(*thank you*)
	/te kédo/	te quiero	(*I love you*)
2;3	/atalalála yaya/	hasta mañana	(*see you tomorrow*)
	/táto tótes/	buenas noches	(*good night*)
2;7	/salúlala/	salúdala	(*say 'hello'*)
	/ñáña nótes/	buenas noches	(*good night*)
	/xálon/	So long!	
	/xái/	hi!	

About the child's second to fourth year, his parents no longer spoke with the high voice frequency they used with him as an infant, and they completely abandoned the nonsense sounds they had used earlier to attract his attention. These years were marked by increased conversation with the child, more moderate voice modulation, and expansion of his utterances, such as:

Papá: ¿Qué te hiciste en el dedo aquí? (*What did you do to your finger, here?*)

Mario: Con el gancho. (*With the safety pin.*)

Papá: ¿Te lo hiciste con el gancho? ¿Dónde está el gancho? (*You did it with the safety pin? Where's the safety pin?*)

Mario: Aquí, gancho. (*Here, pin.*)

Papá: ¿Aquí está el gancho? ¿Y qué es esto? (*The pin's here? And what is this?*)

Mario: Calzón. (*Underpants.*)

Papá: ¿El gancho está en tu calzón? ¿O en tu pañal? (*The pin's on your underpants? Or on your diaper?*)

Mario: (Laughs.)

Papá: Ah, tú, ya no usas pañal. (*Oh, you don't use diapers anymore*).

Mario: ¡No! (*No!*)

Much of adult language was now a socializing force replete with social rules often picked up by the child, becoming part of his own speech:

Mario: ¿El nene toca ese? ¿El nene toca aquí? ¿Pega papá? (*Baby touches that? Baby touches here? Papá spanks?*)

Mamá: Sí, papá te va a pegar si tocas. (*Yes, papá will spank you if you touch.*)

Mario: ¿Ese no toca el nene? ¿Y pega en el potito? No . . . pega, papá. (*Baby doesn't touch that? And he gets spanked on the rump? No . . . spank, papá.*)

In addition, his parents continued to name and label the environment and to direct the child with rules for behaviour. Whereas screaming, crying and jumping up and down, were tolerated earlier, the slightly older child who tried the same thing was often met with negative reactions from his parents. Inappropriate behaviour was tolerated less and some form of punishment was usually given, verbal or otherwise.

Mario's parents also directed him more now in controlling his voice. Tantrums were not tolerated, screaming was not permitted, and Mario was often told to lower his voice. This was especially the case in public places such as in church, in the doctor's office or at the supermarket. Furthermore, not only was volume controlled, but for the first time Mario was instructed not to say certain words which were previously used quite freely. Earlier Mario had been required to separate lexicon according to the language code to which they belonged. Now he was also required to separate specific items *within the same code* for limited use in certain situations. His parents increasingly reacted to words like "pis, caca, tetitas, potito" (words for excrement, or body parts) especially if shouted aloud in public places. These formed the basis for a small core of taboo words. Aware of the special effects they produced when used, he drew upon such words when angry. In addition, he sometimes improvised his own obscenities in spite of increasingly negative feedback.

An analysis of the language used by adults during this period reveals that adults often created a conversational framework into which the child interjected occasional brief responses. This was illustrated in the above passage in which Mario's father expanded the child's responses to full statements. This process also served the purpose, perhaps, of demonstrating to the child how to conduct a normal conversational sequence where there is a give and take of questions and responses.

Adults also used language during this period as a means of highlighting social relationships though the use of proper titles of address and etiquette forms. Mario was repeatedly reminded when he called a neighbour "Hey, Phaneuf!", not to say "Hey" but rather "Mr. Phaneuf", or to say "Señora" when he addressed a shopkeeper in Oaxtepec, Mexico. Likewise he was told to say "Tía Marta" and not just "Marta" when speaking to an elderly friend. Although he protested, "Pero no es mi tía" (*But she's not my aunt*), it was explained "Se dice tía, porque tú la quieres mucho" (*You say aunt to her because you love her a lot*), underscoring their close relationship as the basis for the title.

Language and world view

By five, the language used with Mario was completely devoid of any baby-talk, although it contained many forms of endearment marked by diminutives. It was a language replete with directions, commands, reprimands and explications about the parent's world view. The child seemed curious and interested in absolutely everything and his incessant use of "por qué" triggered lengthier and more meaningful explanations. He was now more rational, and also better able to comprehend much more as his cognitive development advanced. Language about abstract things — things not directly experienced — became topics of discussion. The child used language to learn about nature, languages, the moon, birth, the origin of people, sex, life, old age, and death and immortality (see Appendix B). Through these dialogues on a great variety of topics, his parents imparted aspects of their world view and behaviours which the child should display within that view. Increasing demands were made of the child; imperatives were used more commonly, and negative reactions became more severe if the child transgressed.

This was also a period which increasingly stressed proper verbal interaction — when to talk, when not to talk, and how to talk appropriately with different people. Adults were less tolerant of Mario's interruptions and impatience. He was usually reprimanded whenever he interrupted adult conversation and he was obliged to wait, albeit impatiently, to the end of even lengthy discussions. This conduct was simultaneously reinforced at kindergarten where the give and take of speech among his peers was one of the objectives in preparing him for first grade. Mario was aware of this new system, describing it in this way:

> **Mario:** Y en la escuela, yo tengo alzar (*sic*) la mano . . . y después esperar mu:::cho rato. Y luego la 'teacher' dice: "Now you can speak, Mario", y hace callar a los otros nenes, y dice, "Mario's speaking now." (*And at school, I have to raise my hand . . . and then wait a long, long time. And then the teacher says: "Now you can speak, Mario", and she makes the other children shut up, and she says, "Mario's speaking now."*)

Mario's own curt imperatives were constantly remodelled by his parents. When he said "dáme leche" (*give me some milk*) his parents responded with

"¿Cómo se pide?" (*How do you ask for it?*) as a reminder to say "por favor" (*please*). When he received the milk and said nothing, he was asked "¿Qué se dice?" (*What do you say?*) to which he replied "Ah . . . gracias" (*Oh, thank you*). Etiquette and courtesy expressions were extremely important now. And when the child failed to perform correctly, especially in the presence of other adults, he was told.

Besides being told what to say, Mario was also taught what not to say. For example, he found nothing wrong in making comments about people — pointing to a midget, commenting on a fat woman, singling out someone with a deformity, or making aesthetic judgements about people. Meeting a Bolivian chauffeur whose front teeth were missing — all but the canine — he said in his presence: "El parece vampiro" (*He looks like a vampire*), or seeing a likeness of the Ambassador's wife to a woman on a television movie, he said: "Ella parece la señora de la 'Planet of the Apes'" (*She looks like the woman from the 'Planet of the Apes'*). Seeing an old woman on the street, he pointed to her saying: "Mila (mira) esa viejita" (*Look at that little old woman*). Taking leave of a friend of his parents, he remarked:

> **Mario**: Ella parece una bruja . . . por qué parece una bruja? (*She looks like a witch . . . why does she look like a witch?*)
> (He was duly reprimanded a few moments later, for which he seemed perplexed. He then clarified his original comments.)
> **Papá**: ¿Mario, por qué dijiste eso? ¡¡¡No se dice eso nunca a nadie!!! (*Mario, why did you say that? Don't you ever say that to anyone!!!*)
> **Mario**: Pero no es una bruja. Solo PARECE una bruja . . . pero no ES una bruja. (*But she's not a witch. She only LOOKS LIKE a witch . . . but she's NOT a witch.*)

Norms for language form and use

Attempts to correct the child's language forms intensified by age five and beyond. This changing attitude may have been due to expectations which Mario's caretakers held about his competence at this stage. Whereas previously there were fewer attempts at correction noted, many of the child's errors now became subjected to direct reaction. And although many errors were simply morphological details, they nonetheless attracted increasing attention. Now, when the child said: "la puerta está *abrida*" (*The door is open*), a parent corrected: "*abierta*". When he said: Lo PUNIERON allá" (*They put it there*), he was asked "¿Dónde lo PUSIERON?" (*Where did they put it?*), emphasizing the incorrect word. (It should be noted that both cases involve irregular forms of Spanish verbs.)

Attempts at correction were couched in a variety of ways, from direct instruction to very subtle repetition of the correct form. Some of these techniques are clear from examples provided below: (1) instruction and/or clarification about a specific grammatical point; (2) a correction, followed by a request for the child to repeat the correction; (3) a request for the child to repeat his own statement in hopes that he would self-correct; and (4) an adult repetition of what the child has just said, providing the corrected form but without calling overt attention to the matter. The first technique is evident in the following excerpt:

Age 5;9 — Papá is working at his desk when Mario enters:
Mario: Papá dáme un LÁPI. (*Papá, give me a pencil*).
Papá: ¿Cómo se llama esto? (*What do you call this?*)
Mario: Lápi. (*Pencil*)
Papá: ¿Y estos dos? (*And these two?*)
Mario: Lap . . . is? (*Pen . . . cils?*)
Papá: No, esto es lápiz, y dos son LÁPICES. (*No, this is a pencil, and two are pencils.*)
Mario: ¿Lápices? (*Pencils?*)
Papá: Sí (*Yes.*)
Mario: Lápi . . . ces.

Examples of the second technique are obvious in the following excerpts:

Age 7;2 — Mario is playing and singing aloud:
Mario: I'M been working on the railroad . . . etc.
Papá (correcting him): I'VE been working . . .
Mario: I've been working . . . etc.

Age 8;4 — At the dinner table, Mamá refers to Mario's sister as her little baby. Mario protests:
Mario: ¡No, es guagüita! ¡Ya ES cuatro! (*She's not a little baby. She's four years old!*)
Papá: Ya TIENE cuatro años, Mario. (*She is four years old, Mario.*)
Mario: . . . TIENE cuatro anos. (*. . . is four years old.*)

Age 9;6 — Mario asks for paper to type a letter to his grandfather:
Mario (to Papá): Papá, ¿me das el papel borrador? (*Papá, will you give me some scrap paper?*)
Papá: ¿Para qué? (*What for?*)
Mario: Para la MÁQUINA ESCRIBIDORA. (*For the typewriter.*)
Papá: MÁQUINA DE ESCRIBIR. (*Typewriter.*)
Mario (Repeats): MÁQUINA DE ESCRIBIR.
Papá: Aquí toma. (*Here it is.*).

The following exemplifies the third correction technique which is an indirect attempt to elicit the correct response from the child. It obviously assumes he already has some notion of the correct form:

Age 6;5 — Papá finishes reading to Mario who then says:
Mario: ¿Viste lo que he HICIDO? (*Did you see what I did?*)
Papá: ¿Qué? (*What?*)
Mario: . . . que he HECIDO. (. . . *what I did.*)
Papá: ¿Cómo se dice de verdad? (*How should you really say that?*)
Mario: . . . he HICIDO . . . he HECIDO . . . (*Thinking some more he tries again*) . . . he HECHO!
Papá: ¡Bravo! (*Good!*)

The next example again illustrates the third technique but with the addition of indirect prompting when the correct form is not produced:

Age 10;8 — Both children are getting ready for bed, when papá enters:
Mario (to Papá): Mamá dijo que nos DESVISTEMOS. (*Mamá told us to get undressed*).
Papá (notices the grammatical error and asks in an effort to elicit the correct form): ¿Qué dijo? (*What did she say?*)

He waits while the children try various times to produce the correct verb form. Finally he whispers a simplified answer to Carla without Mario noticing.

Carla (says proudly): . . . que nos DESVISTAMOS! (. . . *that we get undressed!*)
Mario (in disbelief): *¡¡Carla!!*

And finally, the last excerpt illustrates the fourth technique which is simply to restate the child's incorrect form without drawing further attention to the matter:

Age 6;1 — Mario is talking to his caretaker and misuses an irregular verb form:
Mario (to Teresa): . . . MORIDO (*dead*)
Teresa: . . . muerto (*dead*)

Aside from efforts to direct the child's attention to correct speech forms, his parents also began actively insisting on the proper use of the two systems. Mario was not normally allowed to mix languages. Mixing English and Spanish invariably produced a negative reaction, especially from the child's mother who held strong feelings against this behaviour. English was permissible if Mario was roleplaying, quoting someone else, or using phrases which were almost untranslatable. Otherwise mixing produced subtle reactions like:

Age 5;7
Mario (to Papá): Sabes, mi "schoolbus" no tiene un "stop sign". Lo rompieron. (*You know, my "schoolbus" doesn't have a "stop sign". They broke it.*)
Papá (to Mario): Ah . . . ¿quién rompió la señal del autobús? (*Who broke the sign on the schoolbus?*)
Mario: Unos nenes malos. (*Some bad children.*)

Or more obvious ones like:

Age 5;2
Mario (to Mamá): Bueno, y esos van a cantar un "song". (*Yes, and they're going to sing a "song".*)
Mamá: "Canción" se dice, Mario. (*The word is "canción", Mario.*)

Age 5;7
Mario (to Mamá): ¿Dónde está mi "kite"? (*Where is my "kite"?*)
Mamá (to Mario): ¿QUE? ¿Como se dice en español? (*WHAT? How do you say that in Spanish?*)
Mario: Ah, ¡mi volador! (*Oh, my kite!*)

Conversely, the following statement, employing a borrowed item with almost no equivalent in Spanish, caused no reaction at all:

Age 5;7
Mario: Hoy en mi escuela, nos llevaron al "Livestock Show". (*Today at school, they took us to the "Livestock Show".*)

The following incident is also interesting in that it reflects both the "laissez-faire" attitude where culturally bound items were involved (i.e. those having no ready equivalents in Spanish) and strong attempts to thwart borrowings for more obvious and common Spanish words:

Age 6;4 — Mario returns from school and tells his parents about a Christmas project they did that morning in Art class:
Mario: . . . y después ponemos "cranberries" con "marshmallows" and "pipe cleaner" . . . y una cosa donde vienen las medias de mujer . . . un "pinecone" . . . y después se pone el "glitter" . . . (. . . *and then we put some "cranberries" with "marshmallows" and "pipe cleaner" . . . and then the thing (container) in which women's stockings come . . . a "pinecone" . . . and then you put the "glitter" . . .*)
Mamá (interjecting): "Brillo" (*Glitter*)
Mario (continuing): . . . y con "glue" . . .
Mamá: "Goma" ("*Glue*")
Mario: . . . y después lo pintas todo "yellow".
Mamá: "Amarillo" (*Yellow*).

Standards for stylistic variations

As the child gained control over his language systems, the systems in turn exerted increased influence over him, for this child's parents and other adults continued to raise their standards and expectations of his behaviour. Many of the previous examples illustrate precisely this point. Adults not only aided the child in acquiring their system, but they also guided him toward stricter adherence to its norms.

By five, Mario demonstrated mastery of large portions of that system as well as many of the norms for its use. Moreover, his parents continued to demonstrate that the system was not to be learned as a single unit but that it contained innumerable variational possibilities. These options constituted the styles of speech to be used in one circumstance or another. His parents served as both role models and instructors in learning this task, and they intervened in both subtle and at other times, very direct ways. In either case, the goal was the same and that was to enable the child to utilize the forms and to follow the norms as prescribed by their language-culture system.

Socializing efforts were found with considerable regularity in the diary throughout the years which followed. Adults guided the child in mastering increasingly diversified linguistic forms, observing social norms, and in adhering to the rules of conversational interaction. For example, comments dealing with the following areas were found consistently throughout the next five years:

Age 5;6 Directions on rules of etiquette
Age 5;8 Comments on discourse rules
Age 5;9 Prohibition on using certain taboo words
Age 7;1 Attention drawn to differentiating the various forms of direct address ("tú, usted")
Age 8;1 Instructions for softening a request or command
Age 8;4 More on taboo words not proper for public use
Age 8;7 Admonishments to use "usted" as a sign of respect, deference
Age 8;11 Observations on appropriate ways to greet
Age 9;7 Comments on appropriate language etiquette in Mexico
Age 10;7 Observations on appropriate cultural behaviour in Bolivia
Age 10;8 Instruction at school on writing "educadamente" i.e. in an "educated" fashion

In these years, many more adults were responsible for fostering in Mario the differentiated and non-verbal behaviours appropriate to varying social circumstances. The result was that Mario manifested in turn the development of many linguistic styles in his own speech. These will be further examined in the section which follows.

Positive attitudes towards bilingualism

As a developing bilingual, Mario was especially fortunate to have had positive experiences in his use of Spanish and English. He lived in environments where, with few exceptions, he experienced few negative sentiments against either of the languages he spoke. In fact, most people viewed his abilities as something of a phenomenon. Furthermore, he frequently associated with other bilinguals and so observed others switch to languages which he did not always understand. He observed this behaviour both in adults and children and, from his comments about his own bilingual ability, he obviously placed value on this ability. Speaking in other ways was fun. He enjoyed trying Pig Spanish, and guessing at the meaning hidden in words which were spelled or written. He listened intently to Portuguese-speaking children in an effort to carry on their play. And he was quite attentive when Italian was used to tell him stories which interested him.

These experiences were all significant in providing a favourable climate for dual language use. Unfortunately, many more cases are known where other children, also raised in bilingual homes, fail to continue active use of both languages because of adverse social attitudes. Mario never experienced anything like this, although when he first began to use English, he was affected by an inability to say the things he wanted. Initially, his less than fluent English affected his self-confidence and comportment. He was somewhat shy when speaking English, often speaking in a lower volume. Still he had no negative experiences related to his speaking a "foreign" language. And when he gained fluency in English, he was favourably disposed toward speaking either language as the circumstances warranted.

By age 5;0, Mario showed more and more effects from contact with peers. His behaviour, which had been influenced up to this age primarily by his parents, was now affected by the attitudes of others. He became more sensitive about his dress, and he showed distinct preferences for certain clothes, while rejecting others. He chose his own lunch box, requested sandwiches of a specific kind, and insisted on cowboy hats like the ones he saw other children wear. Although he first showed signs of emulating peer behaviour as early as 3;6 while attending nursery school, his feelings were much more definite now.

Summary

Summarizing, we have seen that Mario's parents used different styles of speech with him which varied with his level of maturity. When he was an infant, their primary concerns were to establish contact and to elicit signs of recognition. They also used language to quiet or to amuse him. The language they addressed to the infant was marked by a higher tone of voice and repetitious syllables usually formed by consonant and vowel combinations.

When the infant began to move about, language was used to establish limits, to point out dangers, and to express approval or disapproval. When he spoke his first words, attempts were made to point out things and to provide labels. His caretakers also used language to direct the child and to shape his behaviour. His parents began to direct the child's interaction with other persons and to define his relationship to them.

From the second to fifth years, Mario's behaviour came under increasing control. As he acquired language, he was obliged to use it increasingly in place of other forms of expression; i.e. speaking, instead of screaming, jumping, or tantrums. Mario was required to modulate his voice and lower his volume in certain situations — church, a doctor's office. For the first time he was taught that it was inappropriate to say certain words which became taboo in certain settings. This prohibition provided him with verbal ammunition which he used when angry. He learned that by merely saying these words he produced specific reactions in others. He also learned social relationships through his parents' insistence on the use of titles and proper etiquette terms for greeting, leave-taking, and thanking.

Beyond five, increasing demands were placed on the child. There was little tolerance for inappropriate language or behaviour. Commands were frequent and direct. These were sometimes followed by verbal or physical punishment. There was some alteration between direct commands and attempts to reason with the child. There was increased emphasis on the structure and form of conversation, the give and take of dialogue, and the use of etiquette and courtesy terms. There was also less tolerance for aberrant language, and grammatical errors were usually pointed out by subtle or direct means. Most importantly, code switching with the same interlocutor was not permitted in normal conversation, although it was allowed when quoting, in roleplay, or when a phrase was untranslatable.

The five-year-old child had acquired the language of his parents, and through it, their view of the world in as far as he was able to grasp. However, Mario then entered another world — that of the school and that of an English-speaking peer group. These divergent environments exposed the child not only to two language systems, but also to two different norms for language use and interaction. They presented different approaches to socialization and divergent values. Yet as a bilingual-bicultural individual, Mario seemed to identify what was expected of him in each circumstance. In each case, he was increasingly exposed to standards for stylistic variations in his speech and behaviour. This is true for most children, even monolingual individuals; but in this case, Mario's socializing experiences provided him with limited access to the variations of Spanish and even greater access to the variations of English, the dominant language of his environment. The effects of these experiences on his own speech styles will be examined in the section which follows.

TABLE 2   *Adult language and child socialization*

Child's age	Characteristics of adult language styles and attitudes	Purposes
New-born Infant	Style marked by high voice frequency; use of repetitious syllables, patterned on C+V combinations; high index of nonsense sounds accompany real language	To establish contact and elicit recognition.
0;4	Similar to above, with increasing use of real language	To elicit visible or audible reactions from the child.
0;5	Use of more varied voice modulation (whispering, normal and loud volumes)	To calm, entertain or distract the child.
0;9	Use of repetitive phrases such as "no, no, don't touch, etc." Voice modulates from encouraging tones to discouraging, stern tones, sometimes accompanied by physically directing the child	To delineate boundaries; to point out dangers; to express approval or disapproval; to steer and direct the child.
1;10	Baby-talk, marked by high voice frequency, diminishing use of nonsense words; real language with frequent use of diminutives; expansions of child utterances; frequent directives and commands	To name and label the environment; to express affection; to exchange information through questions-answers; to provide direction, to guide the child's behaviour and interaction with others.
2;0	Normal voice frequency and near-normal intonation; no nonsense sounds; expansion of child's utterances; frequent use of diminutives	To point out social rules; to name and label; to develop conversational techniques; to substitute verbal for non-verbal expression; to control voice volume; to point out taboos; to clarify social relationships; introduce etiquette and courtesy forms; to express affection.
4;0	No baby-talk forms; normalized voice patterns; normal use of diminutives except during	To normalize conversational interaction; to express affection; to conduct rational exchanges.

Child's age	Characteristics of adult language styles and attitudes	Purposes
	affectionate talk; less tolerance of "childish" behaviour; expansions of child's utterances; and occasional direct correction of the child's language	
5;0	Increased rational speech; insistence on etiquette and courtesy forms; stress on proper verbal interaction; correction of child's language; closer adherence to use of the proper code	To delinate proper behaviour and verbal interaction; to establish turn-taking in conversation; to respond to the child's intense curiosity and questioning; to explore abstract ideas.
6;0	Increased demands, directives and reprimands; abundant explanations; adherence to turn-taking; insistence on courtesy forms; control of topics of conversation contingent on presence of audience; relegation of certain topics to private family talk; intensified feedback and linguistic correction; intolerance of language mixing (although limited borrowing allowed); exploration of other codes (Pig Spanish, Italian)	To have child adhere to acceptable speech and behaviour (including what is discussed and where); to conform to social norms; to distinguish public from private speech; to refine his control of language; to enjoy other language forms and to expand his familiarity with them.
7;0	Modelling, guiding and intervening in the child's language and behaviour	To socialize the child toward appropriate stylistic forms of language; and to adhere to the language-culture norms of his environments.

Usage and styles

Thus far we have discussed linguistic and behavioural influences on the child by his principal caretakers and, to a lesser extent, by his peers. What remains to be examined are the outcomes in terms of the child's own behaviour. Language, of course, forms only part of the total behaviour of the developing child, and it is inextricably bound up with other aspects of his comportment. Here, we shall limit our discussion primarily to language — its use and styles.

In a sense, we have already referred to two of the styles present in Mario's speech, Spanish and English. Most researchers, however, treat full code switching separately from the style variations within the same language.[4] Whether bilingual behaviour is considered a code shift or a style variation, it is perhaps the most dramatic evidence that the child is indeed capable of controlling varying sets of linguistic features at a very young age. If he can control two full codes, there should be no doubt that he can control other styles as well. Yet, Berko Gleason's is one of the few other works which has even considered styles in children's language, focusing primarily on children between four and eight. Berko Gleason starts out by affirming: "By and large we were not primarily looking for evidence of code switching or stylistic variation in the children under four." Although children under four were included in the research, she makes it clear that "These children were older children talking to them for evidence of babytalk style." Almost as an aside, she makes the observation that "even the tiniest children make some distinctions".[5] This, in fact, is what Mario did, beginning in infancy.

Communicative styles during the early years

It may be possible to view the infant as possessing two expressive modes: crying or silence. Through his cries, the infant conveyed his various needs — hunger, distress, pain, fear. Ostwald & Peltzman (1974: 84–90) investigated differentiated cries in infants and made similar observations.

Tape recordings likewise show that not all of Mario's crying was alike. In fact, his mother was able to discern different styles of crying, and often she was able to tell by the pitch and intensity of his cry which of his needs was being expressed. For example, a sharp, piercing cry immediately aroused his mother to say something like: 'Ay caray, algo pasa . . . yo sé cuando él está llorando así. Debe tener un gancho abierto." (*My gosh, something's wrong . . . I know when he's crying like that. He must have his diaper pin open.*) Within a few months, and certainly by 0;4, Mario not only cried and screamed, but he also used body motions along with his sounds, waving his arms and legs, and moving his head from side to side. When content, he sometimes cooed, sighed or gurgled. Hence, several distinct vocalizations had emerged, each serving a different purpose.

The following months saw the emergence of many more sounds; however, by 0;9 the infant favoured certain sounds which he repeated more often than others. These were predominantly consonant plus vowel formations. This pre-speech phase concluded when he eventually gained increasing control over the sounds he made so that he could produce specific combinations at will. The appearance of words between 1;4 and 1;10 marked a new stage in the child's progress. Mario emitted two types of vocalizations; some had meaning and others did not. Those with meaning served to communicate with other people; the others (whether they were for self-expression or practice) served no communicative function.

By the end of his second year, Mario had a sizeable lexicon consisting primarily of nouns with which he labelled his surroundings. However, a few other words also extant had a purely social function. Two favoured expressions were "ciao-ciao" (used in the Italian sense so that it served either to greet or to take leave of someone) and "bye-bye". The child usually waved his hand when saying good-bye. However, it was noticed that Mario often fell silent precisely at the moment when he was told to say good-bye, especially with people he did not know well. After the individuals left, he began waving and saying /táw-táw/ (ciao-ciao) several times. This possibly suggests the beginning of another style, one related to the degree of familiarity between the child and the interlocutor. The style shift was vocalization versus non-vocalization; sound and motion as opposed to complete silence.

During this period of limited speech, Mario expressed himself a great deal by pointing, screaming, crying, and jumping up and down. Motions and gestures were more important to the communicative act than language. The early diary, in fact, is replete with contextual comments but few vocalizations. His utterances alone were insufficient to permit us to understand what transpired. However, as language developed, he used language more and more to communicate; besides, there was increasing social pressure for him to do so. After learning sufficient vocabulary, pointing was then met with responses like: "Pues, a ver. ¡Dí lo que quieres; no señales!" (*Well, let's see. Say what you want; don't point!*) The two-, three-, or four-year-old was expected to abandon typical pre-speech behaviour and to use language to communicate. Nevertheless, as long as it was tolerated, the child had two options — linguistic or non-linguistic communication; he used gestures or he used words.

Some of these gestures of course were permitted to continue, but as extralinguistic expressions — expressions which accompanied rather than replaced oral language. At only one point did Mario tend to revert to non-linguistic means. This occurred at about 3;5, when he was immersed in situations where he did not have adequate command of English. At such times he often compensated by acting out with motions and onomatopoeic sounds whatever it was that he wanted to convey.

Another interesting development occurred by 2;7. Mario delighted in creating nonsense sounds which seemed to have several functions: at times they were merely sound play; sometimes they were expressive vocalizations; and sometimes he used them when he was bored, uninterested, or otherwise did not wish to reply to his interlocutor:

Age 2;7 /Silal, luxála, kapála, tistópi, bakók/
/tapála, anís, kopála, tokála, kopíl/
/kakíli, pis:ín, kokála/
/kopála, pinzála, pinsmála, balamkúm/
Age 2;8 /papál, papál, papópu, popópo, popípi/
Age 3;2 /tobíya, stopáka, sisíya, stubíta, búbi/

Although used in a different way and for a different purpose, this style was akin to the language/silence distinction cited earlier. Mario used nonsense sounds for approximately one year, after which they disappeared gradually from his speech. What is surprising is that even though days, and sometimes months, went by before the next use of nonsense sounds, they always preserved a familiar form and rhythm despite their spontaneity.[6] Furthermore, in spite of their originality, these sounds followed the phonological rules of Spanish in almost every detail.

The selective use of whining also took place during this same period. Whining seemed to be a special form of expression used primarily with his caretakers but not with other adults. It involved a sing-song intonation accompanied by higher than normal pitch. It is interesting to note that Berko Gleason (1973: 7) made a similar observation. Mario was observed at times playing happily in the nursery until he caught sight of his parents. Immediately he began to whine no matter what he wanted. The nursery attendant reported, however, that he never whined at other times. Similar observations were made when Mario stayed with other persons — an aunt, grandparent, babysitter. Whining began only after the parents returned, and it was reserved exclusively for them. Consequently, this may be considered a style variation related to specific interlocutors (in this case, the child's caretakers).

Socializing pressures, however, did not permit this style to endure. Beyond 3;0, increasing intolerance was demonstrated so that examples of whining were rare as the child grew older. Whining was noted, for example, once at 5;9 when the child was awakened from a nap in kindergarten when his parents visited. But when the child whined at 8;11, he was met with a stern: "¡Habla bien!" (*Speak properly!*) and thereby made to repeat his statement in an acceptable manner.

A style for intimacy

Linguistic devices to convey affection were evidenced throughout the speech diary. This style was reserved for intimates such as Mario's parents, sister, and also with certain relatives and close friends. It was marked by the wide use of diminutives, occasionally improvised terminations, and occasional terms of endearment. Samples are abundant:

Age 3;1 Papá, papini

Age 3;2 Papapito, mamapita

Age 3;3 Diosito
Señolito (Señorito).

Age 3;6 Fantinito . . . un momentito
Mamapita, papito, papisini

Age 4;6 Carlitita, Carlinina

The samples of endings in Mario's speech were probably more diverse than those found in the speech of other young Spanish speakers due to the varied inputs provided by his caretakers, derived from the morphological systems of several languages.

Another sign of intimacy reflected in Mario's speech was his tendency to revert to Spanish as a special marker of intimate relationships. In various cases when the normal language choice might have been English, the child interspersed communication with Spanish, despite the fact that he knew the interlocutors to be strictly English-speakers. Examples of this behaviour were previously described. Code switching, then, served as another stylistic mechanism which the child had available to him as a way of demonstrating feelings of intimacy with certain individuals.

Mario became increasingly sensitive to linguistic features which conveyed intimacy. He demonstrated this not only by his own use of such features but also by comments which revealed his detection of intimacy and affection in the speech of others. For example, at 5;8 he was recalling experiences he had on a recent visit to Bolivia:

Mario (to Parents): La Teresita de la abuelita Alina me decía "cara sucia". (*Grandma Alina's Teresita — a maid — called me "dirty face".*)

Mamá (to Mario): No . . . "k'ara" cochino. "K'ara" es aymara para decir "niño de la calle." (*No . . . piggy "k'ara". "K'ara" is aymara and it means "a street kid".*)

Mario: No, "cara sucia" me decía . . . pero sólo de cariño. (*No, she called me "dirty face" . . . but only because she likes me.*)

Two months later (age 6;0), while waiting for a neighbour who had promised to buy him a toy for his birthday, he reflected:

Mario (to Parents): Anne me va a comprar DOS juguetes. (*Anne is going to buy me TWO toys.*)

Papá: ¿Cómo sabes? (*How do you know that?*)

Mario: Porque me dice "sweetie pie". (*Because she calls me "sweetie pie".*)

One of the most pervasive markers in adult Spanish — the pronoun *tú* with its corresponding verb forms — was as yet an unreliable indicator of intimacy. Mario, as with many children, even by age 10;0 had not yet been required to employ the contrasting form "usted" consistently, and it was only rarely noted in his speech diary. This distinction — a most interesting linguistic and social development — will be discussed more fully below.

Peer talk

Although Mario had played with children in Bolivia and Mexico, English was most closely associated with peer talk. This was probably due to his intensive contact with English-speaking children at the nursery. The language he used with peers was characterized in distinctive ways, setting it apart from the speech styles used with adults. Peer talk, for example, contained a high incidence of direct commands, many expressive interjections, frequent onomatopoeic sounds, an almost complete absence of courtesy terms and diminutives, imitated utterances, and an occasional interspersing of songs, recitations, and the like. This was certainly not at all like the verbal behaviour he displayed with other people.

Since peer talk was predominantly English, Mario's first speech patterns were often in the form of unmitigated commands in English learned from other children: "Move! Gimme! No!" (meaning: "Don't do that!"), and "My!" (meaning "Give me!" and said while snatching an object from another child). At home, the language of his role playing and play with imaginary friends was filled with the same:

Age 3;4 Get auta here!
Shut up!
Don't do dat! No do dat no more!
My, my! Not yours!

I want this seat! Mus (move)!
Close it! Come on!
Age 3;5 No touch dat . . . is bwoken.
Age 3;6 I punch you right da nose!
Age 4;9 Look me! Look me alot!

Entire dialogues with imagined friends were typically filled with rather aggressive statements. The style, of course, reflected the type of interaction going on between children — often filled with conflict, power plays, attention seeking, possessive behaviour, and sometimes egocentric displays of indifference — reflected in many of Piaget's investigations.[7] This was not the interplay the child had with the adult, and the difference was reflected in language.

Courtesy terms were conspicuously absent from data recorded during peer involvement. Conversely, there was a fairly frequent use of the not-so-courteous "Stupid!" and "Shalup!" (Shut up!). Yet Mario was aware of the potency of this expression and its challenging nature. This became apparent one evening while watching television. Mario misunderstood the sports announcer who said: "The Philadelphia team *shut out* the other", to which he exclaimed with astonishment, "Grampop, he say 'shut up'!!" Apparently, courtesy terms serve little function among children, whose social interaction is forthright, candid and sometimes aggressive. Yet it was obvious Mario knew these terms for he occasionally used them with adults (with some prompting). Furthermore, he sometimes demonstrated his awareness of courtesy expressions during role plays. Pretending to be a playmate, Corey, he sneezed and immediately said to himself: /ga sɛs yu, kówi/ (*God bless you, Corey*).

Peer talk also contained many expressive interjections such as "yuk, hey, bla, gosh, ouch", and the like. Mario copied these and other expressions from his peers often without the least modification of their statements. This repetition was usually done in an echo-like fashion, apparently serving no other purpose. Piaget (1971) provides various interpretations of this phenomenon (see also Chapter 2, in which the author speaks of egocentric speech and collective monologues among children between the ages of 3 and 4).

Throughout his development, Mario rarely used diminutives with his peers, possibly owing to the fact that diminutives in English are generally not as widespread as in Spanish. The few diminutives used were in words such as "doggie" and also in some names such as Bobby and Ronnie. However, these were fairly frozen expressions and they cannot be considered the same as spontaneously created forms. Peer language style contained no notes of endearment. And although Mario had many friends whom he obviously admired (as evidenced by his predilection to assume their role when playing), he did not address his friends affectionately. Yet Mario did use many affectionate expressions with adults who were intimately related to him.

Mario favoured onomatopoeic sounds, whether playing with others or alone. The diary contains numerous examples of sounds made during play, some of which were so amazingly faithful that they were impossible to transcribe. He imitated animals, tractors, aeroplanes, rockets, car brakes, monsters, motors, explosions, sirens, hammers banging and so forth.

Talk with peers was also distinct from other styles in that it contained frequent outbursts of songs, recitations, quotes from commercials, snatches of nursery rhymes, etc. Mario's repertoire included lines from "Cululucucu, Paloma", (Cucurrucucu, Paloma); The Cat in the Hat; Doggie, Doggie, Where's Your Bone?; the A-B-C's; Old MacDonald; Los Pollitos Dicen Pío, Pío, Pío; Intsy, Teentsy Spider; Someone in the Kitchen with Dinah; Poca Fortuna; Mary Had a Little Lamb; Señor Don Gato sobre el tejado; plus many of his own improvised tunes often created around a word overheard while playing.

Peer-talk style evolved rapidly beyond the age of 5;0 when the child began kindergarten. School provided increased contact with other children, and also a norm for interaction within the classroom context.

As Mario grew older he enjoyed imitating the style of his peers and he learned many of the expressions they used; for example, at age 9;9: "Step on it! Step on the gas! Put on the heat! Don't bug me!", and the like. Although adept at this style, however, he never fully incorporated it as his own on any regular, spontaneous basis. Consequently he used these expressions mostly as examples of a peer style when quoting or imitating. In fact, he became increasingly adept at not only imitating peer (and other) speech styles, but also at changing his voice qualities so that he was successfully imitating various character types with considerable skill. For the most part, Mario's peer style was mostly associated with English, the language through which he had most consistent peer interaction. Occasional stays abroad of course produced some stylistic features and expressions common to the place he was in. His tendency to pick up Bolivian or Mexican slang typical of his age group while in either place exemplified such developments. In Mexico at age 9;11 his diary showed increased use of "ándale, qué padre, padrísimo", all typical of his age group. However, these stylistic features did not normally remain on any consistent basis as with those which allowed for full development of a peer style in English. The exception to this of course was the style used with his sister, which sometimes reflected characteristics of his English peer style, but was mostly characterized by the use of a specific code, *viz*, Spanish.

Baby talk: A style for younger children

Mario's parents had used baby talk with him as an infant, but beyond infancy they employed this style rarely and only to express endearment. His mother's baby talk was characterized by extreme variations in intonation, a higher than normal frequency of voice, the extensive use of diminutives (morphologically derived from both Spanish and Italian), the frequent use of certain frozen expressions, and occasional phone substitutions. For example, at 5;0:

> **Mother** (to Mario): Mi chiquitico tan bonito, amorosito. (*My cute little baby, sweetheart.*)

However, earlier as an infant:

> **Mother** (to Mario): ¿Qué pašó mi nenito, mi guagüita tan quiriru? (*What are you doing, my child, my sweet little baby.*)

In the first example, the speech primarily involved affectionate expressions intensified by the addition of the diminutive -ito and the double intensifier -itico (ito plus -ico). In the second, however, there were also various phone substitutions such as /s→š/, /e→i/, d→r/, and o→u/. Apparently, all vowels were levelled to form one of those of the basic traingle /a/i/u/ (which, incidentally, is a common form of interference in Spanish heard among the native Quechua-speakers of Bolivia).

After the birth of his younger sister, Mario began to employ a baby-talk style himself when addressing the younger child. Although in principle he emulated the style described above, he did not copy all of the same features but added many of his own. He adopted the expressive voice pattern and the higher voice frequency, but sometimes inverted whole syllables instead:

Age 4;6 Hola, hermanita . . . tu frentita, Carlitita, Carlinina. Carla, Carla, Carla, . . . oy, su baguicita (barriguita), tengo a (*sic*) taparla. (*Hi, little sister . . . your forehead, Carlitita, Carlinina. Carla, Carla, . . . oh, her little tummy, I have to cover it.*)

Age 5;7 My darling, my darling! La mosicola, mosiquilla, moquilla, moco-silla. (Various forms of endearing terms.)

Age 5;8 Ay Carlina, Carlitita, Carlinina . . . qué monita, qué monita. (*Ay Carlina, Carlitita, Carlinina . . . how cute, how cute.*)

These utterances all shared the typical voice qualities associated with baby talk, plus the extensive use of diminutive (-ita, -illa, and -ina/inina, the latter being Italian forms). "My darling" was possibly learned from television or some other source as an endearment. In the statement made at 5;7, there was also play with the word "mucosa" (used with little children sometimes as endearment; or, depending on the tone of voice, it might also convey hostility or contempt).

None of the examples of Mario's baby talk were at all like his own real baby talk of an earlier age. As a matter of fact, he did not recall anything of his earlier speech. Berko Gleason (1973: 13) also observed that baby talk is learned, not something one retains from earlier years. Once when role-playing a baby, he said only "agú, agú", and nothing else. He sometimes asked his parents out of curiosity how he had said certain words when he was a baby, and he always found it amusing to listen to tapes of his earlier speech. At 8;11 he discovered diary notes of his earlier speech and he read with fascination, with an occasional outburst of laughter: "¿Así hablaba cuando era 'baby'? ¡Qué chistoso!" (*Is that the way I spoke when I was a baby? How funny!*) But he obviously did not directly recall any of his earlier speech. This suggests that the style he adopted beginning at 4;6 for speaking to his younger sister was a new development, a style for a specific instance.

Baby talk was also a transient style, appropriate only for a limited period of time. By 6;3 Mario considered himself too old to be addressed with any features reminiscent of baby talk, even to the point of lexical choices:

Papá (to Mario): Mario, no hagas así. Te vas a hacer chichiu. (*Mario, don't do that, You're going to get a "bu-bu".*)
Mario: No se dice "chichiu", se dice "lastimar". (*You don't say "bu-bu", you say "get hurt".*)
Papá: Ah . . . OK. (*Oh . . . OK.*)

Whereas at the same age Mario prompted his mother to use Bolivian baby expressions with his sister:

Mamá (to Carlina): Carlina, belleza. (*Carlina, sweetie.*)
Carlina: ¿Yo soy bonita, mami? (*Am I a sweetie, mami?*)
Mamá: Sí, amor. (*Yes, dear.*)
Mario (interjecting): Díle "musi, musi", mamá. (*Call her "musi, musi", mamá.*)

Yet scarcely two years later (8;4), Mario considered baby talk inappropriate not only for himself, but also for his sister, now 4;1:

Mamá (to Carlina): Es mi guagüita. (*She's my little baby.*)
Carlina (pretending to be a baby): Las guagüitas dicen "gu-gu". (*Babies say "gu-gu".*)
Mario (protesting): ¡No es guagüita! ¡Ya tiene cuatro años! (*She's not a baby! She's already four years old!*)

From these and similar examples, we can surmise that Mario viewed four to six as the transitional period from babyhood to childhood, requiring a corresponding change in the way individuals of this age be addressed.

A style for adults

When speaking with adults, Mario used a form of speech which was stylistically distinct from that used with peers and with children younger than himself. Because of the fixed relationship between the researcher and the child, this was the most abundantly recorded style. Since it is closest to adult usage, it is easier to describe by the absence of features attributed to other styles plus the inclusion of endearment forms (as appropriate for specific adults), courtesy and etiquette terms, and titles of respect. Here we shall also consider the pronoun/verb markings of Spanish which connote social intimacy or distance. Since endearment expressions have already been discussed, we shall limit our examination to courtesy terms, titles, and other linguistic social markers related to the adult style.

The first courtesy expressions were recorded at 2;2 /ás:yas/ (*gracias*). However, early use of "thank you" was usually limited to purely imitative action prompted by adults; in fact, prompting was necessary for its occurrence for several years. For the child the term probably served a superfluous function in that it was uttered after an action was already completed. De nada (*you're welcome*) fell into this same category. On the other hand, por favor (*please*) was a request for action and, as such, was a requirement, for without it, Mario's parents often failed to respond. Consequently, *por favor* occurred much earlier in spontaneous use, and much more regularly from 2;7 on (appearing first as /palaló/ and later as /pasalól/). Other expressions spontaneously used were:

Age 2;7	/bái bái/	Bye Bye.
Age 2;8	/peyíso/	Permiso.
Age 2;9	/sae lúts/	¡Salud!
	/salút, ĉin ĉin/	¡Salud! Cin-cin! (an Italian toast).
Age 3;7	/gyáŝyas/	Gracias (spontaneous use).

Leave-taking expressions (bye-bye) were usually fun and they were often accompanied by waving. Besides, departures of friends or relatives were usually a lengthy process and the ritual of leave-taking was an exaggerated moment. Much attention was given to the child's participation in this act. Permiso (*excuse me*) and por favor also had functional importance since approval was often withheld until these phrases were uttered. In some cases it was almost guaranteed that a request would be granted if the child added the ending -*ito*, as in *por favorcito* at age 3;8. The addition of the diminutive indicated a special plea meriting special consideration. By 6;0 Mario was well aware of the power of these terms, when properly used, toward the attainment of his goals, as, for example, when he asked to borrow his father's flashlight, an item usually denied to him. Whispering into his father's ear, he begged: "¿Puedo usar tu linterna . . . solo por favor?" (*May I use your flashlight . . . just please?*)

Salud and *cin-cin* were fun in that they accompanied the act of consuming some beverage and were often said while raising glasses in a toast. Other social amenities appeared, such as BUEN PROVECHO (*good appetite*) and CON PERMISO (*excuse me*) at 3;7, usually uttered so rapidly that Mario could not possibly have understood the component words of each expression. Nonetheless, these were ritualistic formulas which obtained permission to leave the table, serving in this way a particular function. However, the spontaneous — yet still sporadic — use of *gracias* made its tardy debut at 3;7, long after many other phrases were already in common use. By approximately 5;0, courtesy expressions had become a rather fixed aspect of the child's speech used with adults, including *gracias*. At age 5;9 his parents were impressed (and pleased) to note that Mario spontaneously thanked his teacher for a cookie she handed him at an open-house at the school. Mario was also fairly consistent about extending his hand when introduced and kissing all adults present upon retiring. Only recently was any hesitancy noted about kissing certain adult males, but mainly in response to the consternation of those persons at being kissed by a nine-year-old boy. Certainly this type of behaviour is rare for the United States, although far more common in Bolivia.

Even though Mario sometimes failed to use courtesy expressions himself at various stages, it was obvious from comments he made when others failed to use them that he knew social amenities formed part of adult speech. For example:

Age 3;6 His mother punished him erroneously for something he had not done. When it became clear that he was not to blame, he said to her (incorporating her own typically Venezuelan expression "epa"): Epa, mamá, ahora dí: "penón" (perdón). (*Hey, mamá, now say: "excuse me".*)

Age 3;7 Requesting a cookie from his aunt, she fails to respond. Mario quickly directs her attention to the proper form of his request by saying:

/Gime a máy kúki . . . ay tel yu plis/ (*Give me a "my" cookie . . . I tell you "please".*)

Age 5;7 A boy comes to the door selling magazine subscriptions. Mario's mother refuses by saying "no, thank you", yet she obviously received nothing. Mario questions this peculiar use:

¿Por qué dijiste "no, gracias"? (*Why did you say "no, thank you"?*)

Age 8;11 Mario sneezes several times. Everyone else is occupied and his sneezing goes unnoticed until he announces:

Yo estornudé cuatro veces y no me dijiste "salud". (*I sneezed four times and you didn't say "bless you".*)

Age 9;7 In Mexico, Mario has just learned it is considered more polite there to respond with "mande" rather than "¿qué?" (*what?*). Moments later he calls to a woman he treats as a grandmother and she answers with "eu" (another typically Mexican response), to which he says:

Mario: Abuelita, no se dice "eu"; se dice "mande". (*Grandma, you shouldn't say "eu"; you should say "mande".*)

The use of titles often reflects position and social distance. Sometimes titles are used to precede a name; in other cases, they substitute for the name in direct address. From the child's point of view, titles as used in the first case were probably superfluous and optional. In the second case, titles were needed when he wished to call someone's attention by substituting the title for the name. In Spanish, more so than in English, it is permissible to use titles such as *señor*, *señora*, etc., without the surname. This is not so for English since ones does not normally address anyone as "Mr." or "Mrs." without also adding the last name.

Señora was the first title that Mario used spontaneously at 3;0. *Señor* plus *tío/tía* (uncle/aunt, used for respect rather than relationship) appeared by 3;7. Other forms of direct address were used unerringly when they were learned upon initial contact as part of a person's name, as with the nursery attendant, Mario's school teacher, the medical doctor, etc. In spite of these developments, Mario preferred to call people's attention by simply yelling "hey", often omitting both titles and names, even up to his fifth year. "Hey" was acquired from his peers and it served a very functional purpose.

In indirect address, too, Spanish requires the referent *señor*, *señora*, etc. rather than *hombre*, *mujer* (man/woman), etc. This is akin to referring to a third party in English as "that gentleman" rather than "that man".

However, titles of indirect address appeared to be bothersome and unnecessary for the child, even if considered appropriate by adults. Despite constant reminders, the following behaviour was typical:

> At 8;2 Mario was sitting in his father's office when the phone rang. His father entered just as the child was hanging up. When asked who had called, Mario responded:
> **Mario**: Ese hombre. ("That man", referring to someone they had seen a while earlier.)
> **Papa**: ¡Señor, Mario, señor!

One of the important social markers of adult Spanish speech — as in most Romance tongues — is the distinction connoted by the choice between the pronouns *tú/usted* (you) and their corresponding verb endings. Brown & Gilman (1970: 252–75) termed these "the pronouns of power and solidarity". To employ this distinction requires mastery of a considerable amount of morphological detail, but more importantly, an awareness of varying types of social relationships. In Mario's dialect, the norm was to use *tú* with his parents (in contrast with some areas where *usted* is employed with parents) and consequently *tú* was the first form to appear in his speech.

The form *tú* was implicit in some of the earliest frozen expressions used by the child at 2;2: dáme, toma, and te quiero (*give me, take, I love you*). It was also implicit in many of the verb forms used at 2;7: ven aquí, papá; alélala (arréglala); ayaya (agarra); ves; salúlala (salúdala), and viste (*come here, papá; fix it; grab; you see; say "hello"; you saw*). However, its first spontaneous use did not occur until 3;0, when it showed up both in the pronominal form as well as in the sometimes accurate verb inflection: ¿Tú no va? (¿Tú no vas?); ¿Qué haces?; ¿Qué comes?; ¿Ya cabate? (¿Ya acabaste?) (*You are not going? What are you doing? What are you eating? Did you finish?*)

By 3;0 Mario had almost completely mastered both the pronoun *tú* and its relevant verb forms for declarative statements, although he still erred in positive and negative commands because of their aberrant patterning:

> *Age 3;0* ¡Tú no cantas! (*Don't you sing!*) (Intended as the negative command: ¡No cantes!) ¿No se va? (*Aren't you going away?*)
> *Age 3;1* ¿No te vas? (*Aren't you going?*) Tú sacate. (Tú sacaste.) (*You took "it" out.*) ¿Qué haces ahola (ahora)? (*What are you doing now?*)
> *Age 4;1* Tú es mi papá. (Tú eres mi papá.) (*You're my father.*)

The alternate form *usted* was implicit for the first time at 3;0, when Mario addressed a maid in Mexico with the phrase: "¿Señora, qué hace? ¿Se va?" (*Señora, what are you doing? Are you leaving?*) Since this utterance was made on the same day when he had told his father "¡Tú no cantas!", it was possible that he fully intended the distinction signified by the addition of -s to the verb used with his father. Later the same month, he used the pronoun *usted* for the first and only time until fully a year later: "usted veye (duerme) aquí" (*You sleep here*). However, this time it was said to an intimate person, and therefore its use was incorrect. Nonetheless, these were at least signs that Mario had begun to notice the form, having used it himself once or twice, even though incorrectly. The distinction apparently served no purpose and *usted* was disregarded.

Yet even by almost ten Mario did not employ the *tú/usted* distinction; *tú* was the form used with few exceptions. One exception was his alternation with the typically Bolivian form *vos*, which requires the same verb forms as *tú* (unlike the Argentine practice). Because this form was frequently used by the child's Bolivian nursemaid, it was commonly used with her and often in direct imitation of her model, as for example at age 7;9:

> Mario's nursemaid had lost her ring and asked the child to help her pray so that the ring would be found.
> **Nursemaid**: Vos puedes ayudar. Reza a San Antonio. (*You can help. Pray to Saint Anthony.*)
> **Mario**: Vos reza porque a mí no me escucha. No me entiende. (*You pray because he doesn't listen to me. He doesn't understand me.*)

Aside from *tú* and *vos* there was a hint that Mario may have temporarily grasped part of the rather complex social rule underlying the contrastive pronouns. At 5;5, while role-playing in La Paz with his parents and grand-parents, he assumed the role of teacher and assigned the others to be pupils. He adopted a rigid posture, crossed his arms and, with a serious face, directed the class. The task he assigned was to translate utterances he gave into English. When his playful students laughed, he called them back to order and, reprimanding his grandmother (now in the role of a little girl), he said:

> **Mario**: Niña, ¡ven acá! ¡Siéntese! (*Come here, little girl! Sit down!*)
> **Grandmother**: (Smiles and laughs.)
> **Mario**: ¡Cállese usted, niña! (*Keep quiet, little girl!*)

Although he was linguistically inconsistent in the first phrase, in which *tú* was implicit in the choice of the verb *ven*, he did use correct forms of *usted* in the two subsequent verbs said in the command form. His spontaneous use of *usted* was correct both in form and in application in this imaginary social situation, suggesting that Mario had some awareness of the pronominal distinction which he had not previously displayed. In spite of what he may or may not have perceived at this age, Mario continued to use *tú* with all interlocutors, without regard for age, role or social distance. Yet adults showed complete acceptance of this form of address from the child, whereas the same would not be true of another adult making an incorrect choice.

In spite of the example just cited, *usted* simply did not re-occur. Its lack of utility for the child may have caused its dismissal from his performance (but possibly not from his competence as well). In several incidents occurring between his eighth and ninth year, he displayed neither linguistic mastery nor a recognized social need:

Age 8;0 A teacher friend was visiting. Because he was interested in Mario's language development, he asked the child to address him with *usted*. Mario was obviously confused by his request:
Mario (to visitor): ¿Cómo estás? (*How are you?*)
Papá (to Mario) (intervenes): No, di lo mismo con "usted". (*No, say the same thing with "usted".*)
Mario: ¿Cómo? (*What do you mean?*)
Age 8;7 Mario began religious instruction in Bolivia, given privately by an elderly priest. Mario used *tú* with the priest even after he was corrected several times by his parents. During all ensuing sessions, *tú* continued to be his only spontaneous form of address for the priest.
Age 8;11 An attempt was made to assess Mario's linguistic control of verb forms corresponding to *usted*. He was therefore asked to change a series of statements from *tú* to *usted*. The child proved to be correct only with the fairly common greeting: "¿Cómo está usted?" In all other cases he merely adopted *usted* but retained the verb ending for *tú*, as in the examples: "Usted fuiste", and "¡Usted *haz* eso!" (*You went. Do that!*)

The child's lack of familiarity with this form was rather surprising. Obviously Mario's experiences up to now had not required this social/ linguistic expression. The question which arises is when do adults expect this formal expression from children, and correspondingly, when do children employ the contrastive social marker in speech? Observations of other children in diverse situations and questioning of Spanish-speakers indicated great variance in both, related to one's social class, type of education, country and regional differences, and so forth. A child of a lower class family, for example, might well begin to use *usted* early by copying the behaviour of his parents in a society where they must address many people formally although they themselves are addressed by *tú* in return (reflecting inferior–superior relationships within their society). On the other hand, children of upper class families use *tú* in many more situations, reflecting also their status in society. As another example, a child attending a rural public school might use *tú* more commonly throughout the elementary levels than a child educated in a religious private school. A child raised in most areas of Venezuela might use *tú* in more situations than would be tolerable in most of Bolivia. With such variance, one might best judge Mario's usage by the reactions of Bolivian speakers in a relationship with him. On this basis, then, his pervasive use of *tú* produced no social awkwardness. Several Bolivian Spanish-speakers of the same social class confirmed that they considered eleven or twelve a transitional period. Puberty seemed to be the critical time for acknowledging social relationships and encoding such information through linguistic markers.

By ten Mario began to display increased sensitivity to this distinction, even before he actively incorporated it into his own speech. An incident which occurred at 10;6 in La Paz reflected such sensitivity. At that time in Bolivia there was much comment about the "Litoral Cautivo" or "captured coastline" commemorating 100 years since their war with Chile. Signs posted everywhere quoted the Bolivian hero, Eduardo Abaroa, who when confronted by the Chilean military and asked to surrender, is remembered as replying defiantly: "¿Rendirme yo? . . . ¡que se rinda su abuela, carajo!" (*Me surrender? . . . let your grandmother surrender, dammit!*) Reading this sign, Mario puzzled, "¿Por qué Abaroa dice SU abuela, no TU?" (*Why did Abaroa say SU grandmother, and not TU?*) This acute observation confirms the *tú/usted* distinction as part of the child's competence at this point even though not actively employed. During this period Mario spent nearly a year in a Bolivian school. Returning from classes one day at 10;7, he reported:

Mario: Le pregunté al profesor . . . "OYE, por qué escribes las blancas palomas y no las palomas blancas? (*I asked the teacher . . . "Listen, why did you write the* WHITE DOVES, *and not the* DOVES WHITE?*)

Papá: Mario, ¿cómo le vas a hablar así? (*Mario, how is it possible that you address him that way?*)

Mario: Porque yo le conozco. (*Because I know him.*)

Papá: Sí, pero es mayor, . . . tu profesor . . . tienes que decirle "USTED, maestro . . . USTED escribe . . ." (*Yes, but he's older . . . your teacher . . . you have to say "YOU, teacher . . . YOU write . . ."*)

Mario: (Unimpressed).

Mario addressed the teacher again with the familiar form of "tú" when questioning the teacher's marked (and therefore poetic) order of the noun-adjective sequence. Yet scarcely two months later (10;9), he quoted his teacher unconsciously repeating even the marked use of the formal "usted" which the teacher had probably employed when angered by one of the students:

> In the car, returning from an excursion to the ruins at Tiahuanaku, Mario narrates the incident:
>
> **Mario**: Casi todos los días el Hermano Eduardo le dice al Castrillo: "¿Por qué usted habla sin permiso? Venga usted para acá . . . !" (*Almost every day, Brother Eduardo (the teacher) says to Castrillo (one of the students): Why are you speaking without permission? Come here . . . !*)
> Y le da un pellizco en la pierna . . . (*And he gives him a pinch on the leg . . .*)
> "Usted no tiene permiso para hacer eso (hablar)." (*"You don't have permission to do that (to speak)."*)

Besides the appropriate uses of *tú/usted*, marked use of either often conveys other meanings. For example, not to use *usted* with adults when it is clearly appropriate is a transgression of social norms, possibly interpreted as an insult, a belittlement of one's social role or position, or simply rudeness. Similarly, parents who address a child as *tú* sometimes switch abruptly to *usted* to produce calculated effects. For example, when Mario's father was irritated or angered by the child's behaviour, he made statements like: "¡Y usted va a marchar a la cama ahora mismo . . . y no me llame más!" (*And you* (usted) *go to bed right now . . . and don't you* (usted) *call me any more!*) This change of linguistic form conveyed much more than the purely literal message of its words. The use of *usted* where *tú* would normally have been employed served to underscore the severity of the message and the anger of the speaker. Mario's speech in his role as school teacher conveyed similar effects. This and other examples demonstrate his sensitivity to this particular usage of *usted*. At 7;1, when his mother got angry with him and addressed him in this manner, he took offence and said:

> **Mario**: ¡No me llames "usted" . . . eres mi gente! (*Don't call me "you"* (usted) . . . *you're my people! (family)*).

Two months later (7;3), when his father entered the kitchen upon return from work and greeted Mario formally, the child reacted in the same way:

> **Papá** (to Mario): ¡Hola! ¿Cómo está usted? (*Hi! How are you* (usted)?)
> **Mario**: ¡No me llames "usted"! (*Don't call me "usted"!*)
> **Papá**: ¿Por qué? (*Why?*)
> **Mario**: Eres mi gente. (*You're my people.*)

Although Mario did not yet acknowledge many dimensions of status normally reflected through the *tú/usted* distinction, he did show an awareness of status in other ways. At age 5;6 he demonstrated cognizance of his role and relationship with the chauffeur and servants in La Paz. This was not detected from his use of *tú* with them (appropriate anyway in this case) but rather from other behaviour — verbal and otherwise. Commands and manner towards the servants were direct and blunt, lacking courtesy terms: "Ven . . . tráeme la mamadera . . . deja eso . . ." (*Come . . . bring me the baby's bottle . . . leave that!*) Naturally he had observed others using similar abrupt and direct commands with servants, often devoid of courtesy modifiers. When his father told him to thank Basilio, or to say please to Irma, he answered: "No tengo a (*sic*) decirlo . . . es mi gente." (*I don't have to say it . . . she's my people.*) Although this statement might make many an English speaker shudder, it nonetheless neatly explains his behaviour, entirely appropriate within the Bolivian context.

The evidence presented of Mario's development and use of the *tú/usted* distinction — or lack of it — touches upon a rather intriguing question: whether linguistic development or social need is more essential for its eventual appearance. Certainly there were signs that he had begun to pick up the form *usted* and its corresponding verb forms at an early age, but for some reason he failed to incorporate these features as a permanent aspect of speech. Furthermore, by five or six he had acquired practically all the morphological requirements of the third person singular, which corresponds in detail to *usted* as well. The only linguistic requirement lacking, then, was to relate *usted* to these third person endings already in use. This would seem to be a relatively minor linguistic feat; hence, social need seems to be the critical factor. One might wonder whether Mario's limited experience in a Spanish-speaking society (and therefore limited interactions with speakers of diverse social backgrounds) might account for the lack of a sociolinguistic rule for usage. However, comparisons with other Bolivian children of similar social background and age rules this out since Mario appears to comply with their norm. Besides, we know that he was sensitive to other sociolinguistic dimensions. He knew, for example, that persons belonging to the same family unit do not address each other as *usted* except as marked behaviour. He knew also quite a lot about the rules of interaction appropriate for use with those in a socially ascribed inferior position. Hence, his lack of a formal form and its use seem to be linked to his particular social role and his current age. When his failure to employ *usted* began to cause his parents discomfort (evidenced, for example, for the first time in Mario's sessions with the priest), their reactions were added to other socializing forces needed to cause Mario to attend to a feature which earlier had not affected him in his role as a child.

One other development deserves comment in our examination of the child's acquisition of a style acceptable with adults. Slowly he is learning to reformulate his requests through the incorporation of linguistic mollifiers. One of the most notable examples in the diary was the appearance of *quisiera*, which gradually took the place of *quiero*. This could be equivalent in English to "I would/should like" instead of simply "I want". This was a fairly recent development, beginning in his eighth year. Initial attempts to have the child soften his requests sometimes met with humorous responses; for example, at 8;2:

> Mario was looking through a listing of children's books which he had brought home from school, when he spotted a particular book he wanted.
>
> **Mario** (to Nursemaid): Marina, sabes que quiero ese libro . . . ése. (*Marina, you know that I want that book . . . that one.*)
>
> **Nursemaid**: Mario, no se dice "quiero" . . . se dice "quisiera". (*Mario, you shouldn't say "I want" . . . you should say "I would like."*)
>
> **Mario:** No, pero yo ESTOY SEGURO que quiero . . . no "quisiera". (*No, but I AM SURE that I want . . . not "I would like."*)

Obviously the child understood the semantic difference between the forms *quiero* and *quisiera*; what puzzled him was this peculiar directive to mollify a request which he was so sure about. However, later on he began to rephrase his statements (especially when met with glaring eyes as a response). By his ninth year, he increasingly used *quisiera* spontaneously as the more acceptable form for communicating his wants — no matter how certain he was of what he wanted, nor the intensity of his desire. This social tactic, accomplished through linguistic means, was a significant development toward participation in the adult world.

Variations for other needs

Besides the styles discussed thus far, still other speech variations were used for other special needs: namely, modifications for certain formal public settings, a narrative style, telephone talk, taboo forms, regional dialectal adjustments, and linguistic accommodation for speaking with those of limited proficiency in either of the languages involved. Stylistic variation was eventually extended even to writing forms. All of these also deserve comment.

One interesting variety involved voice control, without involving other linguistic modifications aside from certain lexical items. Within certain fixed settings, it was necessary to speak more softly than in others. In church, in a doctor's waiting room, in a public theatre or restaurant, Mario was often reminded to speak quietly, sometimes in a whisper. In addition, he was sometimes reprimanded for using certain words. For example, once when his mother spoke to him quietly in a doctor's office, he replied each time with an even louder "¿Qué?" (*What?*). In church he persisted in using the same tone he had used on the street, attracting the attention of everyone around. Furthermore, the content of his remarks was sometimes inappropriate to the setting: "Mira, Diosito está en calzones", observing that Jesus was not fully clothed on the cross; or, "Esos señores parecen indios", likening the dress of the bishop and other priests to Indians in full attire. In other public places, Mario yelled out his toilet needs with complete abandon — "¡¡Pis!! ¡¡Caca!!" Apparently it was difficult to discern the special characteristics of those situations which required a softer voice, for between 2;0 and 5;0 Mario still had not displayed voice control. Voice modulation was a slow development, as well as the knowledge underlying restrictions and constraints on the content of the child's speech. Socialization through school probably hastened this development beyond 5;0.

Among the variations recorded, there was evidence that Mario had adopted a special form for narrations. The style used for storytelling was clearly distinct from that used in dialogue and conversation. Narrative style involved the predominant use of declarative statements, a fairly similar intonational pattern maintained with each utterance, and the beginning of most statements with the Spanish conjunction "y". In addition, the entire narrative was set off with the conventional opening phrase common to Spanish: "Había una vez", (*Once upon a time*), and it concluded with: "Colorín, colorado, el cuento ha terminado" (*Colorín, colorado, the story is over*). Immediately upon conclusion there was a marked shift back to normal conversation style. For example, at age 3;3:

Child's Utterance	*Standard Language*
Aquí stava un nene chitito,	Aquí estaba un nene chiquito,
Y decía "bye-bye".	Y decía "bye-bye".
El nenito tene un bastón.	El nenito tiene un bastón.
Y este nenito stava un nenito aquí con su papá.	Y este nenito estaba un nenito aquí con su papá.
Y este nenito stava con bastón largo.	Y este nenito estaba con bastón largo.
Y este nenito stava y jalava el pelo.	Y este nenito estaba y jalaba el pelo.

(There was a little boy,
And he was saying "bye-bye".
The boy had a stick.
And this boy, this boy
was here with his papá.
And this boy had a
long stick.
And this boy was here
and he pulled hair.)

Although his linguistic talents improved considerably by age 5;5, his narrative style remained substantially unchanged:

Pointing to a demon with big horns he has drawn, Mario narrates the following:

Este es un 'Cuernote''.	*(This is "Cuernote" (Big Horn).*
Es mucho, much malo.	*He is very, very bad.*
Pero él sólo mata Dr Mártins y Drácula.	*But he only kills Dr Martins and Dracula.*
Y no come niños y niñas.	*And he doesn't eat boys and girls.*
Y abajo de él, hay un dragón bueno	*And below him, there's a good dragon*
que es el ayudante del Cuernote.	*who is Cuernote's helper.*
Y el dragón tira fuego por la nariz y por la boca.	*And fire comes out of the dragon's nose and mouth.*
Y también sale humo de la nariz.	*And smoke also comes out of his nose.*
Y también cuando el dragón encuentra niños y niñas se los lleva cargando donde Cuernote.	*And when the dragon finds boys and girls he takes them to Cuernote.*
Y también cuando Cuernote le (sic) habla a los niños y las niñas, le pregunta si le ha mordido el Dr Mártins . . . etc.	*And when Cuernote speaks to the boys and girls, he asks if Dr Martins has bitten them . . . etc.)*

On the telephone, Mario invariably used the proper introductory and closing remarks. In the sense that speaking on the telephone requires certain linguistic modifications, it may be viewed as a limited style for a specific circumstance.

Above we have given a few examples of how the socialization process relegated a small core of utterances into a taboo category. The parents' prohibitions against certain words gave a special aura they did not previously have. Mario used these special words when he became angry or wished to anger others. Although hardly a speech style, the use of this body of phrases was directly related to context. It was a specific social context that gave these words their special power and not the simple act of saying the sounds. As Mario realized what types of words were condemned (principally those related to the sexual organs and bodily functions), he became more imaginative, saying not only things he had learned from direct experience, but also creating his own combinations of potentially powerful phrases:

¡Fastidioso tú, con potito! (*Pesty you, with a fanny!*)
¡Pis y caca en tu cara! (*Pee and poop in your face!*)

Although his taboo repertoire increased rapidly after entering school, so also did his sensitivity about the use of these terms. In fact, he developed such a conservative attitude about the use of certain words that he was reluctant to pronounce them under any circumstances. For example, at 8;4 the following incident was recorded:

Mario had just finished reading a comic book and he was impressed by the number of words uttered by his heroes which he considered unspeakable.
Mario (to Papá): En mi libro hay muchas palabras malas. (*There are lots of bad words in my book.*)
Papá: ¿Ah sí? (*Oh really?*)
Mario: ¿Puedo decir? (*Can I tell you one?*)
Papá: A ver . . . ¿cuáles? (*Let's see . . . which?*)
Mario: Yo no las digo. Sólo las miro y las pienso. (*I don't say them. I only look at them and think them.*)
Mario is obviously reluctant to say the words for his father. When encouraged, he spells them out (in Spanish):
Mario: D-a-m-m-i-t . . . y . . . h-e-l-l . . . Remembering another word he had heard elsewhere, he adds:
Mario: y también . . . G-o-d-d-a-m-m-i-t.

Mario was also aware that the Spanish he heard did not always sound the same; some people spoke in different ways. In fact, when he heard Mexicans, Bolivians, Venezuelans, Uruguayans, Spaniards and others speak, he often showed some visible reaction. In some cases, he hesitated while trying to discern whether they simply spoke a different "style" or whether they were speaking a different language. This occurred, for example, when he spoke with Portuguese-speaking individuals whose speech sounded strange but was similar enough to comprehend. After dealing with persons who spoke other dialects for any period of time, Mario sometimes began to emulate their intonation and expressions. For example, after a summer in Mexico his tone clearly reflected the speech patterns of his caretaker there. He also used typically Mexican expressions such as "popote, qué padre", and "ándale, ándale". When told not to say this, he retorted: "pero Andrés (the maid's brother) dijía (decía) 'ándale, ándale'."

At 5;6, after only two days of play with two Brazilian children he met on a train to Cuzco, his intonation began to reflect theirs, and he already began to say such things as:

> **Mario**: Esta pistola no funciona . . . está quebrada. (Uses *quebrada*, Portuguese for *rota*, and the dental, rather than fricative /d/ required in Spanish.) (*This gun doesn't work . . . it's broken.*)

Later:

> **Mario**: Vamos a brincar arriba. (*brincar*, Portuguese for *jugar*) (*Let's go play upstairs.*)

He was obviously aware of their differing style, and commented on it:

Hearing one of the children reply *não*, he asked:
> **Mario**: ¿Por qué dice así . . . "não"? (*Why does he speak like that . . . "não?" (instead of "no")*)

Or when his friend Alexandro said to his mother:

> **Alexandro**: Limpa a nariz dêle! (*Wipe his nose!*)

Mario, surprised by the construction, laughed and remarked:

> **Mario** (to Papá): El dice "limpia la nariz del". (Apparently focusing on the peculiar contraction and pronunciation and unconsciously changing the verb and noun to Spanish forms.)

In addition, Mario commented on the Castilian pronunciation of a Spanish woman who came to dinner (8;6). In Venezuela, he made remarks concerning the speech of children with whom he played (6;7). He was sensitive even to the detail of an aspirated /s/ in the word "adió" (adiós) as pronounced by a woman from Puerto Rico (9;0). In Bolivia he made observations of a style common to many people there, noting both the verb stress change and pronunciation of the /r̄/ (10;6):

> **Mario** (imitating): . . . llevá . . . dejá . . . aquí en Bolivia hablan así, ¿verdad? (*llevá . . . dejá . . . here in Bolivia they speak like that, don't they?*)

And again the next day:

Mario: Papá, Gustavo dice /žey/ (rey), /tože/ (torre) . . . ponen muchas "zetas". (*Papá, Gustavo says /žey, tože/ . . . they say a lot of "z's".*)
Papá: (amused, he imitates the pronunciation).
Mario: Sí, también dice: dejá, tomá. (*Yes, and he also says: dejá, tomá.*)

As a younger child, his ability to detect the dominant language of others guided Mario in the selection of which of his two languages to use. Often, when he determined that his interlocutor was not sufficiently proficient in Spanish, he changed automatically to English even if the other speaker tried to maintain the conversation in Spanish. However, by 7;0 Mario had learned to accept the attempts of others to speak to him in Spanish even if they lacked sufficient fluency and native pronunciation. In a sense, his linguistic accommodation to such persons constituted the beginnings of another style of speech, one reserved for those who were not native speakers. If his interlocutors switched or mixed codes, he did likewise even though he normally maintained rigid separation of his languages. It was also noted that he often spoke more slowly, sometimes more loudly, and made conscious attempts to enunciate as clearly as possible. These were salient aspects of his style for those whose Spanish was limited.

Aside from stylistic developments in speech, Mario became aware of stylistic variations in writing as well. A diary notation at 9;3 noted his reaction to a sign which spelled a word in abbreviated form. Seeing the word TAC, he commented: "Está escrita mal; . . . falta la 'k' final" (*It's misspelled; it doesn't have the final "k"*). He was told that advertisements often spell words differently, like "nite" and "Xmas", to which he replied:

Mario: Oh . . . they can trick children and then they won't get 100s on their spelling tests.
Papá: Who can trick children?
Mario: The TV and books.

At age 10;8 in La Paz, he sought help one day with his homework. His mother helped by writing something in his copybook, while he cautioned her:

Mario: Pero tienes que escribir "educadamente". (*But you have to write "in an educated manner".*)
Mamá (surprised): ¿Quién dice así "educadamente"? (*Who told you this "educadamente"?*)
Mario: El Hermano Edmundo. (Brother Edmundo, his teacher).

A few days later, he was writing a letter to his fifth grade classmates back in the United States. Occasionally he interrupted to ask: "how do you say?" or "how do you spell?" He asked so many things that the following dialogue ensued:

Mario (to Parents): Hey, I'm forgetting English!

A few moments later he asks:

Mario (to Papá): Papá, ¿cómo se dice así? (*Papá, how do you say like this?*) (With his hands he traces a pregnant stomach.)
Papá: Pregnant?? (questioningly)
Mario: No . . . otra palabra . . . That's not educated . . . Se van a reír todos. (*No . . . another word . . . "That's not educated" . . . Everybody's going to laugh.*)
Mamá (interjects): She is going to have a baby.
Mario (resumes writing): . . . que . . . "my aunt" . . . she's going to have a baby. (Stops and questions the use of "aunt") That sounds like she's old . . . she's an old person.
Mamá: No . . . entonces pon: "my young aunt". (*Then write, "my young aunt".*

Finally, in an example already cited, Mario questioned his Bolivian teacher at age 10;7 concerning the inversion of normal Spanish word order: "¿Por qué escribes las BLANCAS PALOMAS y no las PALOMAS BLANCAS?" Through this example, and others, Mario began to develop awareness, then, not only of the possibility of variation within speech, but in how one communicates through the written medium as well.

Summary

To summarize, we have noted the evolving relationship between language use and linguistic form.

As an infant, Mario used differentiated vocalizations to express varying physical needs. As he became an increasingly social being, his developing speech was continually shaped by social patterns, and he correspondingly modified his linguistic expression in response to varying social needs. Whether the child addressed younger children, peers, or adults; whether his interlocutors were well known, casual associates, or socially distant; whether they were socially superior, inferior, or equal; or whether they were in a formal or informal setting — all were factors affecting the chlid's use of language. His communicative competence included not only an ability to produce grammatical constructs but also to modify these in distinct ways related to each situation. Inappropriate forms of expression were less and less tolerated by adults as the child matured. Negative feedback was provided in various ways when the child did not comply with social expectations. In each case, proper or aberrant verbal behaviour was determined by the social factors present at the moment of speech, with each set of circumstances affecting the child's language output in specific ways.

Although linguists generally agree that children acquire much of their native language by age five, the literature does not comment on the ability of children to differentiate and produce diverse styles. Yet differentiated communicative behaviour probably begins in infancy. And although the younger child does not yet control many of the elements of his language, he nonetheless displays speech variations even with limited language. The bilingual child, in particular, presents convincing evidence of this by his very ability to shift entire codes. Other examples from the data confirm that the child also modifies speech signals in other distinctive ways in accordance with contextual variables.

Speech styles, then, are characteristic not only of adults but of children, too. Occasional clues as to the child's perception of social norms and concomitant styles even when not used in his own speech were witnessed in role-play situations, in his reaction to others when they transgressed social rules, as well as in his own comments. Hence, it cannot be assumed that the child did not possess those abilities he did not display actively. Given the proper circumstances, he demonstrated sensitivity even to several styles not related to his present status. Obviously, certain styles are relevant to a speaker only at different stages of development and are therefore temporal in nature. Such styles come and go in as much as they are contingent upon the differing roles and relationships the child establishes within his developing world. For example, code differentiation was an immediate necessity and was well handled by the middle of the second year; various styles within each language were also clearly discernible before the third. Yet other styles were already discarded before the child was seven: a communicative style dependent primarily on non-linguistic expression (by about 3;6); whining (last witnessed about the fifth year); and baby talk (no longer acceptable by the sixth year in accordance with the child's own judgements). Furthermore, Mario had learned not only to use unmarked language; he employed marked language as well by adopting a given style out of context to create some special effect. Indeed, he became quite adept at invoking styles not normally appropriate for a given situation for a special purpose. In such cases he conveyed much more than the literal message of the grammatical statement.

Two other aspects of stylistic development deserve comment — the relation of style to status and social class, and the relevance of a diversified "society of speakers" to varied speech behaviour. Despite the limitations of a single case study, there is some indication that the individual's ability to control styles, as well as the number of styles he acquires, may be less related to social class in any fixed manner than it is to the need for a child — any child — to behave in the various ways demanded of him. For example, Mario used only one form of address until almost age ten in contrast with demands placed upon servant children younger than himself to employ multiple forms. Secondly, interaction within a diversified group of speakers also seems essential in order for a wide range of speech styles to develop. Speakers of differing ages, sex, role, relationship, social class and so forth, provide variables which foster the development and maintenance of a great range of styles. Conversely, the child who has had limited social interaction is constrained by the reduction of social variables. The bilingual child reared apart from a society of speakers of one of the two languages he is acquiring indeed has less opportunity to experience diversified speech behaviour. Although linguistic development is stimulated and sustained by the child's family, stylistic development may be truncated for want of a more diversified experience. Bilingual-bicultural education programmes, however, may now provide a new source that may help each language to develop with a richness of styles.

Finally, language form and function are intimately related as a dynamic of language use throughout the acquisitional process. As the child advances into a continually expanding world from his base in the family nucleus, so also does his language evolve and change in content and style to meet his new social needs. What began in infancy is a process which continues throughout life — from childhood on into adulthood.

TABLE 3   *Styles and use in child language*

Age	Emerging styles	Characteristics and use
Inf'cy	Differentiated crying	To express basic physical needs.
0;4	Crying or other vocalizations (accompanied by physical motion/ silence)	To express physical needs; contentment; self-expression.
1;4– 1;10	Emergence of speech vs. non-speech sounds	Communication vs. self-expression or linguistic practice.
	Speech (with social terms) vs. silence	Related to interlocutor (known/unknown).
	Oral language vs. physical gestures (pointing)	Socially accepted communication or disapproved (depending on age).
2;0	Developing style with adults (marks the emergence of a vast	Characterized by courtesy and etiquette terms, titles, grasp of some aspects of *tú/usted*. Used with adults for communication; expresses social norms;

Age	Emerging styles	Characteristics and use
	amount of language input)	marks the setting, role, and relationship of participants.
	Beginning of voice control	Related to settings: formal/informal.
	Taboo phrases	Related to interlocutor and setting.
2;6	Spanish/English code distinction	Related to interlocutor and setting.
2;7	Speech vs. nonsense sounds	Speech for communication; nonsense sounds used as self-expression; also reflects boredom, non-compliance.
	Normal speech vs. whining	Whining used with parents only.
3;1	Affectionate language	Marked by diminutives, selected terms, improvised terminations; used only with intimates.
3;3	Narrative style	Formalized beginning and ending; fixed utterances commonly begin with a conjunction.
3;4	Peer language fully developed (begun about 2;2)	Marked by direct commands, expressive interjections, onomatopoeic sounds, no endearment, lack of courtesy terms or titles, few diminutives, frequent eruptions of song and recitations; used with others of same age.
3;6	Cessation of communicative style using only non-linguistic means (begun about 1;4)	
4;6	Baby-talk style	Higher voice frequency, varying intonation, diminutives, some phone or syllable substitutions, selected expressions; used with younger children.
5;6	Style used with servants	Direct commands, lack of courtesy terms; related to social class.
5;6	Increased sensitivity to regional accents, dialects	Adapts some of the features perceived.
5;9	Cessation of whining style (begun about 2;7)	
6;3	Cessation of baby-talk style addressed to the child (upon his request)	
7;0	Linguistic accommodation with non-native speakers	Marked by slower pace, increased volume, deliberate enunciation. Related to interlocutors with foreign accents and/or insufficient fluency.
9;3	Awareness of differing ways to express self through writing	Spelling modifications, poetic devices, and differing lexical choices.

Notes to Chapter 4

1. Burling (1971: 181–82) reports similar reactions on the part of his son "who quickly learned who did not speak Garo and rarely attempted to speak to them . . ." and also that the child was more shy with speakers of other languages than with Garo speakers. Burling felt that his son recognized the existence of two languages as early as 2;2.

2. See Ervin-Tripp (1973: 302–73). Also see an article by Hymes (1967: 8–28) which discusses speech components.

3. Few studies have analysed the effects of adult caretakers on the language of the child. One work which considers linguistic implications is by Brown & Bellugi (1964: 131–61).

4. Ervin-Tripp points out that terms of "registers, styles, marking", etc., are still being developed; most of these terms share the fact that they all involve speech variation. See Ervin-Tripp (1973: 262–301).

5. The reader is referred to a similar analysis done by Jean Berko Gleason (1973). In this paper she also alludes to similar occurrences in children's behaviour.

6. Curiously, few other reports talk about this phenomenon although the use of non-standard words is reported. See Weir (1962) and Leopold (1939–49: 140).

7. Jean Piaget (1971) comments on types of interaction between children; however, his work, *The Language and Thought of the Child*, deals primarily with older children, from four to eleven. In one analysis performed of the speech of 20 children, he speaks of all children having certain functional needs, although "In the domineering child there will be an increase of orders, threats, criticisms, and arguments, while the more dreamily inclined will indulge in a greater number of monologues", (p. 70). In either case, the examples cited of Mario's language were recorded while he played with imaginary friends and it is suspected that much of his language was in imitation of peers, rather than spontaneous language reflecting his own type of interaction.

5 A linguistic profile

General comments

Thus far, several sociolinguistic aspects of bilingual acquisition have been considered. Two other areas are relevant to this treatment of dual language acquisition. The first arises from a natural curiosity at this point about how accurately the child constructs his utterances (in a purely linguistic sense). That is, how does this bilingual child *compare* with monolingual speakers of the same age? The second area of interest arises from the other side of this question, i.e. how does this bilingual child *differ* (linguistically) as a result of his knowledge of two languages? To put the question another way, we are concerned here with language interaction, resulting from the co-existence of two systems within the same individual. This is both a fascinating and complex dimension of bilingual behaviour, a phenomenon which has been known alternately as interference and transference.

Evolution of a concept

Linguists have long recognized that languages interact and affect each other when they co-exist in the same speaker. This interaction was commonly termed "interference", reflecting a view widely held by linguists a little more than three decades ago. Although the concept was immediately useful when first proposed, there was lingering uneasiness with it. First off, one had to distinguish between interference in *language* (in a historical sense) as opposed to interference in *speech* (momentary influences due to the presence of a second language). Basing his distinction on the Saussurian concept of "parole" and "langue", Weinreich (1968: 11) described the difference in this manner:

> "(Parole) . . . is characteristic of a certain discourse, it is momentary, and it is due to the speaker's first-hand knowledge

of another language; the latter is part of the norm, it is a feature of another code that has become habitualized, and it is learned by monolingual speakers in the same way as originally native features of the norm."

Secondly, one recognizes that to define linguistic interaction, identify and describe it, and quantify and tabulate borrowings, are all rather complex problems, and become even more so when sociolinguistic aspects are also considered (see Hasselmo 1969: 122–41). Haugen (1956: 39) described linguistic interference (or "diffusion" as he termed it) as that influence ". . . in which a single item is plucked out of one language and used in the context of another". However, the question remains as to whether "item" refers to a single sound or to a "given stretch of speech". In other words, what is the minimal unit of interaction; and conversely, its outer extensions? Haugen attempted to clarify this by further proposing three stages of linguistic diffusion:

1. *switching*, the alternate use of two languages;
2. *interference*, the overlapping of two languages, and
3. *integration*, the regular use of material from one language in another, so that there is no longer either switching or overlapping, except in a historical sense.

These divisions, however, suggest the possibility of still others. Consequently scholars grapple with a continuum such that as the segment of speech becomes increasingly longer, it becomes more difficult to distinguish clearly linguistic interaction from a code switch. Weinreich (1968: 1) avoided this problem of degree by positing a more general definition of interference, as simply ". . . instances of deviation from the norms of either language which occur in the speech of bilinguals . . . as a result of language contact."

A third aspect of the concept of linguistic interaction has to do with still another continuum — one through time. As linguists considered degrees of interference — whether complete code switching, overlapping, or integration — they usually engaged in synchronic descriptions. The time dimension suggests still another concern, one of language shift, described by Weinreich as ". . . the change from the habitual use of one language to that of another" (p. 68). Although separate synchronic analyses done at different points in time may help to ascertain the direction of language shift, one is again propelled toward a more sociolinguistically oriented approach in order to understand the phenomenon more fully.

Part of the reason the time question may not have been widely treated was because most analyses of linguistic interaction heretofore involved the study of adult bilinguals. Although even adults may undergo linguistic shift, they have usually been viewed in terms of interaction at a given point in time. On the other hand, shifts in language use are so dramatically witnessed in children that they are difficult to ignore. The acquisition or dissolution of a second tongue often occurs within a relatively short period of time. Because of this, one can easily observe the onset of a second language, shifts in language use, and sometimes disappearance of one or several languages over a matter of months (see, for example, Tits, 1948).

Because interaction is a fluid phenomenon, subject to increase or decrease, and shift in direction, it can be best understood in terms of process, and a sociolinguistic one at that. Synchronic treatments of linguistic interaction are simply not adequate to capture such dynamics. Once a process orientation is espoused, distinctions between the synchronic and diachronic are obliterated as the synchronic becomes only a momentary manifestation of the diachronic continuum through time.

Fourthly, many studies of linguistic interaction are indeed purely linguistic in scope, dealing with potential interference arising from any inherent similarities or differences across structures. A common treatment is in the form of contrastive analyses; and in fact, complete series have been produced in an attempt to contrast the linguistic systems of the more commonly taught languages in the United States. These purport to serve the applied linguist, but even classroom teachers quickly realize that not all predictions of interference actually occur in fact. The authors of one such series acknowledge the purely theoretical nature of their work when they state:

> "A theoretical grammar of any type may legitimately be confined to the description of what constitutes a well-formed sentence in a particular language. It must say what a grammatical sentence is, but not necessarily how it is used: in which situations it is appropriate, what its range of synonyms and paraphrases is, and the like. The description of usage, in this broader sense, is not the content of a grammatical study but of something much larger and less well understood." (Stockwell, Bowen & Martin, 1965a: 2).

To consider language in this "broader sense" to which they allude, then, inevitably leads to an examination of interference phenomena in quite a different light.

Before considering a sociolinguistic treatment, we should state a fifth aspect of the concept of linguistic interaction which has moved linguists

beyond the original "interference" viewpoint. Many individuals were un-
happy with the possible social implications of the term "interference" (i.e.
deviation from a norm that implied social judgements). As further study
revealed that bilingual speakers did indeed have a heretofore unexpected
control over their dual language systems, this added to a need to expand the
original concept. Introduction of the term "transfer" or "transference" was
a result. In other words, whereas language interaction was previously seen
as a negative side of bilingual use and one often beyond the speaker's
control, it now was clear that not all linguistic interaction observed was
interference. We now understood that interaction across language systems
in the speech of a bilingual is sometimes a contrived and consciously motivated act which in fact enriches communication possibilities among bilingual
speakers.

Finally, we have already stated that language interaction in speech is
due to the speaker's knowledge of two or more systems, and therefore
peculiar to the bilingual or multilingual person. And as with other aspects of
the speaker's languages, interaction across systems is subject to the impact
of the context of the speech event. Purely linguistic treatments which do not
take this into account therefore fail to capture the phenomenon as a dynamic
process which it is. Weinreich, for one, recognized early on, the influence of
what he called "non-structural" factors when he stated:

> "The forms of mutual interference of languages that are in
> contact are stated in terms of descriptive linguistics. Even the
> causes of specific interference can, in most cases, be determined
> by linguistic methods. . . . But not all potential forms of interfer-
> ence actually materialize. The precise effect of bilingualism on a
> person's speech varies with a great many other factors, some of
> which might be called extra-linguistic because they lie beyond
> the structural differences of the languages . . ." (Weinreich,
> 1968: 3)

He enumerated several extra-linguistic factors, including the speaker's facility of verbal expression, his or her ability to keep two languages apart, the
relative proficiency in each, specialization in the use of each language,
manner of learning each language, and attitudes toward each of the
languages known. Even so, Weinreich was admittedly concerned in his own
detailed analysis of interference with the purely structural causes.

In the past few years, thanks to the research of sociolinguists, we now
have a more explicit understanding of the inter-relationship of language and
context, and along with that, a clearer notion of just how social factors affect
language interaction. Recent studies have examined the social (as well as

linguistic and psychological) factors that trigger the overlapping (intentional or otherwise) of one language on another, which dramatizes the control that bilinguals have over this process. If mixing is indeed under one's control and is produced for a variety of reasons, it would be important to consider both the positive as well as negative aspects. Padilla (1977) attempted to include both by coining the terms *interpolation* and *intercalation*. Many others have preferred the label *transference*. Yet both terms may still be necessary, reserving *interference* for mixing that is beyond the speaker's control and attributable entirely to structural linguistic differences; transference, on the other hand, might be mixing controlled by the speaker (on a conscious or subconscious level) and traceable to environmental and social factors. Both linguistic and sociolinguistic terms may be of continued use in connoting this distinction and are used in this way in this study.

Having referred to nonstructural (i.e. social) causes of language interaction, one might ask how social conditions affect mixing across languages; for example:

1. What specific social variables affect language interaction?
2. Is interaction a predictable outcome of languages in contact, or does it occur only in specific instances in relation to varying social factors?
3. In what direction does interaction occur? Can it go in either direction across languages?
4. In what aspects of language does mixing occur?
5. Does it occur in some aspects more than in others? Are some aspects subject to greater control by the speaker than others?
6. What positive dimensions of interaction (transference) are there in the speech of bilingual children? What are examples of interference?

Language interaction and the bilingual child: Special considerations

Despite increased study of adult bilinguals and their use of two languages, much work is yet to be done with very young children. Bilingual children, in fact, present additional complexities that must be considered when transference or interference is being examined. First of all, one must consider to what extent the child is really undergoing concurrent and dual language acquisition, or when he is more like the second-language learner. One needs only to reflect on the great variety of exposure and acquisitional patterns of bilingual children who have been described in the literature. Truly concurrent and equal exposure appears to be more hypothetical than real. Many children, for example, are exposed to a home language in greater amounts initially than to the language of the larger society. When they are older and begin to interact outside the home, the second language often becomes the principal language of the child. Even in cases in which each parent used a separate language (Ronjat, Leopold, and others), it is easy to imagine that exposure must have varied in kind and in degree, contingent on the interaction and role function each parent performed. Truly simultaneous and equal exposure is probably easier to conjecture than to find in reality.

Bilingual acquisition, therefore (like bilingualism itself), includes a great variety of acquisitional patterns. This is important to keep in mind as we discuss language interaction in one bilingual child. In addition, Mackey (1970: 554) pointed out that with all bilinguals, we must acknowledge not only language dominance but also dominance in relation to various domains of experience. Language dominance configurations are therefore also critical to this view of language interaction.

Second, several researchers have suggested that the child exposed to two languages at a very early age may in fact have only one linguistic system. Swain (1972), for example, speaks of "bilingualism as a first language", suggesting that the differentiation of the single code occurs only later as a result of the social need to create two distinct linguistic sets. Padilla & Lindholm (1976b: 97–142) and I came to the same conclusion through our own research. If this is the case it might be accurate to speak not of interference, but of language separation — a gradual process of language differentiation. What has been called interference may be the residue of an incompleted process. How we view the process affects in part our understanding of dual language development. In either case, it is *differentiated* language use that one recognizes as bilingual behaviour. And differentiated behaviour comes about in response to the demands of a social context that fosters or inhibits mixing or separation. Again, the influence of social context cannot be dismissed in considering either phenomenon.

Third, although the adult bilingual speaker theoretically already possesses two fully developed languages, the child exposed to two systems is involved in the process of developing his first mode of communicating. Consequently it is difficult to ascertain which of his deviations in speech are attributable to mixing because of the co-existence of two language systems within the same speaker, and which are deviations normal in child speech — that is, those deviations commonly present at the various developmental stages in the speech of even monolingual children of comparable ages. It has been demonstrated repeatedly that the child's language at each stage possesses its own internal coherence (see, Slobin, 1967: 106). Sorting deviations caused by mixing from those which are "normal" child deviations from adult language is a most challenging task. The developmental question once again reminds us that we are concerned with a process, subject to change and evolution.

It is also interesting to note that several sociolinguists are of the opinion that all speakers — bilinguals and monolinguals alike — possess more than one variety of speech, and, in this respect, they are quite alike. Whereas the speaker of Spanish and English behaves in two very discrete manners, he is nonetheless not much different from the monolingual speaker who is capable of varying a single code in differing social circumstances, and who, under some conditions, may be just as prone to transfer elements of one variety to another. The difference resides primarily in the fact that the varieties within a single code are often less noticeable, yet they operate in the same way as two distinct codes in that choices are often socially motivated. In this respect some type of mixing may be common to all speakers.

Whatever the case, recent studies have refuted the arbitrariness with which speakers supposedly invoke one form of speech or another. Labov (1966, 1969) documented the interrelationships of specific linguistic elements under varying circumstances in the speech of monolinguals. Hernández-Chávez et al. (1975), Valdés-Fallis (1976: 53–85), and others have likewise recorded and analysed similar patterns in the speech of bilinguals. Whether one is concerned with code-switching, code-mixing, style-shifting, transference, or interference, most speech modifications have plausible explanations that are often — but not always — rooted in the social circumstances surrounding the speech event. Language use, then, is as systematic as language structure itself. The very young child must learn both language structure as well as the sociolinguistic norms for language use (see, Bergman, 1976: 86–96). Transference may occur potentially in either area, leaving the linguist-observer to ponder in which area the child deviated. This is a formidable challenge for the observer of very young children.

Analysis of language mixing

Since code switching has already been examined, this chapter will be primarily concerned with linguistic interaction, examining "deviations" in Mario's speech. Because both languages are still in the process of development, standard adult language obviously cannot serve for norm specification. And although norms derived from other children of comparable ages at each stage would provide the most accurate information, such norms are not always available. Where attainable, however, comparisons will be made. Comparative data provide the first clues in ascertaining the extent of linguistic deviations due to dual systems from those which may be developmental in nature.

Language interaction has been segmented in the traditional categories by examining phonological, lexical and grammatical mixing. These are easiest to detect. However, stylistic and conceptual borrowing are also considered although more difficult to substantiate. These should be of special interest in an examination of bilingual use, especially since few studies have taken these areas into account.

The final section evaluates Mario's language proficiency at various points, obtained through testing instruments and teachers' and other's comments. These evaluations aid both in comparing Mario's proficiency with that of other children, as well as to suggest relative proficiency across each of his two languages.

What is most striking throughout the diary is the small amount of mixing reflected in the child's speech data. Recorded notations reveal relatively few examples, despite this writer's special interest in observing mixing patterns. Part of this is attributable indeed to sociological influences. For one, Mario's pattern of language contact and exposure (see Figures 1–3) shows a high degree of language separateness. In Mexico and Bolivia, he had practically no contact with English, and influence from English to Spanish decreased markedly. Moreover, even while in the United States where both languages were present, causing a corresponding increase in borrowing, mixing was still minimal. The attitude and behaviour of his parents with reference to language use most certainly discouraged mixing in the child's speech as well. These alternating periods of increased or decreased mixing, contingent on setting, reveal clearly the "temporal" and dynamic nature of linguistic interaction.

At five, when Mario entered school, Spanish, his mother tongue, was also his dominant language. However, English gained considerably in the period which followed from five to ten. By ten, he was a balanced bilingual. The direction of dual language development, and possible shift, of course remain to be seen in the years ahead. The continuing influence of education primarily through English (although he subsequently spent nearly one year in a Bolivian school), the impact of peers as he enters adolescence and beyond, and the amount of time spent in Spanish- or English-speaking environments will certainly constitute significant factors. Possibly what will most sustain the child, despite the contact and exposure patterns which ensue, will undoubtedly be the attitudes of those around him and, more importantly, the attitudes and self-image which he holds of himself. In any case, whatever is theoretically hypothesized remains to be tested — in a real context, and in circumstances which the child, now nearing adolescence, is yet to experience.[1]

Phonological development and mixing

General considerations

The child both imitates and creates. Nowhere is this more visible than when the child first begins to articulate sounds. As many recorders of child language have reported, the child often produces sounds foreign to the models he hears; however, many of these earlier vocalizations disappear as the child begins to produce only those sounds common to the languages of his environment. According to Jakobson (1968: 16), two forces shape the child's phonology: his own particularist spirit, and a unifying force which is the natural desire of the child to want to communicate. In so stating, Jakobson alludes to the social function of language.

Various attempts have been made to explain the process whereby the newborn child slowly and gradually acquires his phonological system. One of the most convincing notions is Jakobson's "theory of opposition", which maintains that each new sound is added to the child's inventory in terms of its maximal contrast to other sounds. As Jakobson puts it, ". . . what is important is not single sounds but sound distinctions, and therefore primarily the relation of every sound to all of the remaining sounds of the system." Because of this, there is a relatively fixed order of phonological acquisition which is similar for many of the world's languages, varying among children only in the speed of acquisition. In spite of a rather convincing explanation, the testing of its validity through actual data has still not been widely done.[2]

Aspects of phonological development

Diary notations during Mario's first year were not very extensive; however, recorded tapes provided a fair representation of his utterances during this period.[3] Mario progressed typically through the various stages described by others: cooing, babbling, lallation, and finally, speech.[4]

The differentiation of vowels and consonants was an essential stage in launching the linguistic system. The juxtaposition of the first consonants (/p/b/m/) and vowel (/a/) to appear produced the basis of Mario's first words: "papá, mamá, baba". Usually the consonant changed, but the vowel did not. Jakobson (1968: 84–87) termed this a monophonemic stage, at which point the child's words consisted only of the same syllable, often replicated. Between 1;4 and 1;10 there were several examples of this, including the three words given above. By 1;10, however, Mario advanced to a biphonemic stage evidenced in developments such as: "biba, dedo, mano", and so forth.

There were various times at an early age when Mario showed his recognition and familiarity with the sounds of Spanish long before he was capable of producing these himself. The same was not yet true in English. Examples cited earlier in which Mario spontaneously parroted similar sounds whether they belonged to Spanish or not were signs of his growing familiarity with certain phones. If prodded, he was sometimes persuaded to repeat even unfamiliar sounds, but this was not the same as spontaneous production.

An analysis of Mario's utterances was done to determine their sequential development and also to establish his inventory of vowels and consonants. A glance at Table 4 shows that by 2;7 Mario had all the vowel phonemes necessary for English and Spanish. He acquired the five basic vowels of Spanish (plus a sixth phone which is allophonic) by 2;0 and the additional vowels essential for English between 2;3 and 2;7.

The data likewise show that by 2;0 Mario acquired most of the consonant phonemes for Spanish, excepting /x/ñ/f/rr/r̄/. By 2;7 he incorporated these remaining consonants into his speech with the single exception of the trill/flap distinction, /rr/r̄/. the trill appeared almost instantaneously one morning at age 4;11, and, for two months, it served the function of a single phoneme wherever either a flap or trill was needed. Its appearance was such a glorious moment for the child that he commented on his newfound ability: "¡Mirra, papá, yo puedo dijir (decir)!" (Look, papá, I can say (it)), and he continued to say: "narriz, carra, grrada" (nose, face, stairs) in the same exaggerated fashion for the next months. Eventually, by 5;1, he mastered control of the distinction so that he was able to produce a single flap /r̄/. At this point his words began to sound like standard Spanish. However, even at five, he sometimes lost momentary control of the /rr/, allowing it to alternate initially and medically with /ǰ/ so that words like "rojo, carro" (red, car) sometimes sounded /ǰoxo, caǰo/, thereby resembling certain regional dialects.

The late acquisition of /rr/r̄/ is not surprising, for it is well known to be often the last sound acquired by monolingual Spanish-speaking children.[5] Also it is often a difficult sound for many foreigners learning Spanish. Besides completing his phonemic system, Mario also demonstrated mastery as early as 2;0 of important allophonic variations which caused /b/d/g/ to become /b̄/d̄/ḡ/ intervocalically.

Earlier it was noted that Mario's first use of English lagged more than a year behind his first use of Spanish. In the interim, he completed the entire vowel system as well. It is no wonder, then, that his first words in English were pronounced with distinct vowel qualities of Spanish. Note, for example, his pronunciation in the following, uttered between 2;6 and 2;8:

Child's Utterance	Phone	Standard
/bíli titito/	I→i	Billy chiquito.
/taco bell/	$\begin{Bmatrix} \varepsilon \rightarrow e \\ \textbardbl \rightarrow l \end{Bmatrix}$	Taco Bell.
/grampop/	æ→a	Grandpop.
/luk, luk/	ʊ→u	Look, look.
/ay wanta sangič/	$\begin{Bmatrix} \Lambda \rightarrow a \\ æ \rightarrow a \\ I \rightarrow i \end{Bmatrix}$	I want a sandwich.

Notably lacking are phonemes such as /I/ɛ/æ/ʊ/ʌ/, as well as the final /ḷ/ so characteristic of many English words. However, this period between 2;6 and 3;0 was a particularly crucial time during which Mario rapidly began to manifest most of the phonemes of English, not previously needed for Spanish. These included /š/r/ž/ǰ/z/h/ŋ/ and /ḷ/. Aspiration was also added as a feature of certain phones, a characteristic which does not apply at all to Spanish. By 3;2, then, Mario mastered the phonemic inventory of English with the sole exception of the /ð/~/θ/ distinction, and even by 6;0 he showed no consistent signs of productive use of this phoneme. His rule up to then was usually /ð/→{$\frac{/t/}{/d/}$} and /θ/→{$\frac{/t/}{/s/}$}, depending to a large extent on the position of the sound within a word. This phenomenon is a normal development in that these phonemes are commonly acquired late by most monolingual English-speaking children as well.[6] It is difficult to state with precision when Mario finally incorporated these sounds as phonemes. Signs of /θ/ appeared just after his sixth birthday: "Are you gonna come wi*th* us (our) car" (6;1); but there were no other consistent examples until much later. Signs of /ð/ appeared shortly after his seventh year: "I'm been working on *the* railroad", (7;2), and "He said: 'bug your mo*ther*'." (7;3). However, the first clear statement recorded in which phonemic contrast was accurately employed was at 7;6: "I learned bo*th th*ings at *the* same time." (θ/θ/ð/). What was still lacking, nonetheless, in the child's speech were some of the important allophonic changes which also form part of the phonological rules known to the native English-speaker. Without these, and in spite of a complete phonemic inventory, the speaker reveals a distinct foreign quality in his speech. This will be discussed below.

In spite of mastery of nearly all phonemes required for both languages, there was clear evidence that Mario favoured Spanish sound laws in his early years. This became apparent when his "invented" language or nonsense words were analysed. Examples of nonsense words cited earlier were all recorded between 2;7 and 3;5. In spite of the time spanned, these utterances all followed a distinct pattern; e.g. "kopála, pinsála, pepísi, etc." Most of

TABLE 4   *Development of the phonemic systems (Spanish and English)*

Pre-Speech
Age 0;6   Frequent occurrence of /a/æ/ often in combinatin with /d/l/t/.
Age 1;0   Frequent occurrence of /a/ in combination with /b/d/m/ŋ/k/l/x/.

Speech Sounds

	Vowel phonemes			Consonant phonemes		
Age	Spanish	Either	English	Spanish	Either	English
1;1		a			b	
1;4					p	
					m	
1;5		i			t	
1;9					d	
1;10		u	Glides y/w			
				(v)		v
		o		(đ)		n
		e				
1;11					g	
					č	
2;0				(g)	k	
					s	š
				(b)	l	r (once)
2;3						ž
2;6			Λ (once)			(kʰ)
			I			r
			ʊ			
2;7			ε	x		j
			ɔ	ñ		z
					f	h
2;8			æ			đ (once)
						(tʰ)
3;2						ŋ (seldom)
4;11				rr~j		l
5;1				r̃		
6;1						θ (once)
7;2						đ
7;6						θ/đ (contrast established)

Note: Table 4 shows the order of acquisition of Spanish and English phonemes, and the age at which each appeared. Phonemes are listed in the column under "Either" when they belong to both systems; however, they are listed under the appropriate column when they pertain to only one of the languages. Brackets ( ) indicate important allophones.

these creations were trisyllabic and based on a consonant/vowel alternation except in only a few cases. The words contained only vowels and consonants which were derived from the Spanish phonemic system; none which belonged to English, Also, they followed Spanish stress patterns quite faithfully. For example, all words which ended in vowels stressed the penultimate syllable, whereas words which ended in consonants stressed the last.[7] The only irregularity, perhaps, was the sequencing of several consonants such as /nsm/ and /mk/ found in the words: "pinsmála, balamkúm", and "malumkúm". If these combinations had not occurred across syllable boundries they would have been considered consonant clusters totally out of place in Spanish word construction. However, since their occurrence was across boundaries, only their sequencing was odd. In the first case, Spanish normally requires the vowel /e/ to split the /sm/ combination of "pinsmala" into three syllables, rather than two. If the syllable boundaries are interpreted as "pins-mala", the word becomes more compatible with Spanish, although not common. In the second case, the problem was also one of sequencing rather than clustering since no cases of /mk/ seem to occur in Spanish. Another viewpoint might be to consider the patterning in both cases as influence from English which does permit the sequencing of /nsm/ and /mk/ but, again, only across syllable boundaries as in "kinsman", and "Sam Kernan", /–m+k–/. Juncture is preserved in both cases. (A more detailed account of English phonotactics is contained in Hill, 1958: 68–88.)

Phonological interaction

Given the delayed onset of English, which accelerated only after the Spanish sound system was well set, it was not surprising that many of the child's earlier English words were couched in Spanish phonology. For a while it appeared that Mario's lexicon was expanding more rapidly than his phonemic inventory and consequently his first English words were pronounced within the limited system available to him. The result was a fair degree of phonological interference, i.e. until he eventually expanded his inventory to the point where he incorporated the additional sounds required for English. Consider the following examples recorded between 2;6 and 3;0:

Age	Utterance	Shift	Standard
2;6	/tésas/	ɛ→e	Texas
	/soš/	ǰ→s	George
	/bíli/	I→i	Billy
	/só:so/	ǰ→s	Jo-Jo
	/disé:t/	ʌ →i	dessert
	/grámpap/	æ→a	grandpop

Age	Utterance	Shift	Standard
	/ápo/	æ→a	apple
	/tis/	ɖ→t	this
		I→i	
2;7	/afítiz/	I→i	Fix it!
	/vɛts/	w→v	wet
	⎰ /hái/ ⎱ /xai/	h~x	hi
	/si/	iy→i	see
	/xávits/	h→x	Have it!
		–t→ts	
	/xéles/	h→x	Here it is!
	/yʌ/		yeh (yes)
	/polónts/	–t→ts	Vermont
2;8	/muf/	v→f	move
	/jani/		Johnny
	/sáiyɛts/	š→s	Sharon
	/bébi/	ey→e	baby
	/slips/	iy→i	sleep
2;9	/wač/		watch
	⎰ /luk/ ⎱ /lʊk/	ʊ~u	look
	/dis/	ɖ→d	this
		I→i	

Although we see the appearance of many English vowels (excepting /I/ɔ/æ/), we also note that several vowels were not always accurately pronounced. This was a period of considerable vacillation and a period in which many adjustments were being made in the child's phonology to accommodate the intrusion of new phonemes. Throughout there was a tendency to assimilate English vowels to the nearest Spanish vowel phoneme, in the following manner:

$$\varepsilon \rightarrow \left\{ \begin{matrix} e \\ i \end{matrix} \right\} \qquad \text{/tésas/disé:t/}$$

I→i   /bili/tis/afítiz/xávits/
æ→a   /ápo/xávitz/

There was some alternation between /ʊ/~/u/. And diphthongs were assimilated to the dominant vowel:

iy→i   /si/slips/
ey→e   /bebi/

Where consonants were concerned, the following observations can be noted:

ǰ→s	/soš/so:so/
đ→ $\left\{ \begin{array}{c} t \\ d \end{array} \right\}$	/tis/dis/
h→x	/xai/xávitz/xéles/xalo/, but /hai/
v→f	/muf/
š→s	/sáiyɛts/
–t→ts	/xávits/polónts/

Of course /ǰ/đ/v/ and /š/ do not exist as phonemes in Spanish, and there are restrictions which prohibit the occurrence of many consonants in a word-final position, including /t/. The closest sound to /h/ in Spanish is /x/ which possibly explains its alternation with /h/. This analysis, although brief, is sufficient to substantiate evidence of interference in Mario's early pronunciation; that is, until he integrated the necessary additional phonemes into his system and eventually made finer articulatory differentiations than previously needed. In most cases, interference was one of under-differentiation, a problem almost entirely eliminated by age five.

Speech samples taken only after a few months after those given above show that already the child had made considerable improvement, and phonological deviations decreased notably. The following recorded between 3;0 and 3;6 provide examples:

/gɛt/	get
/rákɛt/	rocket
/fInIs/	finish
/pIgi/	piggy
/béybis/	babies

Here Mario demonstrated increasing mastery of English vowels. Consonants, however, developed somewhat more slowly. And even when they began to appear it was clear that there was still lingering difficulty with consonant pronunciations in certain positions, especially finally, where Spanish restricts the occurrence of many consonants which English does not:

Age	Utterance	Substitution	Standard
3;6	/ɛsmɛl It/	+e	smell it
	/lub/	–v→b	love
	/bɛri/	v→b	very
3;7	/áuts/	–č→ts	ouch
	/gas/	–š→s	gosh
	/débɛd/	–v––→b	David

Age	Utterance	Substitution	Standard
3;8	/fri/	θ→f	three
	/sɛbɛn/	–v––→b	seven
	/kaéfi/	θ→f	Cathy
	/eskíyel/	+e	squirrel
4;1	/xar/	h~x	hard
	/ɛstúdi/	+e	study
4;6	/telebišion/	–v––→b	television
	/fInIs/	–š→s	finish
5;1	/báytamIns/	v––→b	vitamins
	/espún/	+e	spoon
5;7	/da kaet In da haet/	đ→d	The cat in the hat
5;9	/wIt tIs/	θ→t	with this
		đ→t	
6;0	/múbis/	–v––→b	movies
		–z→s	
6;1	/da báeli/	đ→d	the valley
		v––→b	
7;2	/đu/	d––→đ	do

When analysed, these words highlight some of the lingering pronunciation problems between the fifth and sixth years, attributable in part to Spanish influence, and in part to the normally late development of certain sounds by most children. Interference most probably caused by influences of Spanish phonology were the following:

1. Spanish restrictions upon the occurrence of various consonants in word-final positions causing the assimilation of /-š/, (/-z/) and /-č/ (as in "finish, gosh, movies, ouch") to /s/, which is permitted.
2. The English phoneme /v/ tends to be pronounced as /b/ due to under-differentiation since a /b/~/v/ distinction is not relevant to Spanish (as in "David, seven, vitamin, valley").
3. There is a tendency to pronounce /h/ as /x/ since the former is non-existent in Spanish (as in English "hard, head").
4. The addition of an epenthetic /e/ to English words beginning with the common cluster of /s/+C, since Spanish does not permit the clustering of /s/ with other consonants in initial positions (as in "study, smell, squirrel").
5. Finally, Mario's dialect of Spanish (Latin American) does not contain /θ/; and although it contains /đ/, it exists only as an allophone of /d/ in intervocalic and word-final positions.

Only the last rule of Spanish cannot entirely account for the mispronunciation of English words with /θ/ and /đ/ since these are late sounds often missing in the speech of his monolingual English-speaking peers. Nonetheless unmistakable interference was witnessed due to differing allophonic variations and clustering patterns of Spanish phonemes.

At age 5;0 phonemic tests were used with Mario to substantiate observational data. Their results supported the conclusion that Mario's interference was due primarily to differences in consonant clusters, differing allophonic variations of similar phonemes across languages, the over-differentiation of /x/, and differing restrictions on the position occurrence of certain consonants. In a perceptive test designed to examine ability to perceive English phonemic distinctions (see Wepman, 1968), Mario demonstrated that he correctly perceived all phonemic distinctions contained in minimal pairs, including /θ/đ/ with only one error. Furthermore he perceived these differences whether or not they occurred initially, medially, or word-finally, as witnessed in the following items:

thimble/symbol	/θ/s/	lash/lath	/–š/θ/
bass/bath	/–s/–θ/	clothe/clove	/–θ/–v/
thread/shred	/θ/š/	sheaf/sheath	/–f/θ/
vow/thou	/v/đ/		

Mario's one error involved the variants /f/θ/ pointing out his single greatest difficulty in perception, as in "fie/thigh". Since /f/ and /θ/ are both voiceless fricatives with the sole distinguishing feature being their place of articulation (and somewhat close at that — labiodental versus dental) it is understandable why this remained a discriminatory problem. In any case, the problem was clearly more one of production than of recognition, as shown through another instrument which tested productive talents (see, Skoczylas, 1971). An item analysis of the errors made in this test revealed the following:

Utterance Required	Error	Phone Substitution
That's the way	dats	/đ/→/d/
She lik*ed* it	like	final /t/→∅
I *th*ink it's good	sink	/θ/→/s/
Runni*ng* is fun	runnin	/ŋ/→∅
The tu*b* is clean	tuf	final /b/→/f/
He use*d* a book	use	final /d/→∅
It's the tru*th*	trut	final /θ/→/t/

Other deviations noted, but not specifically tested for, were:

I li*v*e here	lib	/–v/→/b/
That's *th*e way	da	/đ/→/d/
It's up *th*ere	der	/đ/→/d/
Yes, I wan*t* it	wan	final /t/→∅

These substitutions may be summed up in the following rules:

1. initial /d̪/→/d/
2. initial /θ/→/s/
3. final /θ/→/t/
4. final /t/ŋ/d/→∅
5. final /b/→/f/
6. final /v/→/b/

Examining these rules, we conclude that rules 1, 2 and 3 were due to the child's lack of productive ability of an important English phonemic distinction (/d̪/~/θ/), no matter in what position these occur. Spanish influences, however, stood out clearly in rules 4, 5 and 6. Rule 4 follows a Spanish rule which does not permit full stops to occur word-finally, and, of course, /ŋ/ does not exist at all, hence their disappearance from English words in this position. Rule 5 may have resulted from the fact that Spanish permits at least some fricatives to occur word-finally, but no stops (as in "ciudad" /θ/, "casas" /s/, and "reloj" /x/); consequently /b/ changes to /f/ instead of completely disappearing. Finally, rule 6 seems to be a clear case of under-differentiation of English phonemes due to the fact that Spanish does not maintain the /b/~/v/ distinction, and possibly also to the fact that the phoneme /b/ in Spanish has the allophones /b/ƀ/ and sometimes even /v/, depending upon its position and the speaker's dialect.

Hence, in spite of his mastery of most English phonemes (with the two exceptions cited), we note that at age 5;0 Mario did not have total control over allophonic variations. Part of his phonological deviation, then, was due to the under-differentiation of the /b/~/v/ distinction, part to his inability to produce the sounds /θ/~/d̪/, and part to the influence of allophonic rule variations native to Spanish. The result was that Mario's pronunciation retained a slightly, but not entirely distinct, foreign quality which disappeared entirely by his eighth year.

Phonological borrowing, of course, may occur in either direction — from Spanish to English as well as the reverse. Since Spanish was his dominant tongue, it is to be expected that interference would be greater in the direction of English. This was certainly true on the level of phonology although, as we shall see later, it was not also true in other areas of language. (See also, Hasselmo, 1969: 128). In any case, English phonology exerted practically no effects on Mario's pronunciation of Spanish, but with rare exceptions. Examples are so scarce that no real patterns emerge:

| Age 3;1 | /se k^hae/ | se cae |
| 3;6 | /se k^hae | se cae |

Age 3;8	/eskúla/	escuela
	/ospitáu/	hospital
	/elicátʌ/	helicóptero
	/tʰengo/	tengo
3;9	/teleƀišyón/	televisión
4;2	/pʰepʰito/	Pepito
5;8	/máunstro/	monstruo
9;6	/tʰío/	tío
10;9	/kaθedral/	catedral

In several words there is aspiration of certain consonants; aspiration, of course, is not natural to Spanish. And in English it is often a free variant, occurring most frequently when one is asked to repeat a statement. In almost all cases recorded, aspiration interference also occurred in repeated utterances. The other words listed are all cognates which may explain why interference occurred precisely in these words and practically no others.

Summary

In summary, Mario had nearly completed the development of his phonological system of Spanish by the time he began uttering English words. The first words in English were couched therefore within the phonemic system as it existed at that time, which was predominantly Spanish, lacking several phonemes required for the proper production of English. Within a few months, however, he added most of the remaining phonemes needed so that by his third year he had completed the phonemes required for bilingual speech. Therefore, by five, interference was minimal, and it decreased even further beyond this age. When it occurred, it was primarily due to under-differentiation of one or two phonemes in English, Spanish phonological restrictions on the occurrence of certain word-final stops, and/or Spanish rules concerning allophonic variations. Mario's late sounds both in Spanish (/rr/r̄/ acquired between 4;11–5;1) and English (/đ/θ/ acquired between 6;1–7;6) were characteristic of late acquisitions of other children. And phonological interference proceeded primarily from Spanish to English, giving his pronunciation a slightly foreign sound.

Interference from English to Spanish was rare and almost never occurred. The few instances where interference was noted involved the addition of aspiration and borrowings from cognate words. It is doubtful that this small degree of interference in Spanish was even detected by other native Spanish-speakers. More importantly, there was no evidence that his slightly aberrant pronunciation of English interfered in any way with communication, or with his relations with others.

Finally, sound interference seemed to be an area of language that was primarily linked to the developmental process and largely beyond the conscious control of the child. One indication of this is that it was generally uniform, occuring usually in the same direction and in the same areas regardless of context (except the few rare examples of aspiration of certain Spanish consonants listed above). He either perceived and was capable of articulating certain sounds, or he was not. There was no clear relation to external social factors. In this sense, one may speak primarily of an evolving phonological system or systems to meet the needs of a rapid lexical growth, or, if one is impatient, of phonological interference across languages. Because his sound systems were still in development, the same might not necessarily be true for the older speaker. However, Mario, who had now fully completed his acquisition of both sound systems, showed virtually little interference in either language. Although phonology seemed less linked to environmental factors, the same cannot be said of other areas of language.

Lexical development and borrowing

General considerations

Early on the road to language, children acquire meaning for the sounds they utter as well as knowledge about the social basis for verbal communication (see Gumperz & Hymes, 1972). Lexical analysis provides another way of looking at this development. Many case studies treat the growth of vocabulary through a statistical reporting of words in terms of word lists, word counts, and by grouping lexical items into categories (i.e. parts of speech, semantic groups, etc.). Whatever the treatment, lexical analyses incur difficult problems since adult language criteria are not necessarily accurate guidelines. Clearly, child language has its own internal coherence at each stage of development, whether we consider phonology, lexicon, or grammar (see Brown, 1973).

A more difficult undertaking would probe why and how lexicon evolves. To do so requires an acceptable theory within the field of semantics itself (see Chafe, 1970), which is often beyond the scope of linguists in that it leads beyond the purely linguistic formation of words and into cognition.[8] Even so, any examination of word development cannot help but recognize that much of word meaning is derived from the context of the speech event and cannot always be accounted for by the utterances alone. Anglin (1970: 6) alludes to the social dimension of word meaning when he describes the word as a social tool, stating that it is ". . . a social phenomenon, a part of the culture, and relatively useless unless it means the same thing to different speakers of the language." It is clear that context contributes significantly to word meaning and to communication in general. Nonetheless, the social setting is often ignored in terms of its impact on the process of communication and interaction (see also, Clark, 1973: 66–110; Brown, 1958). Considerable work is yet to be accompished, not only through contributions from psychologists and linguists, but also from sociolinguists. Their combined efforts might produce a framework for understanding better the inter-relationship of linguistics, cognition, and the social aspects of the communication act. The previous chapter dealt with some aspects of the sociolinguistic dimension. In this section, we shall look at Mario's word development and lexical borrowings across languages, and social factors affecting both.

Aspects of word development

Mario's first visible recognition of a speech sound occurred at 0;11 when he reacted to the utterance "Bimba" (his dog) by turning his head in the direction of the animal whenever the sound was said. His reaction was so distinct that the word was often uttered to distract him from crying. Other early signs of recognition were apparent, but his reactions were not so consistent as to assure comprehension. At 0;10 he even said the name once himself when the dog entered the room (/dida/), however he failed to say any other word until fully four months later.

Almost predictably his first words were "papá" and "mamá", (see Jakobson, 1971b: 212–17) uttered at 1;4 and used consistently from then on. In the ensuing months his repertoire increased by only a few items:

/papá/	papá	(papá)
/mamá/	mamá	(mamá)
/áta/	agua	(water)
/títi/	diente	(tooth)
$\left\{\begin{array}{l}\text{/katún/}\\\text{/gatún/}\end{array}\right\}$	gato	(cat)

It was not until 1;9 that a sudden burst of vocabulary growth was witnessed and rapid development continued thereafter.

By contrast with children described in other case studies, Mario might be considered a "late talker". The onset of his native language was tardy by comparison with Leopold's reports of his daughter's progress. By the completion of his second year, Mario used 21 words in active speech in contrast with 337 words used by Hildegard, the subject of Leopold's study (1939–1949: 149). Comparisons with other children also reveal greater fluency and wealth of vocabulary than that manifested in Mario's speech (see Figure 5

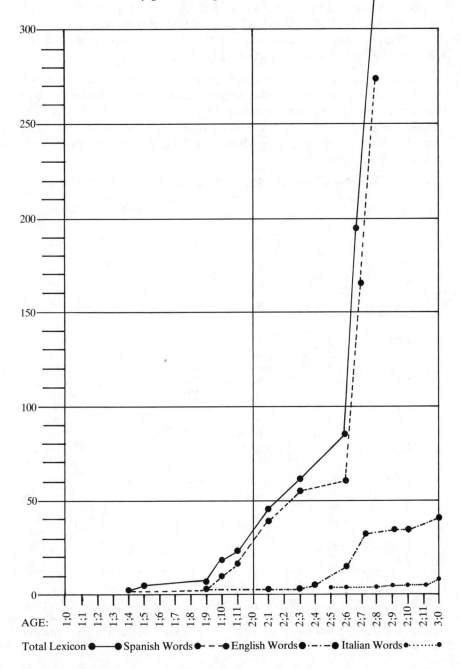

FIGURE 5   *Vocabulary growth to age 3;0*

Total Lexicon ●———● Spanish Words ●– –● English Words ●–·–● Italian Words ●······●

and Table 5). To what extent this was caused by the changing pattern of exposure and contact which Mario had with English and Spanish can only be left to conjecture. Yet it seems likely that alternating language contact might have required more time initially for the child to sort linguistic inputs, thereby slightly delaying productive skills.

It is well known that comprehension precedes production, and in fact there were many indications that Mario's comprehension far outweighed any active use of language. Months before uttering his first words, he was capable of pointing to parts of the body, various objects, and of identifying people when the appropriate words were said. He also reacted occasionally

TABLE 5 *Vocabulary growth compared with children in other studies*

Age	Mario	Carla	Smith	Doran	Leopold
0;7		1			
0;8		3			1
0;9					3
0;10		5	1		8
0;11		8	1		10
1;0	1	8	2		20
1;1	1		2		32
1;2	1		2		36
1;3	1	13	19	61	43
1;4	2	16	19		53
1;5	4	17	19		75
1;6	4		22		106
1;7	4				138
1;8	4	32			176
1;9	6	34	118		201
1;10	16	62			266
1;11	21	81			377
2;0	21	81	272	455	377
2;1	46				
2;3	60				
2;6	82				
2;7	193				
2;8	315				
3;0	503				

Note: Statistics from studies by Smith and Doran are reported in Leopold, 1939–1949: 159. Smith's figures are compiled from the averages of 100 samplings. However, all words, active as well as inactive, are included. The figures for Carla, Mario's younger sister, are compiled based on speech data up to 2;0.

to adult conversation in a manner which suggested that he had understood the topic of conversation.

There are several possible areas of discrepancy in comparing word counts of children. First of all, it is difficult to ascertain when a word becomes a word. Does a sound become a word when it is recognized by the adult, or when the child first uses a single sound consistently for the same meaning? Leopold emphasizes that care must also be exercised to include only those words which appear spontaneously and not those which are merely produced out of direct imitation or mechanical echoing. Furthermore, there is a question whether all words ever uttered in meaningful context should be reported, or only those which become a permanent part of the child's lexicon. In some cases words are used once or twice and may not be used again for months. Hence there is considerable mortality among early words used by children. Even if accurate reporting were theoretically possible, there is still no way to account for the child's passive lexicon. There are certainly many cases known of children who do not utter a word for two or three years; to assume no functioning lexicon would be false. Finally, reporting becomes increasingly difficult and unreliable as the child's vocabulary expands beyond the first few hundred words.

Mario's crucial period began after his second birthday. Between 2;0 and 3;0, his vocabulary grew from scarcely 21 items to more than 500 recorded words, besides others that probably escaped documentation. Furthermore, he progressed rapidly from the use of single words to two-word utterances and then to more complex structures almost within the space of two months, moving toward a phase of recombination and creativity with language. Mario was soon able to converse about a variety of things — his wants and needs, commands, dislikes, memories, and future wishes, as well as to tell lengthy narratives.

Analysis of the child's lexicon from the onset of speech to age 3;0 revealed a total productive lexicon of about 503 items. Their distribution by part of speech was as follows:

Nouns	266
Verbs	127
Adjectives	37
Adverbs	18
Pronouns	7
Interjections and others	26
Prepositions	2
Total	503

Nouns constituted about 57% of the total lexicon; verbs about 25%; adjectives 7%; adverbs 4%; and the remainder was formed of pronouns, prepositions, interjections and other expressions. This was the state of word differentiation at the time when Mario was fully into three- and four-word utterances.

Brown & Bellugi (1964: 155–57) maintain that categorization and differentiation are required to form words into functioning parts of speech. This occurs through progressive differentiation of privileges of words which causes their divisions from one general category (at the one word stage) into smaller and smaller classes as utterances increase in length. That is, one syntactic class is distinguished from another when the members of one class have combinational privileges not enjoyed by the members of the other. In one of their studies, these researchers show through examples taken from children's speech the various combinational possibilities which occur. For example, articles and modifiers appeared in front of nouns. But before this could occur, it demanded the recognition on the part of the child that "a" and "the", for example, can be combined in ways in which other words cannot. Aside from the development of differentiated words by parts of speech, it is also interesting to note that in the case of bilingual children, words originate from two different language sources. Of the total words Mario used at this age, 445 were Spanish, 48 English and only 8 Italian, reflecting clearly the direction of the child's dominance.

The child's words were documented the moment they were actively used for the first time and substantiated by a second spontaneous use. When words recurred in novel phonetic form, they were also noted. In this way, besides serving as a compendium of words, the lexical chart reflected also the evolution of their phonetic development. It was also interesting to note which words were actively used, reflecting periods of contact with English or Spanish and the various domains of experience.

Lexical borrowing

Borrowing may occur across languages in either direction, from Spanish to English or from English to Spanish. Since Spanish was Mario's dominant tongue, it is natural to expect greater borrowing in the direction of English as was the case with phonology. However, just the opposite occurred. Examination of the lexicon shows that Mario actually used more English words when speaking Spanish, than the reverse. English words were incorporated most commonly when Mario spoke with his parents, probably because he knew they understood English as well as Spanish and so he could use both. Even so, mixing was possibly less than it might have been owing to their insistence against mixing. Practically no mixing occurred when Mario spoke to monolingual speakers. In other words, he knew that when addressing people who spoke only one language, he was constrained to express his thoughts without the added convenience of transference. The result was that the *direction* of lexical transference, and whether it occurred at all, were factors related to interlocutors; whereas the degree of transference was tempered by their attitudes. Interference, on the other hand, was presumably beyond the speaker's control and therefore far more impervious to social context (except possibly during total shifts of environment, from the United States to Bolivia).

Lexical mixing was of two types: (1) pure borrowing, that is, when a word in language X was used in language Y, retaining all of its native features; or (2) adjusted borrowing; for example, an item borrowed from language X adapted phonetically and/or morphologically into the system of language Y. Both types were found in Mario's speech; the latter, however, occurred ony rarely and is examined more fully later. Table 6 confirms that most mixing involved pure borrowing of English words into Spanish statements. In most cases pronunciation of the source language was preserved, and the child usually indicated awareness of borrowed items by setting them off with some form of verbal quotation marks, such as pause, or a change of pitch or stress (see Weinreich's explanation of this phenomenon, 1968: 73–74).

TABLE 6 *Lexical borrowing*

Early Stage	
Age 2;6	No differentiation of many lexical items according to their appropriate language system; words often used indiscriminately regardless of the interlocutor; few synonyms.
Age 2;7	Initial sorting of languages and lexicon; utterances sometimes formed with words from either system; typically:

Dis e yoto.	*This* es (está) roto.
Dis más *dis*.	*This* más *this*.
See patatina?	*See* (la) gelatina?

Age 3;0	Separation of languages; borrowing minimal from this age on, as described below.

Age	Interference in English	Interference in Spanish
3;1		¿Quién es ese con *glasses*?
3;2		Quiero *down*.
3;3	Múfete. (Move)	
3;5		Mira, es un /wáblt/ (rabbit).
		Es un *rocket*.

Age	Interference in English	Interference in Spanish
3;6	I'm *sak*ing (sacar) my nose.	Un juguete para el *baby*.
	Das (that's) *maní*	Yo ví un honguito afuera en la
	I wanna no go no *lo(s) nenes*.	*outside*.
	Look (X) (*mira*) my police car.	No, lo(s) *babies* no hablan.
	Let's go play *in* (en) da floor.	Mis *snacks* . . . ¡ay se me comiste
		todo!
3;7		Se cayó en lo(s) *steps*.
3;8	*Su* nose, hey, look (*X*) *su* nose!	De la *escula* (school).
	Hey, look it /*ospitál*/ (hospital).	Es un /*hóspitau*/ (hospital).
	I gotcha horses der *in* da table.	Mira, es un /elikátʌ/ (helicopter).
	Don('t) /*pika*/ (picar) da nose.	Uses frequent interjections of:
		Hey! Ouch! Yuk!
		Yo ví lo *eskwíyels* (squirrels).
		Es uno de los *rʷáketIs* (rockets).
		Mira un eskíyel (squirrel), y *bites* a los
		nenes.
		Yo tengo *free* (3) bullets.
		Mamá, ¿qué *parl*as (parlare, It.)
		Sta mangiando (mangiare, It.)
		Frequent interjections of:
		Help! Watch! Look! Yeh!
		Yo besé a *baby*.
		No está *sick*.
		Yo comí fideos, *beans*, y pan con
		peanut butter.
		Mamá, un *baby* con un *bottle* de leche.
		¡No 'sta *big*!
3;9		Comí comida, *applesauce*, *beans*, pan
		y agua.
		¡Ay! Muchos *balloon*-es (balloons).
		Papá, yo quiero un *ball*-e así para
		jugar.
4;1		Yo tengo /*lápitaps*/ (lollipops).
		No tene (tiene) más *fleas*as (fleas).
4;2	Marta, *look all da time*.	Y no le compres *peanut butter cup*.
	(todo el tiempo).	¡Blueberries! . . . Y hay miel también.
		Vamos a hacel (hacer) *kákon*
		(popcorn).
4;5		Mira, los /ælɛrgétɛrs/ (alligators).
		Esto es *mía* pelota (It.)
4;6	Oh, many lights! (Oh, muchas luces).	Esto es *el mío* tenelol (tenedor),
	I'm *seeing* television.	(It., il mio)
	(Spanish, mirando).	*snor*car (English, "snore" plus
		Spanish verb termination).
5;1	Das (that's) a *hipopam*	Un nene trajo a la escuela un
	(Sp. hipopótamo).	*Indian corn* . . . un maíz indio.
	Pam, can you *desen*tie (untie) this?	Bueno, y esos van a cantar un *song*.
	(Sp. morpheme for "undoing").	Quiero un *drink*.

Age	Interference in English	Interference in Spanish
5;2		Giacomo (/ɟákomo/) subió y vino un *gigante* (/ɟigante/) (It.) Tenía tres fagiolinis (/fáɟiolinis/) mágicos (máɟicos/) (It. plus Sp. plural morphemes).
5;6		Ya apúrate porque estoy muy *excited*.
5;7		Estoy jugando con *tinker toys*. Voy *slide . . . boarding slide*. ¿Dónde está mi *kite*? Pero tú puedes comprar con *Master Charge*. El azul va con cuál va . . . su *partner*? Hoy en la escuela nos llevaron al *livestock show*. Sabes mi *school bus* no tiene un *stop sign*. El no me llevó a los *rides*.
5;8		Papá, voy al otro lado del *sidewalk*. Voy a subir al *merry-go-round* como ese nene. Estoy llamando Carla con el *puppet*. Viene con un *stick*. Estoy haciendo . . . *pretending* que es una grúa. Hoy, yo era *line leader*, en mi escuela. *Pretend* que es una grúa. El está en *first grade* . . . en grado. Yo me llamo el *jet*, ¿oíste? ¿Viste ese *dump truck*?
6;0		Se parece ese *egg* un fútbol. No le vas a decir que *canal*. (*clase*/kind)
6;2		Se va a *get in trouble*, ¿verdad?
6;3		Yo lo voy a *lok*ar. (cerrar/lock)
6;4		Ponemos *cranberries* y *marshmallows* y después se pone el *glitter* y con *glue*. Y después lo pintas todo *yellow*.
7;1		Está *for sale*. Tiene un *gate*. Si yo fuera al . . . *nursery*.
7;2		No eres *mágico*; soy *mágico*. Con *ribbon*. No *correct*as.
7;3		Un *lobster* . . . que gigantéstico (sic).
7;4		Quiero *calculation paper* (papel de calcar/tracing paper).

Age	Interference in English	Interference in Spanish
7;6		Yo estoy *allergic*.
		Vas a *sender* una carta para *order* más.
8;11		Y después on *stage* cuando empiezan,
		y abre el *curtain*, y los *spectators* . . .
9;3		¿Duele más un *heart attack* o un
		tiburón?
9;6		*migeto* (enano/midget)
9;8	Let me *re*freshen up your mind.	
10;1		Voy a *trade comic books* con él.
10;2		Yo llevé esto al *waterfall* por si acaso.
10;6		Es de otro *hunted house*.
10;9		Más lejos de la *cathedral*.

Many borrowed words shared in common the fact that they were culturally and semantically related to the child's experiences in a specific milieu. The following words, for example, were all related to cultural experiences in the United States:

snacks	rocket	peanut butter	cranberries
applesauce	blueberries	popcorn	glitter
peanut butter	Indian Corn	tinker toys	nursery
cup	first grade	livestock show	lobster
Master Charge	line-leader	rides	allergic
school bus	(a kindergarten	(amusement	comic books
dump truck	term)	park)	
marshmallows			

The more culturally bound an item, the less likely the possibility of a ready synonym in the other language. This explains the intrusion of these English words into everyday Spanish. Conscious or intentional transfer of such words may also account for the fact that most culturally bound words were not integrated when borrowed. Curiously, culturally bound words were not also borrowed from Spanish. This is probably related to the fact that Mario seldom spoke of his experiences in Latin America *in English*. When reminiscing with his parents, it was done in Spanish; and conversations about Bolivia or Mexico with English-speaking playmates were unlikely. Were he to speak of life in Mexico or Bolivia, however, it is conceivable he would have had an equally difficult time providing English equivalents for terms such as "cholo, chuño, ekeko", and "lluchu". Other Spanish words, such as "taco, tortilla, llama, fritos", and "nacho", on the other hand, already enjoyed widespread use in the United States.

In other special cases, we see examples of non-cognate homophonous words across Spanish and English, which evoked different meanings. One incident which occurred at age 5;0 will help to explain what is meant. While he was playing with his cousins, Mario's mother called suddenly from the other room to inquire as to his whereabouts. He replied "aquí, aquí" (*here, here*). Overhearing this, his English-speaking cousin asked: "Mario, what does '/akí/' mean?" Mario looked at him, puzzled by the apparent simplicity of the question, and said: "Something for to open da door." Returning home to Vermont with his parents later that day, his father asked again in English: "Mario, what does '/akí/' mean?" The child answered unhesitatingly, "aquí, aquí, Vermont" (pointing at the same time to the ground to stress location). In this case, the conceptualized meaning of /akí/ was contingent not only on sound, but also on interlocutor with the latter serving as the primary determinant. Given the differing variables, the sound /akí/ evoked either a notion of location (aquí) or object (a key) depending on who asked the question.

All in all, interference was rarely evidenced throughout the speech diary. Some examples of borrowing found in the chart which seem most likely a form of interference are the following:

I'm *sak*ing my nose	From Spanish, "sacar"
De la *scula*	From English, "school"
¡Ay! Muchos *balloon*es	English "balloon" plus Spanish plural morpheme
*ball*e	English "ball" plus Spanish phonetic accommodation
*snor*car	English "snore" plus Spanish infinite verb ending
Can you *desen*tie this?	Morphemes derived from Spanish
*fleas*as	English "fleas" plus Spanish plural termination
hipopam	Not knowing how to say "hippopotamus" in English, he created this based on Spanish "hipopótamo", abbreviating the Spanish form to satisfy his English intuition
*lok*ar	From English "lock" plus Spanish infinitive verb ending
*correct*as	Modelled either on English "correct" plus Spanish second person verb

	ending, or on Spanish adjectival form "correcto"
calculation paper	Modelled on Spanish "papel de calcar", or "tracing paper"
*send*er	From English "send" plus Spanish infinitive verb ending
migeto	Modelled on English "midget" plus –o; correct Spanish word is "enano"
*re*freshen (meaning: freshen)	Possibly modelled on Spanish *re*frescar
cathedral (for: catedral)	Modelled on English "cathedral" and pronounced /kaθedrál/ for Spanish "catedral" /katedrál/

Immediately apparent is the fact that most of these examples show attempts to adapt the source words morphologically to the target language. Because of this, most of these instances will be further discussed in the section which follows.

Mario also used another group of words in speech which, although basically "foreign" to the system in use, were not also classified as interference. These were mostly expressions learned from his parents who had already incorporated them into their own speech. Consequently Mario learned some obviously foreign terms as part of the language norm just as he did the other features of his native Spanish:

drink (noun)	unhuh	ciao-ciao (It.)
O.K.	salute (It.)	mamma mia (It.)
baby	Kleenex	buona notte (It.)
nonno (It.)	nonna (It.)	bubu (It. dialect)
Scotch tape	mangia (It.)	cin-cin (It.)
chiacchierone (It.)	zitto (It.)	mi piace (It.)
lascia il naso (It.)	meter/poner[9]	guardalu (It. dialect)
kali nikta (Greek)		

These, plus more English and Italian words — particularly brand names, place names, greetings, sayings and expressions having no adequate translation — were all part of the family's language and therefore not interference in Mario's individual speech.

Few cases of borrowing from Italian occurred: "¿qué *parl*as?" modelled on the Italian verb "parlare"; and "sta mangiando", a direct loan. Other examples were recorded once when the child recounted a story to his sister which he had originally heard in Italian. The result was phonetic and morphological adaptations of several key elements:

Giacomo subió, y vino   Spanish is /xigante/;
un /jigante/   Italian, /jigante/
    (Jack went up, and a giant came)
Tenía tres /fajiolinis/ /májikos/   Italian /fajiolini/ plus Spanish plural
                                    morpheme; phonetic adaptation of
                                    Italian /májiko/ plus Spanish plural
(He had three magic beans)

Since Italian is often similar phonetically and morphologically, its diffusion into Spanish requires few accommodations. Because of this, it would not have been surprising had there been more borrowing from Italian except that Mario had limited productive ability.

Summary

The task of tracking vocabulary growth in children is a challenging one. This is partly due to the difficulty of accounting for receptive as well as productive vocabulary, and ascertaining when a child's utterance is indeed a word. Mario's first word occurred at 1;4 and his vocabulary remained comparatively small until just past two when he began to show rapid growth. In this sense, he appeared to be a late talker, possibly because of changing language environments during his early years.

As his vocabulary expanded in both Spanish and English he showed surprisingly little borrowing on the lexical level. Although borrowing may occur potentially in the direction of either language, Mario appeared to borrow mostly from English when speaking Spanish, and seldom the reverse. Since he spoke Spanish primarily with his parents, also bilinguals, this type of borrowing was characterized as transference, used to enhance communication possibilities by drawing on both source languages. This was constrained, however, by the models and the attitudes which his parents demonstrated towards such behaviour and mixing remained quite limited. Lexical interference, conversely, was practically non-existent.

From examples found in the diary, Mario's lexical borrowing was mostly of the unintegrated type, that is, words directly loaned into Spanish, generally preserved in original form. Few cases were noted where he attempted to adapt or integrate them into the target language. This is confirmed by his use of verbal quotes when incorporating borrowed items. The highest incidence of borrowed words, moreover, was the type which were culturally bound and for which appropriate translations were not readily available.

It was further noted how word meaning is related not only to the utterance of sounds but also to the context of the event. An example was provided illustrating how both setting and interlocutor directly influenced meaning, in addition to the phonic shape of the word. This underscores again the sociolinguistic dimension of developing speech behaviour. Not only is meaning affected by context, but also lexical borrowing — its type, direction and degree. Some of the variables cited were setting, interlocutor and topic, the latter becoming increasingly relevant to word borrowing as the child progressed through the educational system.

Finally, another group of words of obvious foreign origin was not treated within the types of borrowings already cited (whether transfers or interference. These were extraneous items used as part of the family's language norm and which the child learned as part of the system. In this sense, these may be viewed as "creolized" words rather than as borrowings, resulting from the interaction of dual languages in the developing speech of a bilingual child.

Emerging grammar and syntactic borrowing

General considerations

Just as Jakobson was cited for his contributions to the advancement of phonological theory, Chomsky is to be cited for his impact on syntactic theory. Chomsky's work (1957), *Syntactic Structures*, outlined the basis for a generative-transformational theory of grammar. As a result, many scholars subsequently developed new approaches for examining grammatical acquisition by children (see, for example, Bloom, 1970; Chomsky, 1969; Anglin, 1970). However, even before the Chomskyan theory was formulated, linguists were aware that the processes involved in the acquisition of syntax were substantially different from those involved in the learning of vocabulary and sounds (see Leopold, 1939–49).

In spite of many developmental studies on the acquisition of syntax, McNeill (1970) points out that "The process remains one of the major mysteries in the acquisition of language." And some of the prevailing notions which attempted to explain the processes involved in syntax acquisition have been widely discussed, and sometimes discarded.[10] There is now heightened awareness that a purely linguistic approach is inadequate for explaining the process. Brown (1973) and Slobin (1973), in their works, have each pointed increasingly toward semantic *and* grammatical determinants which affect the order of syntactic acquisition; highlighting "cognitive prerequisites for the development of grammar".

Most investigators today are committed to the view that child speech reflects underlying mental structures of some sort. The child does not simply transfer what he hears from adult grammar, but he is an independent "linguist". Slobin (1967: 106) states that:

> . . . the basic facts, in regard to the ontogenesis of grammar, are: that combinations of words and parts of words in child speech seem to be systematic rather than random, and productive rather than merely imitative or rote learned. (It appears) . . . that child language is structured from the start, that it soon takes on a hierarchical structure, that it tends to be regular, that the structures change with age, and that they do not always correspond to adult structures.

Still the main concern seems to concentrate primarily on the acquisition of linguistic structures. Hymes (1971: 23) calls for a broader theory which shifts the emphasis from linguistic structures to social life as the starting point of language so that social functions guide and linguistic structures follow. Others have also called for a wider approach to the child's learning. To reflect this broader view, scholars introduced the term "communicative competence" (see, for example, Slobin, 1967). Cazden (1973: 348–50) has used the term "language socialization" to include the acquisition of all aspects of communicative competence. And although we can indeed view the child as "linguist", we cannot overlook the fact that he is also an "ethnographer", and that what he is learning is "communication", not just a set of grammatical rules.[11]

Aspects of emerging grammar

At the onset of speech, Mario's utterances consisted of only one word. Although it is possible to speculate about possible knowledge of underlying grammar at this stage, examination of the rules is obviously inaccessible (see, Ingram, 1971: 888–910). It is not until the child joins two words in some relation within the same utterance that most linguists speak of the ontogenesis of grammar (see, Slobin, 1971: 3–14).

During the initial stage, single words served Mario's communicative needs. Single words were used to express his wants, to identify items, to ask questions, and to make statements. Holophrases constituted the sum linguistic externalization of his thoughts and expressions. These consisted mostly of nouns, albeit with varying meanings.[12] Eventually adjectives, adverbs and interjections were also used as single word utterances. Verbs were limited initially, and were normally a later development. What Mario lacked in vocabulary and syntax was frequently made up for through vocal expressions and extralinguistic means. Questions and imperatives were easily distinguished by the accompanying intonation. However, sometimes even guessing was required. When the wrong guess was made, Mario often made his frustration known, and another interpretation was sought. Since linguistic aspects of speech were extremely limited, much of meaning at this stage depended on the context of the speech event. Situational context was crucial to an understanding of one word pronouncements.

An excellent example of the varied meanings which were conveyed through the use of the same word was recorded in the following instance. Mario opened his mother's purse and happily discovered a chocolate bar. Using the same word repeatedly, but with differing expression, he communicated the following meanings:

Utterance	Interpreted Meaning
¡Talalate! (for Spanish "chocolate", exclaimed with a surprised expression)	Ah! Here's some chocolate!
Talalate . . . talalate . . . talalate . . . (whining, imploring expression)	Please, give me some chocolate.
¡Talalate! (now screaming, demanding)	I want some chocolate . . . now!
Talalate . . . (receiving the chocolate, smiling, pleasant voice)	Ah! Wonderful, delicious chocolate.
Talalate. (satisfied, eating and pointing to the candy)	Look. I'm eating it. See?
Talalate. (pleased, rubbing his tummy)	Baby likes chocolate.

Words were grammatically undifferentiated during the holophrastic stage. For this reason syntactic analysis usually begins when two words are joined which do not belong together but which, when joined, represent separate units of thought — expressions which in some way contrast with each other yet are related by some kind of coherence. At this time we can begin to speak of subjects, objects, verbs and so forth. It is for this reason that Leopold (1939–49: 166–7) warned about giving undue importance to a classification of the child's vocabulary by parts of speech in his earlier phrases.

Mario's holophrastic stage lasted for at least nine months.[13] Even though some apparent two-word utterances were used, a closer look revealed that these were merely imitated expressions, requiring no knowledge of underlying syntactic rules. The proof of this was seen in his consistent use of certain word combinations without altering sequence, using either word independently, or combining either with other single words. For example:

Age	Child's Utterance	Standard Language	
1;11	/ón ta?/	¿Dónde está?	(Where is it?)
	/áy ta!/	¡Allí está!	(There it is!)
	/tá tʌc!/	Don't touch!	
	/dá me!/	¡Dáme!	(Give me!)
2;2	/te yé yo/	Te quiero.	(I love you.)

The components of "dáme", for example, were never used separately or recombined with other words. The entire phrase served as the child's command, meaning simply "give!" (and often "take!"), without reference to the person denoted by the morpheme "me". Hence the mere positioning of two words side by side did not necessarily constitute syntactic progression. Two words used in sequence, like "chocolate" followed by "dáme", often still constituted holophrases; this was usually the case when each word received primary stress and terminal intonation contours. Only when Mario joined separate words in original patterns can we be sure of the beginning of syntactic patterning. Two-word utterances then were characterized by the fact that only one of the two words received primary stress.

The earliest suggestion of syntactic patterning was recorded at age 1;10. Mario learned to say "ciao ciao" (*bye-bye*) when his father left the house each morning. Once, when both parents were about to leave, he began to cry, saying repeatedly, "/no taw taw, no taw taw/" (no ciai ciao, no ciao ciao). Mario often used either "ciao" or "no" previously, but the combination of the two in the same negative utterance was definitely original.

Most of his two-word utterances continued to be quite primitive, usually amounting to the joining of a vocative with a noun. This was a useful device which Mario often used to call the attention of a specific individual by name, followed by his request:

/mamá, lála/	Mamá, leche	(Mamá, milk)
/papá, datór/	Papá, tractor	(Papá, tractor)
/dúcis, mamína/	Dulces, Marina	(Candies, Marina)

Other than this construction, the two-word phrase often consisted simply of a predicate, the subject implied by the context of the situation, or it was a noun accompanied by an adjective. Eventually Mario joined a verb and a noun, making significant progress toward conventionally complete sentence types.

Mario's two-word phase began about 1;11, lasting only a few months, after which he suddenly began to form longer utterances of three words. At this point he demonstrated increasing ability to join words in novel ways, moving forward in the direction of organized sentences. It was also at this point that he began to mix morphemes from both Spanish and English. By 2;7 four-word utterances were common, marking the upper limits of sentences produced during his first three years, with occasional five-word utterances appearing toward the end of the third year (see Appendix 2 for examples).

Increased sentence length was related to the child's progressive differentiation of parts of speech. In a sense these are concomitant developments since word differentiation allows for increased syntactic complexities. Following are the ages at which each new part of speech appeared for the first time, each stage comparing roughly to the increase in utterance length:[14]

Age 1;4   Single nouns (mostly proper names at first, followed by names of objects).

Age 2;3   First use of nouns as the subject of an utterance: /bima ʋn tásal/ "Bimba está en su casa" (*Bimba is in his house*).

Age 2;3   First objects expressed with a verb: /vamos al autos/ "vamos al auto" (*Let's go to the car*).

Age 2;3   First use of a predicate in a sentence: /ven tasa/ "Ven a casa" (*Come home*).

Age 2;4   First use of an adverb: /ven akí papá/ "Ven aquí, papá" (*Come here, papá*).

Age 2;7   First use of adjectives and demonstratives: /tis e yoto/ "This está roto" (*This is broken*).

Hence, by age three, Mario had fairly well differentiated the parts of speech. Some of his utterances formed complete sentences containing a subject and predicate; others were only partial sentences containing a noun phrase or predicate verb phrase, or sometimes simply a prepositional phrase. Mario had learned to express questions and negatives almost before he had a well-developed syntax. This was possible with the aid of intonation and the addition of the simple negation "no". The addition of the conjunction, prepositions and other function words also began to appear toward the beginning of his third year, although a few prepositions were already in consistent use as early as age 2;3.

Aspects of morphological development

Morphology was the last aspect of language to emerge. Even by age three, morphology was still at an incipient stage. But once begun, it developed rapidly. Initially the relationship of words to each other was purely a syntactic one, reminiscent of isolating languages like Chinese. Mario simply placed words side by side without any formal inflectional modifications. The rest was inferred by the listener.

The importance of morphology varies to a greater or lesser degree in accordance with the language. Standard Spanish relies fairly heavily on morphological devices, especially in the inflection of verbs. In spite of its late development, Berko (1961: 359–75) demonstrated that by school age children generally mastered most of the morphological detail not yet apparent in their pre-school utterances. Berko, of course, dealt with English-speaking children; however, other studies showed that even where highly inflected languages, like Russian, were concerned, children gained fair control over morphological complexities by at least age six (see, Slobin, 1966: 129–52; Popova, Zakharova & Bogoyavlenskiy, 1973: 269–94). Hence the critical time is between about 2;6 or 3;0 for the onset of morphology, and five to six for near mastery, depending on the degree of complexity in the language concerned. These findings are compatible with Mario's case as well.

Mario began to show signs of devoting increasing attention to verb inflections and noun endings by about three. By age 5;0 he spoke a fairly accurate and fairly standard Spanish, including morphology. He erred occasionally, but only with irregular patterns which present the greatest challenge even to adult learners.

In part, mastery of morphology requires that the child discern patterns from large numbers of varied examples. The patterns, of course, do not always apply to all words in the same way; often there are subclasses and exceptions. Fairly well developed powers of abstraction are needed which may partially explain the reason morphology is a late development.[15] Another reason may be that morphology is often a redundant feature of speech. Word order often ensures that a message gets across properly even without the useful, but not always totally indispensable, endings which form part of some languages. The low perceptual salience of word endings (in that they are often unaccented) may also contribute to their later development.

It is widely recognized that the child at first often uses high frequency, but irregular forms correctly as a result of direct imitation. However, as he begins to generalize the more-consistent patterns, he regularizes also the irregular forms, be they nouns, verbs, or other parts of paradigms. Each time the child applies incorrect analogical forms, he demonstrates his developing awareness of the norms of adult language.

Two aspects of Spanish which require inflections are nouns and verbs. In standard speech, Spanish nouns fall into two categories — masculine and feminine gender, expressed primarily by their articles. Nouns are also inflected to denote plurality through the addition of either -s, or -es, depending on whether the word ends in a vowel or consonant. Verbs are considerably more complex; these separate into three classes (-ar, -er, -ir), each forming a separate paradigm of five endings (in Mario's dialect) in accordance with the subject, and each having an indicative and subjunctive mood. There is also a core of high frequency, irregular verbs plus another group which changes its stem in addition to its ending. Tense, which is also expressed through inflectional endings, further complicates the picture by requiring separate paradigms for each tense expressed. The task seems fairly challenging, yet the process which was still at a rudimentary stage by three, was nearly completed by 5;0.

As an example, let us first consider the acquisition of morphemes expressing noun gender and number. At 2;3 Mario began using an unidentifiable morpheme in front of some nouns. These occurred irregularly and were somewhat inconsistent in shape (see Table 7). This sporadic and irregular usage continued until age 2;7 at which time Mario introduced an article before all nouns without differentiating gender. By whatever chance, he seized the feminine form "la", which he incorporated into his speech as the sole article for all nouns. This, despite the fact that adult speakers divide nouns into two classes — feminine signified by "la" and masculine by "el", each with its corresponding plural form. Words lke "el pie" (*the foot*), "el cielo" (*the sky*), as well as "el papá" (*the father*) were all preceded by a feminine article. Mario did this consistently with only two exceptions where "a" (instead of "la") was used before "puerta" (*door*) and "seco" (*dry*).

TABLE 7   *Development of articles, prepositions, and plural markers*

Age	Child's version	Feminine/Singular Standard language	English	Child's version	Masculine/Singular Standard language	English
2;7	la tasina	la cocina	the kitchen			
	la tasa	la casa	the house			
	la uya	la uña	the fingernail			
	la papá	el papá	the father			
	la pákel	el parque	the park			
	la siya	la silla	the chair			
	a seta	el seco	the dry one			
	la taye	la calle	the street			
	la myánya	la mañana	the morning			
	la bama	la cama	the bed			

Age	Child's version	*Feminine/Singular* Standard language	English	Child's version	*Masculine/Singular* Standard language	English
	la fala	la falda	the skirt			
	la me:sa	la mesa	the table			
	la pie	el pie	the foot			
	la selo	el cielo	the sky			
2;8	la auto	el auto	the car	el gatito	el gatito	the kitten
	la vopa	la ropa	the clothes	el soyól	el señor	the man
	a peta	la puerta	the door	el dotól	el doctor	the doctor
	la bayón	el camión	the truck	el tólo	el toro	the bull
	la pyato	el plato	the dish			
	la felelo	el sombrero	the hat			
	la felulelo	el basurero	the trash basket			
	la pananina	la vitamina	the vitamin			
	l'ayón	el avión	the aeroplane			
	la duča	la ducha	the shower			
	la tololón	el cinturón	the belt			
	la abwezita	la abuelita	the grandmother			
	la baño	el baño	the bathroom			
	la manalela	la mamadera	the baby's bottle			
	la siyita	la sillita	the chair			
	la patetela	la maletera	the trunk			
3;0	la nena	la nena	the girl			
		Other			*Plurals*	
2;3	ʋn tásal	en casa	at home			
	al autos	al auto	to the car			
	na la tésas	en Texas	in Texas			
2;7	nel ayón	en al avión	in the airplane			
	en na árwol	en el árbol	in the tree			
	na buka	en la boca	in the mouth			
	en na tyénya	en la tienda	in the store			
	na nene	del nene	the boy's			
	na papá	del papá	the papá's			
	ʋn pas	a La Paz	to La Paz			
2;8	lo potito	el potito	the rump	dos baiyóne	dos camiones	two trucks
	al osito	al osito	to the bear	dos patato	dos zapatos	two shoes
	nel potito	en el potito	in the rump	dus ayones	dos aviones	two planes
	en la sesa	en la ceja	on the eyebrow			
	en la bayíya	en la barriga	in the stomach			
	en la sala	en la sala	in the living room			
2;11	a la kasa	a la casa	to the house			
3;0				dos pistolas	dos pistolas	two guns
				dos tatáiyas	dos guitarras	two guitars

Within a month, however, the second article began to appear in a few instances such as "/el soyól/" (el señor/the man), "/el dotól/" (el doctor/the doctor) and "/el tólo/" (el toro/the bull), but "la" prevailed with all other masculine nouns.

It is difficult to determine to what extent the process is imitative and to what extent cognitive, since word gender is not always linked to the form of words. For example, there is some relationship with respect to words ending in -a, which often take a feminine article; and nouns ending in -o or consonants (other than "d") usually take a masculine article. Words ending in -e, however, may be of either gender. The inherent physical sex of a living being sometimes influences the choice of article, over-ruling the shape of the word, but not always. Then there are also many exceptions to all of these categories, complicating the system even further. By whatever strategy used, however, Mario began with the feminine form as the sole article for all nouns. The masculine form appeared initially in a few cases where a word and its modifier were acquired jointly. By age 5;0, Mario practically mastered the entire gender system for all Spanish nouns (it is interesting to compare these results with the process involved in the acquisition of Russian gender, described by Popova *et al.* 1973: 269–80).

Where articles were preceded by prepositions, Mario tended to blend both into one morpheme. This, of course, does not occur in standard Spanish, although it is a common phenomenon in most other Romance tongues. Hence various combinations of prepositions plus articles resulted such as "nel" or "na". By 2;8, contractions of this sort were used less, being substituted by the separate forms "en el" or "en la".

No number distinction was apparent in Mario's speech until 2;8, at which time he formed his first plural. This occurred only with words terminating in final consonants. The rule was to add -es, hence "baiyón" (camión/truck) became "baiyónes" and "ayón" (avión/airplane) became "ayónes". No plural form appeared yet for words ending in vowels so that "patato" (zapato/shoe) remained "dos patato" when pluralized. By age 3;0 Mario also began adding a plural morpheme to words ending in a vowel. The addition was a simple -s rendering "dos pistolas" (two pistols) and "dos tatáiyas" (dos guitarras/two guitars). However, none of the plural forms was as yet accompanied by the plural article "las" or "los".

In summary, then, no distinctive article was used at first. Eventually various sounds preceded nouns, usually occurring after, or in conjunction with, a preposition. Later the feminine article "la" was introduced and generalized for use with all nouns. Toward the end of the second year the masculine form appeared in a few isolated cases. The fact that there was no free alternation between the feminine and masculine forms suggests that the masculine article was acquired directly along with the noun it modified. Mario also combined some articles initially with prepositions but toward the latter part of the third year he differentiated the two so that they were no longer combined.

An examination of verb morphology is even more complex than that for nouns. Mario used verbs for the first time by 1;11. However, for several months, they were used only within frozen expressions; consequently their form was still of no importance morphologically:

Age 1;11	¿Dónde está?	(Where is it?)
Age 2;1	Dáme.	(Give me.)
Age 2;2	Te quiero.	(I love you.)
Age 2;3	Ven (a) casa.	(Come home.)
Age 2;4	Ven aquí, papá.	(Come here, papá.)

By age 2;6, however, Mario began to use verbs as isolated items, and by 2;7 as part of longer utterances. All verbs both in Spanish and in English, were used without an explicit surface subject. Although this is incomplete in English, it is permissible in Spanish and it is frequent in adult speech. Verb termination normally reveals the actor; however, Mario's verbs were morphologically undifferentiated. Patterns began to emerge first among verbs belonging to the -ar class, which are also those of highest frequency in the language. In addition to the third person marker of -ar verbs, Mario also used an isolated gerundive form, an imperative form, and two markers of the past tense. Barring thse exceptions, all other verbs were inflected with the marker of the third person singular, no matter what the referent was. For example:

Age 2;6	šaka	saca	take out
	kita	quita	take away
	toma	toma	take
	ayaya	agarra	hold
	salúlala	salúdala	greet (her)
	vite	viste (preterit)	you saw
	se kayó	se cayó (preterit)	he fell
Age 2;7	alsa	alza	lift
	saltando	saltando (gerund)	jumping
	séntate	siéntate (imperative)	sit down
	lola	llora	cry
	sal	sal (imperative)	leave
	oye	oye (imperative)	listen
	pon	pon (imperative)	put

This suggests the adoption of a highly frequent morpheme which he extended initially as the single termination of all verbs.

Beyond age 2;7 verbs appeared regularly as part of longer utterances. The most frequent ending continued to be the third person present indicative; however, in Table 8 we can see that although most verbs were formed on the model of the -ar type (Section I) we can also note the beginnings of a second class of verbs belonging to the -er/-ir type (Section III) with words terminating in -e.

Verbs in which the vowel of the stem is normally diphthongized when inflected were not yet identified and these were also modelled after either of the two developing classes (Sections II and IV). Section V contains a variety of imperative forms, both regular and irregular, in both Spanish and English. These forms, which show little similarity in terms of common patterning, again suggest the possibility of direct imitation of high frequency, irregular patterns from adult language. The same can be said of irregular, negative commands. However, regular negative commands were formed very simply by patterning the verb after regular indicative -ar and -er verbs and placing the negative "no" before them. Hence the child produced "no/bute/" from "escupe" (to spit), and "no pisa" from "pisa" (to step on).

In general, verbs were inflected only with the third person morpheme with few exceptions where a first person morpheme was employed. This suggests the beginning of differentiation between the third and first person endings and the introduction of the latter. All verbs were inflected only in the present tense until the last months of the third year, when Mario began to use past forms of regular and irregular paradigms (Sections VIII and IX). All regular forms followed the same pattern for indicating past tense by adding -o, and shifting stress to the final syllable. However, irregular forms were so devoid of any common pattern that it is possible these resulted from direct copying. In the last month of the third year Mario twice used a morpheme of the imperfect which became the third tense to emerge.

One interesting development, possibly as much for its psychological implications as for the linguistic, was the appearance of the first person ending correctly employed in the statement: "Aquí estoy" (Here *I* am). Although the first person marker had previously appeared with some verbs, this was the first time it was used with the correct referent. Mario had formerly referred to himself by saying: "*Nene* no toca eso" (*Baby* doesn't touch that).

By grouping the nouns and verbs listed in Tables 7 and 8, it is easy to see emerging patterns as well as exceptions to the patterns. In some cases, the

TABLE 8 *Morphological patterning of verbs at age 3;0*

Child's utterance	Standard language	English
I. *Regular -ar verbs*		
šaka	saca	take out
kita/kito	quita	take away
toma	toma	take
alsa	alza	lift
lola	llora	cry
peƀwa/peva	pega	hit
i va	se va	go away
kanta	canta	sing
pasa	pasa	pass
tota	toca	touch
buta	busca	seek
pawa/ayaya	agarra	hold
bata	baja	go down
abafa/abaso	abraza	hug
está	está	is
veya	lleva	carry
pema	quema	burn
manexa/manesa	maneja	drive
deka/dexa/gexa	deja	leave
empuxa/apuxa	empuja	push
evanta	levanta	raise
yusta/guta	gusta	like
salta	salta	jump
mata	mata	kill
tansa	alcanza	reach
pika	pica	bite/sting
kamina	camina	walk
avla	habla	speak
aóga	ahoga	drown
apawa/apava	apaga	extinguish
pyena	prende	light
meta	mete	place (in)
II. *-ar verbs with stem change*		
wela/vela/bela	vuela	fly
šeye/seyo/siéya	cierra	close
III. *-er and -ir verbs*		
fuve	sube	raise
abve	abre	open
tyáe	trae	bring
pone	pon	put
oye	oye	listen
yiye	ríe	laugh
taye/tae/kai	cae	fall
ase	hace	do
coxe	coge	take
come	come	eat

Child's utterance	Standard language	English
III. *-er and -ir verbs*		
yompe	rompe	break
vivi	vive	live
IV. *-er and -r with stem change*		
peyo/peye	puede	may/can
tene	tiene	have
yeve	llueve	rain
tyéyo/tyéye	quiere	want/love
V. *Imperative*		
alélala	arréglala	fix it
salúlala	salúdala	greet (her)
abyočače	abróchate	fasten
aprétate	apriétate	squeeze
séntate	siéntate	sit
sal (also for 3rd. ind.)	sal	leave
pon	pon	place/put
ven	ven	come
pónla	pónla	put it
dáme/máme	dáme	give me
afítiz	fix it	
huač/wač/vats	watch	
si	see	
muf	move	
open	open	
VI. *Negative commands*		
no vói/no vaya	no vayas	dont go
no aya	no hagas	don't do
no bute	no escupas	don't spit
no pisa	no pises	don't step on
VIII. *Various forms*		
is	is	
xéles	here it is	
e/es	es	is
ai	hay	there is/are
van	van	they go
ečayo	echado	lying down
saltando	saltando	jumping
VIII. *Regular preterit forms*		
se taiyó/se kayó	se cayó	fell down
apakó	apagó	went out (extinguished)
apagó	acabó	finished
yegó	llegó	arrived
se quedó	se quedó	remained/stayed
IX. *Irregular forms*		
vite?	viste?	did you see?
nene puse?	nene puso?	baby put?
f:we	fué	went
vino	vino	came

Child's utterance	Standard language	English
X. *Imperfect tense*		
estava (2;11)	estaba	was
se yía (3;0)	se reía	was laughing
XI. *Present-first person*		
estói (2;11)	estoy	I am

exceptions are externalizations of the incorrect application of generalizations made by the child. Viewed in this way, "errors" show a child's ingenuity in deducing latent structure; it is in the overextension of the patterning where he has gone too far.

An interesting detail of morphological development was the derivation of the singular of some words from their plural form. Generally we tend to think that children create the plural by deducing the appropriate morpheme to be added to the singular form. There was evidence, however, that the reverse also occurred in Mario's speech. For example, the singular form of the Spanish words "pencil" and "light" were "lápiz" and "luz" respectively. In these words it was easy to see why Mario understood them to be plural forms. Basing himself on other pluralized words which end in -s/-es, he mistook the final /s/ of lápis/ as a plural morpheme; and therefore he derived the singular /lápi/ by dropping the /s/. (The "correct" plural for pencils is "lápices" pronounced /lápises/.) In the same way, Mario derived /lúse/ from /lúses/ and /nuése/ from /nuéses/ by simply omitting the final -s, instead of the conventional singulars "luz" and "nuez". These derivations apparently made such obvious sense to Mario, being consistent with a normal pattern, that he persisted in saying "lápi, lúce", and "nuéce" almost to 6;0 in spite of occasional correction.

In most cases, Mario correctly used the third person form of -ar verbs. In only two cases did he incorrectly apply the final -a ending to verbs of the -er class. These were "meta" (*to put into*) and "prenda" (*to turn on*) instead of the standard forms "mete" and "prende", respectively. It is probable that the reason he grouped these words with other -ar verbs was because he usually related them to their opposites: "saca" (*to take out*) and "apaga" (*to turn off*) when speaking about the tape recorder or television. Consequently it appears that he gave both verbs the same ending because of their association in speech.

Finally, the morphology present in Mario's speech by age three was clearly very limited and quite rudimentary. It amounted to a few plural endings, the differentiation of only two verb classes, an incipient distinction between first and third persons, some command forms, and the beginning of preterit and imperfect verb endings. Syntactic constructions at this age were certainly more advanced than the morphological devices to indicate them.

Yet, two to three years later, Mario had nearly completed the morphological system of Spanish.

Syntactic and morphological interference

In the areas of syntax and morphology, we can most clearly see evidence of interference. Like phonological interference, utterances noted in the diary seemed to be primarily of the type made without conscious thought or control. Nonetheless, syntactic and morphological borrowing documented throughout the case study is surprisingly low. This, despite the fact that contrastive studies of the systems suggest considerable potential for interference in both areas (see, Stockwell *et al.*, 1965; Stockwell & Bowen, 1965). Table 9 lists interference examples documented during this ten year period. Their small number dramatizes the separateness of Mario's dual systems and his control of each.

As previously noted, a brief period of mixing occurred in both directions at the onset of English. Borrowing took place frequently in all aspects of language from about 2;6 to 2;8, evidenced in utterances such as:

/bili titito ʋpstés/	*Billy* chiquito *upstairs.*
/dis es la siya/	*This* es (de) la Zia.
/dis mas dis, otéy?/	*This* más *this, okay?*
/xe lésita/	Here it is. (pronunciation)
/si patatina?	*See*, gelatina?
/dis e na mones/	*This* es la molde.
/bili titito n xávits/	*Billy* chiquito *can't have it.*
/ay don si mamá/	I don't see mamá. (pronunciation)

However, by 2;8 mixing ceased. As a consequence, all examples of borrowing occurring beyond this point of language separation were treated as interference. Grammatical interference was grouped into four categories: (1) the transfer of morphemes; (2) the transfer of grammatical relations; (3) word positioning; and (4) the integration of loan-words. Other types of grammatical interference identified by Weinreich (1968) did not occur.

The direction of borrowing is interesting to note. From the examples listed in Table 9, we note that the direction of interference was heavily toward English in the early period from 3;3 to 6;3, with only ten incidents of borrowing in the direction of Spanish. Of the latter, moreover, nearly half were caused by interference from Italian, not English. Interestingly enough, this corresponded to the period when it was customary to use Italian for storytelling. Beyond the seventh year, however, a shift in direction of

TABLE 9 *Grammatical Borrowing*

Age	Language affected	Child's utterance	Observation
3;3	E	Mu*fete*!	Move + *e* + *te*; English "move" plus Spanish verb ending plus reflexive.
	E	I'm *sak*ing. (I'm taking it out.)	Spanish "*sac*ar" plus English morpheme -ing.
	E	I *no have* hungwy (hungry). (Yo *no tengo* hambre).	Modelled on Spanish syntax.
	E	You *no have* it. (Tú *no* lo *tienes*.)	Modelled on Spanish syntax.
	E	I *no* going. (Yo *no* voy.)	Modelled on Spanish syntax.
	E	Look (X) my police firecar.	"at" consistently omitted after "look", modelled after Spanish "mirar".
	E	Let's go play *in* da floor.	"in" assumes function of both "in" and "on" due to single Spanish preposition "en".
	E	I have too many*s* car*s*.	Unnecessary plural agreement between N + Adj. modelled on Spanish morphology and syntax.
3;8	E	Is come a car (Viene un auto.)	Modelled on Spanish syntax.
	E	I gotcha horses der *in* da table.	Same as above example of "in".
	S	Mamá, ¿qué *parl*as?	Verb stem based on Italian "*parl*are".
	S	Es su comida, sta *mangiando*.	Based on Italian verb form, "mangiare".
	E	I have toy*s* horse*s*.	Unnecessary N + Adj. agreement, modelled on Spanish morphology and syntax.
	E	/rwáket*Iz*/ (rockets)	Plural based on Spanish; C + es = plural.
	E	*All-i-body* quiet*s*.	Possibly modelled on Spanish equivalent, "todo el mundo", or "toda la gente", and plural morpheme "quietos".
	E	I told you you quiet*s*. (¡Les dije: quietos!)	Plural marker modelled on Spanish "quietos".
3;9	S	Ay, muchos *balloon*es (balloons).	Plural based on Spanish; C + es = plural.
4;1	S	No tene más *fleas*as (fleas).	Integration of English loanword "fleas".
4;2	E	Look *all da time*.	Possibly modelled on Spanish "todo el tiempo".
4;5	E	He's going away *da* car. (Se va *del* auto.)	Possibly modelled on Spanish "Se va del . . ."

Age	Language affected	Child's utterance	Observation
	S	Esto es *mía* pelota.	Modelled on Italian possessive "mia".
4;6	E	Where you are? (¿Dónde estás?)	Word order based on Spanish question form: Where + subj. + verb.
	S	¿Por qué tene la *yoto pyena* (*pierna rota*)?	Word order based on English "broken leg".
	S	¿Dónde est *el mío tenelol* (tenedor)?	Possessive modelled on Italian "il mio".
	S	*snor*car	English "snore" plus Spanish infinitive ending.
	E	*I'm seeing* television. (Estoy mirando televisión.)	Verb form modelled on Spanish "mirar", — "to look at".
	E	Oh, *many* light! (¡Ay, *mucha* luz!)	Modelled on Spanish
	E	Glue put mamá.	Modelled on Spanish word order: "La goma puso mamá".
	E	*Watch me dress me.* (Mírame vestirme.)	Modelled after Spanish pronoun case and syntax.
	E	Look (X) me alot. (Mírame mucho.)	Modelled on Spanish verb "mirar + me".
	E	I gonna leave on da porch dis. (Voy a dejar en el porche esto.)	Possibly modelled on Spanish construction; although not common, it is acceptable within his dialect.
5;1	E	Pam, can you *desen*tie dis?	Modelled on Spanish morphemes: *des* + *en* + VB, as in "*desen*ganchar".
5;7	E	How (X) it happen?	Modelled on Spanish ¿Qué pasó?
5;8	S	Allí en la escuela hay un libro de *japoneses nenes*.	Word order based on English, as in "Japanese children".
	E	You being rude!	
	S	Vamos rápido a *poner el fuego afuera*.	Modelled after English "to put the fire out".
	E	He doesn't do *nofing*.	Possibly modelled after Spanish "no hace *nada*", although also an error common to many English-speaking children.
5;9	E	Das my /favoríta/ "Cheeta" in da whole wide world.	Correct English syntax but form and pronunciation are

Age	Language affected	Child's utterance	Observation
			Spanish, with feminine gender to agree with "Cheeta" (a chimpanzee).
	E	I don't know to swim but I *know to swim* wit tis.	Modelled on Spanish "Yo sé nadar".
6;1	E	An' *has* to go dis way	Modelled on Spanish verb form obviating the explicit pronoun "it".
6;3	E	An' *one body* makes noise . . . in na second musam (museum) where I got dat.	Modelled on Spanish "una persona".
7;2	S	¡No *correct*as! (corrigas)	Possibly modelled on English "correct", or Spanish "correcto".
7;6	S	. . . *de* mías (mías)	Modelled on English "*of* mine".
	S	. . . cuando termines de *pintando*	Modelled on English, "to finish *painting*", hence use of a Spanish gerund instead of the infinitive.
	S	. . . si voy *en* cárcel.	Modelled on English "*in* jail".
	S	Necesito más lápices *de tuyos*.	Modelled on English, "of yours".
	S	Vas a *send*er una carta para *order* más.	Modelled on English "send" plus Spanish infinitive -er.
8;0	S	¿*Tú vas a*, papá?	Modelled on English, "Are you going to, papá?" lacking second verb.
8;4	S	Ya *es* cuatro años.	Modelled on English, "She *is* four years old".
9;2	E	*Pass me them.*	Spanish syntactic order: "Pasa/me/los".
9;6	S	*Una otra* señora estaba en la biblioteca.	Modelled on English "another".
9;8	S	Yo fuí *nadando* . . . hay otra (clase) de *disparando*.	Modelled on English "I went swimming" and a "shooting class". Uses Spanish gerunds instead of infinitive forms.
9;8	E	How do you *put that on?* (the lighter)	Modelled on Spanish "¿Cómo se prende?" instead of "How do you light that?"
10;9	E	Someone's gonna *copy me* the work.	Uses Spanish syntactic order "copiar/me".

interference from English to Spanish seems to have occurred with more cases of borrowing into Spanish than the reverse. This new trend corresponded to attendance at school which most certainly will continue to have further impact on the child's language behaviour in the years ahead.

Considering, first of all, interference in English, we can easily find examples which illustrate each of the four types of interference described above:

(1) Transfer of morphemes:	Can you *desenti*e (untie) this?
(2) Transfer of grammatical relations:	I have too many*s* cars. (Unnecessary plural agreement.)
(3) Word positioning	Glue put mamá.
(4) Integration of loanwords:	I'm *saki*ng. (From Spanish "*saca*r", to take out.)

Examples of all four types of interference in the direction of Spanish can also be found:

(1) Transfer of morphemes:	Esto es *mia* pelota.
(2) Transfer of grammatical relations:	. . . cuando termines de *pintando*.
(3) Word positioning:	. . . hay un libro de *japoneses nenes*
(4) Integration of loanwords:	Vas a *sender* una carta . . .

Even though all four types of interference occurred, examples of the first two types were quite rare. In fact, the example of the first type cited above reflects interference from Italian, rather than from English. Other examples of type (2) interference, occurring mostly between ages seven to nine were:

Age 7;6   . . . *de* mías
           Necesito más lápices *de* tuyos.
Age 8;0   Tú *vas a*, papá?
Age 9;8   Yo fuí *nadando* . . . otra de *disparando*

These statements show a clear carry-over from English grammatical patterns; nonetheless their occurrence was self-limiting and most did not exist for long in the child's speech. The single exception, perhaps, was a tendency to use the gerundive form in Spanish where the infinitive is obligatory: "pintando" for "pintar", "nadando" for "nadar", and "disparando" for "disparar". The source of interference is transparent when English structure is considered. English uses gerundive forms in these instances: When you finish *painting*; I went *swimming*, etc.; whereas Spanish expresses these thoughts through the infinitive construction. A Spanish rendition in English would read: When you finish *to paint*, I went *to swim*, etc.

Examples of the third type of interference — word positioning — were more obvious to detect and slightly more recurrent:

Age 4;6   ¿Por qué tene la *yoto pyena*? (Por qué tiene la *pierna rota*?/ Why does she have a broken leg?)

Age 5;8   Allí en la escuela hay un libro de *japoneses nenes*. (Allí en la escuela hay un libro de *nenes japoneses.*/In school there is a book about Japanese children.)

Both examples follow English construction in which the adjective is normally placed before the noun it modifies rather than the reverse, as in Spanish. There were, however, several similar examples which occurred at an earlier age:

Age 2;8	/yoto yayayíyo/	cigarrillo roto	(broken cigarette)
	/yoto tása/	casa rota	(broken house)
	/yande totól/	doctor grande	(big doctor)
	/buta yoto ayónes/	¡Busca (los) aviones rotos!	(Look for the broken planes!)
	/yande yayayíto/	caballito grande	(big horse)
	/yande talaláte/	chocolate grande	(big chocolate)

However, a month later, Mario inverted this order along the lines of standard Spanish:

Age 2;9	/blusa mala/	bruja mala	(bad witch)
Age 2;10	/oxo ceyáyo/	ojo cerrado	(closed eye)

Although at first it appeared that aberrant word order was due to English influence, this was unlikely since Mario had not yet begun using adjectives with nouns in English (except for "Billy chiquito" which he learned together as the complete name for his cousin). Yet on two succeeding days Mario used both sequences of "casa rota" (*a broken house*): /tasa yoto/ and /yoto tasa/, revealing his vacillation.[16]

This unusual order of adjective-noun sequences appeared to be due to at least two influences. First, Mario had already learned and correctly used demonstratives and adverbs, both of which precede the noun as in "oto pío" (otro pío = pájaro/*another bird*); "ese tren" (*that train*); and "/dos xyaxyaxyía/" (dos policías/*two policemen*). When adjectives appeared, it was possible that he followed the same patterns at first. Secondly, it was possible that a transformational rule was required to invert the adjective-noun sequence. This rule may have been acquired between 2;9 and 2;10 when Mario began using the inverted pattern as in "bruja mala" and "ojo cerrado". It was not until about one month after his third birthday that conventional placement of nouns and adjectives appeared fixed in Mario's speech. Beyond 3;1, then, later inversions must be considered interference from English. The context of the utterance often proved this was so. For example, in one case Mario had just heard the English sentence on television: "She has a *broken leg*". He turned at once to his mother and asked: "¿Por qué tene la *yoto pyena*?" (*Why does she have a broken leg?*) preserving the word order of the original statement. In any case, occurrences of aberrant word order were so few as to be almost inconsequential.

Examples of the fourth type of interference in Spanish involved integration of several English loanwords (*balloon*es, *flea*sas, *snor*car, *rocket*es), and the direct transfer of English expressions into Spanish: "to put the fire out", or quite literally, "poner el fuego afuera", as Mario said. This unusual rendition would be almost incomprehensible to a monolingual Spanish-speaker, who would express this thought by saying "apagar el fuego". Hence, not only was there a word by word transfer of English expression into Spanish, but the original word order was also preserved. This was especially surprising because of the spontaneity of the utterance and not a case where Mario was groping for words. Yet such examples were also rare, and, all in all, both grammatical and morphological interference were unusual events in the speech of this bilingual child.

Other areas of borrowing

Aside from phonology, the lexicon and grammar, borrowing may also occur in other areas of communicative behaviour. Evidence in these areas is often less visible than that found in structure. Yet borrowing occurs across dual systems at the stylistic, interactional and conceptual levels, leading naturally to the larger context of cross-cultural differences.

One source of evidence of borrowing at the conceptual level is reflected through time expressions. For example, Mario invariably preferred to express time in English even when conversing normally in Spanish: "Mamá, no tenemos clases *on Monday*" (Mamá, we don't have classes *on Monday*).

Most other time expressions were likewise stated in English: "in the fall", "at 4:00 p.m.", "on Saturday". At first glance this might be construed as simply lexical borrowing. However, the motivation was more certainly derived from the manner in which Mario learned notions of time. When one considers that Mario was socialized, insofar as time concepts were concerned, through an English-speaking world that involved school hours and days, television schedules, and the learning of days, dates, months and seasons primarily in the classroom, it is easy to understand his preference for expressing time notions through English. By ten, he still doubted the reliability of Spanish equivalents even though he produced these upon request. The fact remains that he felt more natural, more precise, and more certain when time statements were said in English.

At the interactional level (i.e. the strategies for interacting and relating to others), in many ways Mario seemed to operate in a mode more appropriate to Spanish speakers than to English speakers. Most assuredly he copied this as well as other interactional behaviour from his models at home. Yet there is evidence that such behaviour patterns were utilized even when operating in English, resulting in interference. Comments from his teachers — beginning in kindergarten throughout several years of elementary school — indicated that his voice control and participation in group conversation were not entirely suited to the school situation. "He still has a lot to learn about the give and take of conversation", said one teacher, alluding unwittingly to underlying differences in conversational strategies between monochronic and polychronic cultures (see, Hall, 1976: 14). In addition, Mario continued to greet visitors to the home by extending his hand. When retiring at night, he kissed all guests, female and male alike, often surprising many men unaccustomed to being kissed by a boy of nine or ten.

It is at the interactional and also stylistic levels where many bilinguals entering school probably encounter problems. Labov (1972) speaks of "language in the inner city" and the styles of speech that Black students use in school settings. In similar fashion, Mario seemed to have transferred speech styles used with a Bolivian maid to his first schoolteacher. It was obvious enough to cause his teacher to remark on one occasion "My student teacher assistant seems to think you must have a maid at home". When asked why she inquired the teacher referred to the way Mario requested things of her and others (as though they were in a caretaker role). Fortunately the child eventually sensed the differences in his new situation and made the needed stylistic adjustments. However, until adjustments were made in interactional strategies or speech styles, inappropriate interference can result in misunderstanding between school teachers and bilingual-bicultural children at various stages of development.

Summary

To summarize, there was relatively little grammatical interference in Mario's speech, in spite of the potentially great degree possible on the basis of contrastive analyses. Early examples of language mixing occurred during the child's first contact with English when both systems were fused. Consequently, true examples of interference did not arise until after language separation had taken place (2;8). Subsequently, the direction seemed to parallel the child's varying degrees of contact with each of the three languages concerned. For example, interference occurred initially from Spanish to English; during periods of story-telling in Italian, Italian forms were incorporated into the child's speech, affecting Spanish uterances; when the child began school and English exposure increased, the direction of interference reversed slightly from English to Spanish.

Four types of grammatical interference were noted and classified and examples of each were found in English and Spanish, although not in equal distribution. Few cases of morpheme transfer and transfer of grammatical relations were evident, as contrasted with a higher incidence of word positioning transfers and loanword integrations. All in all, the degree of grammatical interaction recorded over a ten year span was indeed insignificant, revealing a strong command of separate language use.

The direction of borrowing was somewhat at variance within each of the language aspects considered. In phonology it was noted that Mario demonstrated greater interference from Spanish to English, probably because the Spanish sound system was nearly intact at the onset of English. Once phonemic systems were complete enough to serve the sound production needed for both languages, phonological interference all but disappeared. Lexical borrowing presented an altogether different picture. Lexical mixing was more clearly a question of conscious transference, used to enhance communication with other bilinguals. Whereas phonological interference diminished until virtual disappearance, lexical borrowing increased as the child's semantic needs broadened and as his intellectual pursuits deepened through education in English. Grammatical borrowing appeared less contingent on conscious control when it occurred. Its directionality was affected by varying exposure and contact patterns, while the degree was constrained by other social variables. Other borrowing within the communicative competence of bilinguals may occur at the interactional, stylistic and conceptual levels.

Finally, language interaction — whether transference or interference — appeared contextually motivated, or at the very least, affected. Transference is indeed an easy pattern for bilinguals to take up, using and mixing inputs from two sources as best they serve communication needs. Yet it is apparent that social factors may also exert sufficient influence to counteract potential borrowing at most levels. One can see these forces in operation when the language norms and attitudes of those surrounding the child are considered. Even interference, although somewhat less amenable to conscious control, was affected by contact and exposure with each of the languages involved, and by the pattern of socialization which he experienced. Hence, any consideration of languages in contact which seeks to understand their interaction must go beyond theoretical analysis to examining actual use. Social dimensions clearly affect the extent, direction and type of borrowing which actually occurs. And although the circumstances for each speaker vary, the process, if it is to be understood, must ultimately account for both language structures in contact and the social and individual arenas in which they come together.

Indices of proficiency

Mario's language development has been considered thus far from two perspectives — linguistic and sociolinguistic. The sociolinguistic investigated aspects of language use, including language differentiation, code selection, socialization patterns and resultant speech styles. The linguistic investigated aspects of phonological, lexical and grammatical development, along with linguistic interaction across systems. At this point, it would be of interest to know something about the child's proficiency in each language as compared with that of monolingual children. In other words, how did his knowledge and use of Spanish and English differ from, or resemble, that of monolingual speakers?

Indices of proficiency were sought in several ways: (1) through formal language testing devices; (2) from school reports commenting on areas relevant to language development; and (3) from subjective comments provided by teachers and others who knew the child in one language or the other.

Formal language testing devices

The search for formal testing devices capable of providing the indices desired is a difficult one. Some areas of interest considered in this search were: availability of paired instruments for evaluating both Spanish and English, capacity to test both receptive and productive skills, ability to provide indicators of both general proficiency and also specific instances of language deviation, existence of norms, to permit comparison of this child's results with that of larger groups of children, and finally instruments geared for the proper age level of the child. Few tests speak to all of these points. Consequently various instruments were used in combination to assess Mario's proficiency. The pattern which emerged was sufficient to establish some basis for describing Mario's verbal skills in Spanish and English in contrast with those of other children of a similar age. Since most tests were paired with equivalent versions in each language, the discussion which follows treats paired tests together so that his ability across languages, as well as his comparative ability with peers, may be seen. All the formal assessment instruments used (see Table 10) were administered between the child's fifth and sixth years. Indices of the child's proficiency at other stages are provided from school reports and subjective comments in the section which follows.

Auditory Discrimination Test — English (Wepman, 1968). This test is designed to determine the child's ability to differentiate English phonemes, measuring only receptive skills. It does this by providing a list of 30 minimal pairs in which the phonemic distinction being tested occurs in different word positions. The main purpose of this test is to permit the selection of children most likely to have difficulty learning to read through a phonics approach. The test is geared to older five-year-olds and younger six-year-olds. Unfortunately there is no Spanish counterpart.

Mario scored 36 correct responses out of a total of 40 items, erring in responses to the following word pairs containing same/different sounds:

Item A. fie/thigh
Item B. pen/pin
Item C. tall/tall
Item D. pose/pose

The test separates responses into two columns providing X and Y scores. Y scores are responses to ten pairs which are the same. These items are not used in the determination of the level of auditory discrimination, but rather to judge the validity of the test. Therefore Mario's score of X items is actually 28 out of 30. The test describes "inadequate development" as X errors greater than six. This norm is derived from scores of 533 unselected first-, second- and third-grade children from both urban and non-urban communities.

It is interesting to speculate about reasons for Mario's incorrect items. It is not surprising, however, that he missed the pair fie/thigh. Even though he demonstrated ability elsewhere to differentiate /d/~/Ø/, he was incapable of active production himself. It is possible that the other errors were related

TABLE 10 *Assessment instruments used*

Tests used	Skill tested (Receptive/Productive)		Language aspect tested	Age group	Permits item analysis	Norms
Spanish						
1. Spanish Phonemic Test (Skoczylas)	X	X	Phonology	K–C	Yes	No
2. Vocabulary Test		X	Vocabulary	5	Yes	No
3. Auditory Test of Language Comprehension (Carrow)	X		All	3–7	Yes	No
4. Tests of Basic Experiences (Moss)	X		All	K	Yes	Yes
5. Kernan/Blount Morphology Test	X	X	Morphology	5–12	Yes	Yes
English						
1. Auditory Discrimination Test (Wepman)		X	Phonology	5–8	Yes	Yes
2. English Phonemic Test (Skoczylas)	X	X	Phonology	K–5	Yes	No
3. Vocabulary Test		X	Vocabulary	5	Yes	No
4. Auditory Test of Language Comprehension (Carrow)	X		All	3–7	Yes	No
5. Tests of Basic Experiences (Moss)	X		All	K	Yes	Yes
6. Berko Morphology Test	X	X	Morphology	4–7	Yes	Yes

to the fact that the test administrator, being from the Southwest, tended to diphthongize vowels. Whatever the case, Mario compared favourably in his perception of English phonemes with his monolingual English-speaking peers.

Spanish/English Phonetic Unit Production Test (Skoczylas, 1971). This test has equivalent versions in Spanish and English. It is designed for use with learners from kindergarten through college. The test measures the subject's ability to produce certain Spanish or English sounds which have been identified as crucial to proper control of each language. This is accomplished by having the person tested repeat a variety of utterances. Specific sounds contained in each utterance are considered in scoring. There are two versions of this test (form A and B) and both were used with Mario.

Mario scored 38 correct items in Spanish out of the total of 40, erring with /r̄/~/rr/ distinction in the following items:

Item A. Viene el to*r*o.
Item B. El pe*rr*o ladra.

In English, however, he achieved only 65 of the total 72, losing points on the following errors:

		Response
Item A.	*Th*at's the way.	Dat's
Item B.	She lik*ed* it.	like
Item C.	I *th*ink it's good.	sink
Item D.	Runni*ng* is fun.	runnin
Item E.	The tu*b* is clean.	tuf
Item F.	He use*d* a book.	use
Item G.	It's the tru*th*.	trut

Mario's problems in Spanish stemmed from his still inconsistent use of the /r̄/~/rr/ distinction. In English the problem was his inability to pronounce the /đ/~/θ/ distinction in any position. No valid comparison can be made across languages given the fact that the phonemic inventory of each language is different. Nor can we make comparisons with other speakers since no norms exist for this instrument. However, the test is useful in determining Mario's phonemic inventory and assessing the extent to which he handled allophonic variations. At five, then, inventory was normal for his age in both languages based on observations and knowledge about other five-year-olds. Where Mario deviated, however, was in his lack of control of allophones in English, essential for correct native speech.

Oral Vocabulary Test. This test was prepared by the author with aid from three sources (Cornejo, 1969; Thorndike, 1921; and Keniston, 1938) and was based on various centres of interest related to the child's environment. These included: toys, animals, parts of the body, modes of transportation, common household items, clothing, school items, foods, plants, insects, tools and basic jobs. The test was designed to assess Mario's vocabulary in each of his languages as related to his surroundings. Since the test was especially prepared, no norms exist.

In Spanish, Mario correctly named 144 of the 156 pictures, missing only 12 items. In English, however, he named only 102 of the 156 items, missing 54. He missed seven of the same items in both languages; these were:

envelope	sobre
bucket	cubeta/balde[17]
snail	caracol
secretary	secretaria
waiter	mesero/mozo (see Note 15)
student	alumna/estudiante
student	alumno/estudiante

The last four items were in the category of basic jobs, an area with which Mario had least familiarity. The results also supported expectations that the child's vocabulary would be broader in Spanish than in English because of his more extensive experiences in the former at this point.

Auditory Test of Spanish/English Proficiency (Carrow, 1971). This test also exists in equivalent versions for Spanish and English. It is designed to permit assessment of children's productive skills in each of these. The test is geared to children between ages 3 to 7, and it consists of 100 pages, each containing a set of three drawings. The test administrator utters a phrase, and the child responds by pointing to the picture which best describes the phrase. The pictures represent referential categories and contrasts that are signalled by form classes and function words, morphological markers, grammatical constructions and syntactic structure.

In the Spanish version, Mario scored 96 correct out of a possible 100. The items missed were the following:

Item A. Un *par* de canastas. (A pair of baskets.)
Item B. Distinguishing *left* from *right*.
Item C. El la empuja a ella. (He pushes her.)
Item D. Si eres la maestra, marca el perrito; si no eres la maestra, marca el osito. (If you are the teacher, point to the dog; if you are not the teacher, point to the bear.)

In the English version, Mario also scored 96 correct items, missing the following:

Item A. Point to the *second* one.
Item B. Distinguishing *left* from *right*.
Item C. *Easily.*
Item D. *In front of the car.*

Some of the drawings were questionable, however. For example, the drawing used to depict *easily* was consistently interpreted by Mario as expressing the distinction between *heavy* and *light*. The picture showing a series of men pushing heavy to light objects, with difficulty or ease, actually expressed two possible concepts. In a second case, the phrase *fast* was accompanied by drawings of a donkey, an elephant and an airplane. Mario selected the elephant which he judged ran quite fast based on his observations during a Tarzan movie on television. Aeroplanes, he insisted, go quite slow, based on his own travel experiences. He explained that when looking out the window, the plane flies over the land below very slowly (illustrating the approximate speed of the plane flying over the earth by moving his hand across the table, very slowly!).

The Carrow test shows that Mario has almost equal command of the grammatical aspects tested in each language. It should be noted, however, that the English version was given after the Spanish version and that both tests employ many of the same drawings. Consequently, it is possible that Mario was favourably influenced when taking the English test. Since there are no published norms for either language, no comparisons of Mario's results can be made with those of other children.

Test of Basic Experiences (TOBE) — English/Spanish (Moss, 1970). This test deals with ". . . such basic language concepts as vocabulary, sentence structure, verb tense, sound-symbol relationship, and letter recognition. It also contains items pertaining to listening skills and perception of symbols as the carriers of meaning . . . and (it) makes use of 'nonsense' words . . . (so that) the child must derive their meaning from the context of the sentence in which they are used" (p. 7). Equivalent versions exist for Spanish and English.

In the Spanish version, Mario scored 25 correct items out of the total possible 28. He missed the following.:

Item A. Izquierda/derecha (left/right distinction).
Item B. Marca el que estará lastimado. (Mark the one which will be hurt.)
Item C. Marca el libro que está listo para ser leído. (Mark the book which is ready to be read.)

Although the Spanish test does not have norms as does the English, local norms were under development by the Southwest Educational Development Laboratory based on a sampling of 31 Mexican-American children attending Day Care Centres in Austin, Texas, which assumes some amount of formal instruction in Spanish. Their mean score was 18, so that Mario fell approximately within the 89th percentile,[18] even without any formal instruction in Spanish.

In the English version of the TOBE Language Test, Mario scored 26 correct items out of a total possible 28. The items missed were:

Item A. The smat will break. Mark the smat. (smat = glass).
Item B. Mark the one that starts with a "bee" sound.
(Answer = bottle).

His results placed him in the 96th percentile as compared with national norms for his age group.

Looking at Mario's errors, it is now quite clear that he did not know his right from his left, having missed this item in both the Carrow and TOBE tests, in Spanish as well as English.[19] The other items missed in the Spanish version were two rather awkward grammatical constructions ("estará lastimado" and "ser leído") which are not common in daily speech. Equivalent constructions like "se va a lastimar" and "se va a leer" are more natural, and consequently there is some suspicion of possibly poor test items. In the English version, Mario missed Item B because he searched for a word which "sounds like" rather than "starts with" a "bee" sound. This would seem to be a natural tendency for most children since the two preceding items ask for words which "rhyme with", thereby conditioning the child to do the same with the third item. Technically, there is no basis for comparing Mario's percentile score of 89 in Spanish with the 96 percentile in English. In any case, the child compared favourably with monolingual children of his same age group.

Berko Test of English Morphology (1961). This test is designed to discover what children know about the morphological rules of English. It utilizes nonsense materials (both words and pictures of unfamiliar creatures) to elicit morphological markers of plurals, possessives and verb endings. The test is used with children ranging in age from four to seven. Percentages are given for the number of children who scored correctly in the original Berko experiment on any given item, separated by age groups. Hence an item by item comparison is possible. No total scoring system is provided for comparing global results since the test is designed as a linguistic experiment rather than a placement or diagnostic tool.

The first impression gathered during the administration of the test was Mario's insistence on defining the kind of creature viewed. His persistence in classifying animal types often interfered with the testing process. His behaviour is apparently at variance with that of the children whom Berko tested and described as willing and co-operative subjects. Mario's most typical question was: ¿Qué es, papá, qué es? ¿Díme, por favor, qué es? . . . ¿un dinosauro? . . . ¿un pulpo? . . . ¿qué?" (*What is it, papa, what? Tell me, please. What is it? a dinosaur . . . an octopus . . . what?*)

In spite of Mario's concern with the classification of the strange creatures, he scored in a fairly average way with a few exceptions. This judgement is based on the fact that most of his correct responses were also those correctly answered by between 58 to 79% of his peers, varying with the item. In one case he also correctly provided a past tense marker which was answered by only 36% of his peers. In items where he erred, his peers also erred greatly, with only 14 to 32% correct responses. There was one area of exception, however, where Mario's peers did consistently better, ranging from 47 to 73%. All these cases involved tense markers for the past and third person of the present, as in "ricked, glinged, binged, nazzes", and "loodges". This points up one area of weakness in Mario's knowledge of English morphology. The second area of weakness has to do with possessive forms. The first time Mario was asked the question: "Whose hat is it?" he sidestepped the problem by responding simply "mariachi" (referring to Mexican musicians) since the hat looked like a Mexican sombrero. However, the second time elicitation of the possessive came up, he admitted to lack of knowledge of the form by saying: "No puedo decir 'de ellos'." (I don't know how to say "de ellos".)

Kernan/Blount Test of Spanish Morphology (1966). Kernan & Blount adapted the Berko test to Spanish which they used in a study which tried to determine what native Spanish-speaking children know about the morphological rules of their language. This test was also given to Mario, who seemed more amenable to the Spanish version than to the English one. On the other hand, because he was already acquainted with many of the same drawings, a decline in interest was noted. The authors of the test readily pointed out that in their study they experienced considerable difficulty in eliciting answers on the basis of nonsense figures, and they therefore preceded each question with an example (Kernan & Blount, 1966:3). This was a helpful procedure in getting Mario to respond as well.

A difficult problem sometimes was to elicit precisely the form of the marker being tested. For example, in trying to elicit a diminutive ending for a nonsense word like "fetor" Mario responded with "chiquito fetor". The cue was further exaggerated by giving the example, "un fetor muy, muy pequeño", to which the response was "un fetor muy, muy chiquito". However, the form sought was the diminutive added to words ending in a consonant.

Mario did considerably better with Spanish morphology than he did with English morphology. He responded incorrectly to only two items in the Spanish test, both items involving tense markers. In the first case Mario created "sostado" instead of the more commonly given response "sosteado"; and in the second, he formed the imperfect "totaba" instead of totiaba". In neither case, however, was there an overwhelming percentage of correct responses by his peers — 57% answered correctly to the first, and only 47% to the second. Since Mario scored correctly on almost all other items he was often substantially better than many of his peer group, ranging from 23% to 100%.

The test also pointed out Mario's lack of a future tense formed by a verb infinitive plus future marker. Mario has not yet employed this form in spontaneous speech, using a more common future construction formed with the verb "ir" + a + verb. Apparently this was fairly common also with the five-year-olds tested by Kernan & Blount since only 27 to 33% of the children they tested produced the first type of future expression.

Finally, one other area deserves comment. Whereas 40% of Mario's peers created agentive forms such as "pretero" and "ticador", Mario created other forms like "pretor" and "ticor" in the same way one forms "pintor" from "pinta" ("to paint", third person). Since Kernan & Blount based their test items on norms derived from adult language within a given area of Mexico, it may be possible that Mario's responses would appear to be less at variance if he were compared with norms derived from his own parents' speech. Nonetheless, his formations were acceptable in standard Spanish, and they did, in fact, demonstrate knowledge of how to form the agentive from a verb form.

To summarize, the picture which emerges from these tests supports earlier descriptions of Mario's proficiency. The tests show that Mario between five and six was an individual who controlled Spanish and English on about the same level as the average monolingual child of the same age in each of these languages. On a phonological level, he did not have complete control of allophonic variations of English phonemes although he distinguished all the phonemes of each language. He produced those phonemes commonly produced by most children of the same age. He appeared to be slightly stronger in his knowledge of Spanish vocabulary than in English. He also had a fairly good command of the grammar of both languages. He was probably more advanced in Spanish morphology than his peers; however, the same was not true in English where he lacked certain tense markers and the possessive forms.

School reports

School reports which helped establish a basis for evaluating Mario's language development were essentially of two sorts: actual report cards (in areas related to language skills), and standardized tests given at various times throughout the educational process to monitor students' development in several areas. Both were helpful in assessing the child's ability in English. This is less so for Spanish, obviously, since most of his schooling during the first 10 years was done in the United States.

One of the earliest standardized tests to which Mario was subjected was preliminary to kindergarten entrance. At age 4;9, he was given the Peabody Picture Vocabulary Test (see Dunn, 1959) on which he did quite poorly. He obtained a raw score of only 47 which ranked him in the 29th percentile according to estabished norms. The tester was well aware of the child's dominance in a language other than English which she indicated by noting on the completed test form that ". . . his ability is much better than indicated . . ." A day or so later, the same test was administered in Spanish and Mario's raw score nearly doubled to 84. Naturally no norms existed for placing this score within a percentile rank.

The next standardized tests were given several years later when the child was in fourth, sixth and eighth grades (ages 9;9, 11;8 and 13;9). Although the last two fall beyond the scope of this study, they are interesting to note in that they illustrate the direction of the child's language development since his first test experience just prior to entering school. The tests given in all three cases were the California Achievment Tests (C.A.T., 1977). Sections relevant to language performance are indicated below:

	Grade Level: 4.8			Grade Level: 6.7			Grade Level: 8.8		
	NP	LP	OGE	NP	LP	OGE	NP	LP	OGE
Reading Vocabulary	87	76	7.4	87	77	—	97	85	12.9
Reading Comprehension	99	98	11.0	87	74	—	93	77	12.9
Total Reading	98	98	10.0	89	78	—	96	84	12.9
Spelling	99	98	12.2	93	91	—	98	96	12.5
Language Mechanics	80	78	7.7	90	83	—	87	69	12.9
Language Expression	91	83	9.0	95	83	—	97	91	12.9
Total Language	89	83	8.5	96	88	—	96	86	12.9

To explain further, results of the child's performance were first compared with National Norms, hence this score is expressed as a National Percentile (NP) rank; and secondly with Local Norms, giving a Local Percentile (LP). In all cases, and at the various grade levels, Mario compared extremely favourably with his monolingual English-speaking peers in the various aspects of language expression tested. Finally, the child's "On Grade

Equivalent" (OGE) is cited expressing the level at which the child is performing. By this measure, the child at eighth grade performed at a level comparable to monoglots at the twelfth grade level.

Two separate report cards were issued for the child during his tenth year owing to the fact that he commenced the school year in the United States and completed it in Bolivia. These reports are interesting in that in one the child's performance was judged through English, and in the other through Spanish. Extrapolating from these reports in those areas related to language performance, letter grades (on a scale ranging from a high of A to a low of F) from the American school at mid year were:

Reading   A
Language Arts:
   Language   A
   Spelling   A –

By the end of term of that same school year, Mario received the following grades (number grades ranging from a high of 7 to a low of 1) from his school in Bolivia:

Lectura (Reading)   5
Escritura (Writing)   5
Lenguaje (Language) 5
Inglés (English)   6

Based on the first report it is clear that he excelled in language-related areas (taught through English) while at school in the United States. It should be kept in mind that by this time he had already experienced nearly six consecutive years of education in the American schools. The second report reflected his first real educational attempt in a Latin American school setting in which all subjects were taught in Spanish. Despite this very novel experience, he did average to well. Curiously, he did not attain a top grade even in English, taught as a foreign language subject in the Bolivian school.

Subjective evaluations

Finally, one other type of indicator is relevant to an assessment of language performance and development at various stages throughout this period. These were subjective comments made by various teachers who worked with the child as well as others who knew him in either English or Spanish. Although these assessments are the least reliable statistically, they are nonetheless highly reliable in terms of the judgements which other monolingual speakers made of the child. Admittedly, most native-speakers have a great capacity for perceiving non-native or foreign deviations when it comes up in their native tongue.

Age 5;7 From his kindergarten teacher, Vermont: "Mario . . . got along well with the other children. He expressed himself verbally quite well. At times he would pause and say 'how do you say that?' or words to that effect. He seemed to understand what I told him and directions that I gave him and responded in an appropriate manner. For the most part, Mario did not appear to be hindered by any language problems."

Age 5;9 From his kindergarden teacher, Austin: ". . . he speaks clearly and with good diction."

Age 6;2 From his gym teacher: ". . . thinks through what he says . . . speaks clearly . . ." From the special education teacher (speech therapist): "Mario should attend therapy to correct speech variance."

Age 7;1 From his second grade teacher: "Mario is a bright boy . . . he reads everything . . . I'm amazed (by his English). His first grade teacher said he was away in Bolivia this summer."

Age 8;5 His third grade teacher expressed surprise that Mario speaks any language other than English. In almost disbelief, he tried in several ways to see if Mario could say something to him in Spanish.

Age 8;7 At a Bilingual Education convention held in New Orleans, the child was introduced to a prominent figure in bilingual education who had recently completed a bilingual dominance test which he administered right on the spot at the booth. At the conclusion, he exclaimed: "He's got an even score of 13–13 which means he's a perfectly balanced bilingual."

Age 9;3 His fourth grade teacher did not know he spoke another language. When told, she recalled an incident: "Mario was speaking, he hesitated, thought, groping for a word . . . then asked: 'What's the opposite of husband?' I thought to myself what a strange question for a little boy."

Age 9;9 From Mexican friends whom the child was visiting (translated): ". . . he's definitely not Mexican. He seems more 'españolado' (Spanish-fied), because he pronounces the /s/ a lot. He has a different intonation, he sings his sentences. Seems like he's from somewhere else in South America."

Age 10;2 From his fifth grade teacher: ". . . unusually clear, precise in his speech . . . pronunciation."

Age 10;6 From his aunt from Bolivia: ". . . habla bien no más."

From these comments, his development becomes quite clear. By third grade (age 8;5), his English was as native-sounding as that of any other child in the same school, so that his teacher was almost in disbelief upon learning that the child spoke Spanish at home. Two months later, Mario tested out as a perfectly balanced bilingual. And the reaction of most people beyond that point when asked about the child's language ability was one of consternation since there was no hint that he was a bilingual speaker. His ability in each language was taken for granted as with any other child. There is not much to say when an individual is taken as a native speaker. Hence, the only significant comment the teacher contributed was that he spoke unusually clearly and precisely; just as his aunt made the simple comment about his Spanish: ". . . habla bien, no más" (*He speaks fine, that's all*).

Taken together — formal language tests, school reports, and comments from various observers of the child — the picture which emerged was one of a child who had successfully developed dual language systems. By age ten, he had demonstrated talents as linguist and ethnographer so that he was judged an acceptable and competent member of each of two cultures and two societies.

Notes to Chapter Five

1. Dell Hymes (1971: 3–32) suggests the broadening of linguistic theory to include sociolinguistic aspects.
2. Two investigators who examined phonological acquisition within Jakoboson's framework are Moskowitz, 1970: 426–41; and Contreras, 1961. Each arrived at different conclusions.
3. A tape recorder is more reliable at this stage because of the unintelligibility of many of the early sounds. Leopold commented on a similar difficulty, ". . . the quality of those early sounds is so indistinct and unconventional that they defy transcription and almost description." See Leopold, 1939–49: 17.
4. The reader is referred to excerpts from the Speech Diary in the Appendix of this report for examples of the child's early phonology.
5. It is common experience among Spanish-speakers that children are not normally capable of producing the $/\tilde{r}/\sim/rr/$ distinction until almost five, although isolated exceptions are also known. Mario's mother, for one, is reported to have produced trill and flap sounds by about three years of age. Jakobson (1968: 90–91) also comments on their acquisition.
6. This fact is well known to linguists, but it was also substantiated by the observations of one Elementary School Teacher, Brenda Willis, Allison Elementary School, Austin, Texas, who commented that more than half of her first-graders were still unable to pronounce the $/\theta/\sim/d/$ distinction. In some cases, the difficulty persists into second grade as well; also see Jakobson, 1968.
7. For a more explicit account of Spanish stress rules, consult Stockwell, Bowen & Martin, 1965: 19–34.
8. Several persons have worked specifically on cognition and language, most notably Piaget, 1954, 1963, 1971. Also see Vygotsky, 1962; and Sinclair-de-Zwart, 1969.
9. Mario experienced confusion with the proper use of these words in Spanish, owing to the fact that his father sometimes confused the two because of inter-

ference from Italian. In Italian, "mettere" conveys what is expressed through two different words in Spanish, each with a slightly different conceptual meaning.

10. Some of the more widely discussed processes were advanced by Brown & Bellugi, 1964: 131–61; also the notion of "contextual generalization" discussed in an article by Braine (1971: 242–43).

11. An excellent work which focuses on the "ethnography of communication" is that by Gumperz & Hymes (1972). Also see Sherzer & Darnell, 1972: 548–54.

12. Leopold, Brown and Bellugi all made note of this fact. Leopold suggested that since the semantic peak and phonetic stress do not put function words in relief as much as content words, this may explain their later acquisition; see Leopold, 1939–1949: 3. Brown & Bellugi also demonstrated that the stress pattern placed greatest emphasis on content words, thereby attracting the child's attention at first to these; see Brown & Bellugi, 1964: 141.

13. Leopold notes that his daughter, Hildegard, had a period of at least eight months of purely one-word utterances, although her onset of speech was considerably earlier than Mario's. See Leopold, 1939–1949: 2.

14. Brown uses sentence length (calculated in morphemes) as a productive measure of syntactic progression as well as to compare children of varying chronological ages. This serves as an index of grammatical development in that almost every new kind of grammatical knowledge invariably increases sentence length. See Brown, 1973: 53–54.

15. Leopold remarked that the learner's first steps into the realm of morphological patterns provide a valuable index of the growing powers of abstraction and progress from pure imitation to freer handling of structural devices and that the intellectual maturity needed for these first steps is normally not reached until the turn of the third year. See Leopold, 1939–1949: 269–80.

16. Leopold also observed several examples of non-standard word order in his daughter's speech which could not be readily explained; see Leopold, 1939–1949: 70–72.

17. Alternate forms are used by Mario's parents.

18. Norms for the Austin Mexican–American children were provided by Murray A. Newman, Coordinator, Thinking and Reasoning Program, Southwest Educational Development Laboratory, Austin, Texas. Newman also computed Mario's percentile score based on these norms.

19. After learning this fact from the tests, Mario was shown left from right and he was able to make this distinction himself only a few days later. Because of this, it may be assumed that his problem was not cognitive in nature, but merely linguistic.

6 Summary and conclusions

This study has attempted to examine the language development of one bilingual child, from infancy through his tenth year. The research was based on data obtained through taped recordings and a speech diary collected throughout this period. This documentation permitted tracking the child's language acquisition of Spanish, English, and to a lesser degree, Italian. The perspective throughout was sociolinguistically oriented, considering the relationship between dual language development and social variables extant in the child's milieu.

The study began with a description of the project, its objectives and methods. A review of relevant studies dealing with bilingualism, especially infant bilingualism, and with advances in sociolinguistic research, was conducted. Specific aspects of the child's circumstances, his caretakers and the settings in which he lived, were described as relevant to the study, as well as his pattern of contact and exposure with the languages in question.

This background set the stage for an investigation of bilingual acquisition, considering first the sociolinguistic dimension. This included attempts to ascertain the process of language separation, a prerequisite to the child's awareness of his own bilinguality. Social factors impinging on this process were identified, and the approximate period of occurrence was ascertained. Once systems were differentiated, environmental cues affecting choice of each code were identified. When and how these cues combined in varying contexts to affect language use were discussed. The influence also of caretakers and others was considered in terms of their effects on the child's verbal production, shaping his world view and guiding his comportment throughout the socialization process. Lastly, as part of this sociolinguistic analysis, the child's usage and styles of language were of interest. The specific ways in which the child learned to vary and modify language output, leading toward distinctive styles of speaking, each related to specific social circumstances present at the moment of speech, were identified and described.

The linguistic dimension of this study included consideration of several aspects of linguistic development — the acquisition of the phonemic systems, lexical growth, and morphological and syntactic development. The primary emphasis, however, was on the effects of dual language use, producing language borrowing across systems which is typical of most bilingual behaviour. Within this area of concern, the changing notions of interference and transference were reviewed. Both phenomena were examined with regard to the social context as a determinant affecting the degree, type and direction of borrowing. Finally, various testing results and other reports were utilized in an effort to provide indices of the child's proficiency in English and Spanish, as well as to provide a comparison of his language development with that of monolingual children of similar age.

Obviously any case study contains its own intrinsic characteristics which make the experience of each individual different from that of any other individual. Yet what may be extrapolated are possibly some insights about the process and the inter-relationship of the component parts. Future researchers will help to determine to what degree these extrapolations may be part and parcel of a more common human experience.

Observations on language differentiation and bilinguality

1. Linguistic differentiation was an on-going process as long as the child was in contact with two or more language systems. It was evident in the child's behaviour from the onset of his second language, although there were indications that differentiation had begun even earlier, judging by his reaction to familiar and unfamiliar sounds.

2. Language differentiation appeared to be related to the social need to talk and to be understood. The child sorted linguistic signals into proper sets until communication was accomplished. The degree of separateness of language use was determined by the norms of the participants.

3. Use of distinct and separate language systems was observed by age 2;8. This early differentiation occurred in spite of delayed and only occasional contact with the second language.

4. The separateness of environments in which each language was acquired and the consistency of language use within each of these environments were probably significant factors which facilitated early and successful language distinction.

5. Knowledge of more than one language appeared to be a factor which

contributed to Mario's general curiosity and interest in other forms of human expression.

6. Differentiated language use helped the child's formation of the abstract concept of "language" possibly earlier than for monolingual children. In fact, he was unable to label either of his languages by name until he had cognitively grasped the significance of his ability to group linguistic elements into "sets".

7. The use of dual language systems helped the child to learn how to use metalanguage (i.e. how to use language itself to learn more about verbal expression) as a productive learning technique. He not only asked how to say things, but he also asked for equivalents and translations.

8. The co-existence of two languages was a factor which permitted the child to become aware that there were various verbal possibilities for expressing the same concept, and a continuing interest in other language codes.

9. The acquisition of Spanish and English depended not only on sufficient and prolonged exposure but also on the child's social needs. Where the social need was slight, so too was his productive use of the system (as with Italian). Periods with little or no language contact caused this system to fall quickly into disuse.

On language choice and social variables

1. The interlocutor appeared to be the principal determinant affecting language choice. When the interlocutor's language was not known, Mario was guided by other factors (such as physical appearance) in determining proper language choice.

2. The setting of the speech act seemed of secondary importance in affecting language choice (when the act occurred in an environment in which both languages were in use). Other considerations were the form and function of the speech event.

3. Social factors which had an effect upon language choice were hierarchically arranged in order of importance: interlocutor, setting, and form and function. The topic of speech became significant to code choice as the child became specialized in domains of language use through public education, becoming apparent toward his ninth year. However, when the child used language for any purpose other than as a purely representative device (e.g. expressive or evocative purposes as in roleplay, song, etc.), this hierarchy was disregarded, and the function of the speech act became the primary determinant of choice.

4. Mario was capable of complete code switching by 2;8; from that time to the present he has been capable of switching rapidly and appropriately in

relation to changing contexts. The child behaved "normally" in either language.

5. Switching was orderly and purposeful, rather than haphazard.

On language and socialization

1. Mario's parents (and other adults) used different speech styles with him in accordance with his level of maturity at each age and in accordance with their own beliefs about his abilities.

2. Speech styles — identified by combinations of linguistic features such as intonation, pitch, selection of specific phones and morphological devices — were detected in the speech of adults and recreated by the child.

3. During his infancy, Mario's caretakers used language to establish contact and to elicit signs of recognition from him. Once he became physically active, they used language increasingly to point out dangers, establish limits, and to express approval or disapproval, thereby shaping his pre-speech articulations.

4. As Mario matured, his caretakers used language to exert increasing control on his behaviour. They also demanded that he respond through language rather than through the non-linguistic means which earlier they had permitted.

5. Mario's caretakers provided negative feedback to inform him when he behaved inappropriately, linguistically or otherwise. They guided him in regulating the volume of his voice, in the context of his remarks (thereby fostering the beginnings of taboo language), and in the mechanics of conversation (when to speak or not).

6. The child's parents taught him social roles and relationships through their use of etiquette and courtesy terms, through insistence on titles, and through other indices inherent in their language system.

7. As Mario demonstrated increasing control of his language, adults showed less tolerance of aberrant language and grammatical errors.

8. The attitudes of the caretakers were an important factor affecting the appropriateness or inappropriateness of code switching.

9. The child's initial attitudes toward his languages and language use were strongly influenced by the examples of his caretakers. His parents also used language as a medium through which they conveyed their world view to the child.

On usage and styles

1.From infancy Mario used differentiated cries to express varying physical needs. As he matured and became a social being, he used different language styles in accordance with social circumstances present during the speech act. Styles were marked by consistent patterns of linguistic modifications related to specific social contexts.

2. Patterns noted in the child's speech included a style of speech he used with adults, a peer style, a style used with younger children, a narrative style, and a style used with socially inferior interlocutors.

3. There was evidence (in one specific case at least) that the child perceived speech patterns, even when he did not necessarily use these in his own language. Style identification was related to the child's ability to perceive patterns in linguistic variations; his use of a style, however, was related to his social status.

4. As the child matured, and certainly by age five, his performance was increasingly judged by others both in terms of its grammaticality and social appropriateness.

5. Speech styles appeared to be rooted in the social context, reflecting social interaction between Mario and other speakers. Mario's styles changed even during the few years observed, suggesting that specific usage and styles were not permanent features but rather that they change in accordance with changing roles and relationships. Consequently, styles were adopted, modified or discarded in relation to social needs at any given time.

On linguistic borrowing

1. Language interaction was ascertained by comparing developmental data with language norms for monolingual children of comparable ages. This was done to determine which deviations were caused by the co-existence of dual systems, and which were "normal" deviations from adult speech characteristic of children under five.

2. Mixing increased during periods approaching equal contact with both languages; it decreased when language use during a prolonged period was almost totally Spanish or English.

3. In spite of initial phonic interference, Mario mastered the complete phonemic systems of Spanish and English by age 5;0, with the exception of phonemes which are normally late acquisitions for most children (such as /ð/~/θ/ in English, and /ř/~/rr/ in Spanish).

4. In spite of nearly complete phonemic systems, interference persisted on a phonetic level, especially where allophonic patterns differed in the two systems (e.g. the /b/~/v/ alternation in English based on the Spanish allophonic pattern).

5. Borrowing was greatest in the area of the lexicon, possibly reflecting the child's separate direct experience with each language. Loan-words usually ceased when a synonym was acquired which replaced the borrowed

item. In cases where no equivalent was learned, the borrowed item persisted in the child's speech, as was the case with many culturally-bound expressions.

6. Mario usually demonstrated his awareness when introducing borrowed words into an alternate language system by setting these off with "oral" quotation marks and retaining phonetic aspects of the word as pronounced in the source language.

7. Borrowing occurred in various aspects of the communicative act. It was not restricted solely to structural aspects lke phonology, morphology and syntax, but occurred as well across speech styles, interactional strategies, and at the conceptual level.

8. Whereas interference was structurally derived, transference was socially motivated. The occurrence, direction and degree of linguistic borrowing were directly affected by social aspects of the child's milieu — setting, interlocutor and the attitudes of the participants.

9. The child exercised surprising control over his dual language systems. When transference was allowed to occur, it was for calculated reasons related to language use: social identification, marked speech, emphasis and so forth. Whatever the reasons, the child was normally aware and sensitive of circumstances that demanded monolingual speech and to those which permitted the utilization of elements from two systems.

10. Borrowing must be viewed as a process — appearing or disappearing, increasing or decreasing, and reversing direction, always in response to changing contexts in which the child found himself at the moment of speech.

On proficiency

1. Test results showed that Mario's language ability compared favourably with ability norms for monolingual speakers of Spanish and English of similar ages.

2. By five, Spanish, the language of his home, was definitely Mario's dominant tongue. Nonetheless, his verbal skills in English were ranked "average" when tested along with monolingual English-speakers entering kindergarten, and better than average on other tests.

3. By ten, Mario demonstrated through his proficiency and language use that he was able to master two languages on a par with his peers, as well as to acquire receptive skills in a third.

In conclusion, the process of dual acquisition was not observably different from that involved in the acquisition of only one language. It is true that Mario acquired more phonemes, more lexicon, and more syntactic rules than would have been required for only one language; the *process*, however, remained inherently the same. In a similar way, Mario was exposed to at least two cultural patterns.

What differed was language use. Mario had to learn the signals in his environment which triggered the use of one or another of his two languages. In similar fashion he learned to recognize the social factors which required corresponding style modifications. When styles are viewed in this way, it becomes obvious that all speakers learn to use linguistic alternatives in relation to differing contexts. Hence, the process of learning the rules of co-occurrence or co-variation between linguistic elements and social factors remains inherently the same, whether for the bilingual or monolingual speaker.

Language is the child's passport for entry into a social group, or a cultural community. Two languages permit the child to enter into and acquire the world views of two communities. The desirability of two world views appears to be primarily a question of one's attitude. However, for these views to exist in harmony rather than in conflict, favourable attitudes on the part of those who surround the child are essential to permit him to grow up a well-adjusted individual, comfortable in either community. Unfavourable attitudes in either social group in which the child participates may produce conflict or force him to choose one type of verbal behaviour to the exclusion of the other. Thus far, Mario has been fortunate in having had positive experiences in each of the communities in which he has participated.

It seems possible that an individual, exposed to at least two languages and two world views from early childhood, may emerge a double beneficiary. Furthermore, dual membership impresses upon the individual the variety of possible behaviours of human beings. In any case, no matter what language or languages are spoken by an individual, his use of language reflects much information about his roles, his relationships to others, and his views of the world. Yet language is only a part of his system of communication and interaction, and therefore it cannot be studied in isolation. Language must be contemplated within a social perspective. This is what this study has tried to accomplish.

Further Reflections

In retrospect, it should be recalled that this study was not an experiment, but a case study. It concludes with no hard facts on the general subject of language learning. Despite many years of observation and hundreds of books on the subject, one is struck with the little we know about the actual *process* of language acquisition. One can record content, devise charts, count morphemes, and ascertain stages, but process still proves elusive. One can account for what the child says and when he says something, but it is more difficult to account for how he acquires the ability to do so. It has been recognized that linguistics alone cannot provide the answer, nor can psychology, biology, or any other discipline. A multidisciplinary approach is needed for a better understanding of language acquisition processes.

Bilingual acquisition has often been viewed as a special phenomenon. Yet from a generative-transformational viewpoint, the developing bilingual is little different from the child learning only one tongue. If it can be assumed that phrase structure rules are universal to all language systems, then speakers of different languages must differ primarily in the distinct sets of transformational rules which they acquire, specific to the language of their environment.

Theoretically, whether the child is exposed to one or more languages, the process of rule acquisition remains intrinsically unaltered. The child exposed to two or more systems simply acquires more transformations, and possibly different transformations, but the basic process of rule formulation is the same. On the other hand, if the bilingual child is to communicate properly, he is faced with an additional task — that of sorting out which rules belong to each code, and which rules are appropriate for use in each set of circumstances. Ultimately, then, it is the social context which requires rule differentiation and produces bilingual behaviour.

Within linguistics, approaches to child language have often been based on too narrow a view. Linguists have been primarily concerned with the acquisition of linguistic elements, overlooking the fact that language is only part (although a significant part) of a broader communicative system. When it is viewed in this way, we are forced to look not only at language, but also at language use and the social context in which language unfolds. We are ultimately concerned with all forms of human interaction once a wider view of verbal behaviour is considered.

Whereas linguists often commence the study of language from the onset of the first words, interaction commences at birth. From the moment of his first cries and the first responses of others to the child's cries, social inter-action has begun. All forms of human contact communicate meaning; and this is precisely the area which language and other forms of interaction share. What one says, the manner in which it is said, how one uses body movements, and whether one says anything at all — all communicate. It is not surprising, then, that researchers are increasingly examining the semantic component of language as an important determiner of the order of acquisition, constrained, perhaps, by cognitive aspects. As Hymes has indicated, form follows function, and not the reverse.

In reviewing Mario's speech data, many examples were noted which showed how often words alone were incapable of preserving the meaning of a given speech act. Without contextual notations, it would often have been impossible to reconstruct the message conveyed by the child's words alone. Recreation of the setting and the social interaction of those present through contextual notes were crucial to understanding the meaning behind words in so many cases. Children reared away from a social enclave do not learn language. The child articulates sounds, but it is the presence of others which is required for the sounds to become meaningful words. But even before words are formed, the child has learned to communicate with others through social interaction. Consequently the child learns to derive meaning from many sources; often they reinforce each other, sometimes they are at variance.

Furthermore, language is a developing and continually evolving communicative device. We can witness its fluidity in dramatic fashion in the young child; this fluidity is not so easily seen in the adult speaker. Since language conveys information about the user's social status, role and relationships with others, it must certainly change as these factors change. We have seen how the individual at a very early age is already capable of code switching (if bilingual), and of using different speech styles. If language styles are related to the social status of the user, then obviously styles change as these factors evolve from the moment the infant becomes a social being and throughout life. The fact that language can be so affected by various external social factors and the fact that each speaker possesses several styles raises questions concerning a theoretical notion of competence as an abstract notion. Attempts must be made to broaden linguistic theory to include sociolinguistic variants which form part of everyone's speech.

Many researchers now view the child as "linguist"; we must also view him as "ethnographer". What he learns is one form of human behaviour which comprises his language, and he also learns all other aspects of behaviour which are part of the culture of his community. He develops a sense of grammaticality as well as a sense of social appropriateness for the use of language. And through language, as well as through all of his experiences as linguist-ethnographer he forms a view of his world.

How all of this is accomplished remains a mystery. Obviously the process of language acquisition is affected by various factors and constraints: biological, maturational, psychological, conceptual and cognitive, and circumstantial (social). Yet the specific strategies involved are no different from those used by an individual to learn almost anything else. We read of imitation, induction of latent structure, pivot grammar, problem-solving, hypothesis-forming and differentiation and generalization. Of all these strategies, the themes of differentiation and generalization appear to be important building blocks of learning. And apparently they are two aspects of the same process. That is, since no two items are ever identical in time and space, to be able to generalize requires that one must be able to ignore the fact that any two items are different along some dimensions. Similarly, to differentiate requires previous generalization over a multitude of concepts. One sees how differentiation and generalization form part of many aspects of learning language, especially since maximal contrast appears to be the first point of focus for the child. In learning to pronounce, the child first differentiates and uses the two phonemes of greatest contrast. In distinguishing colours a similar process seems to occur, permitting the child to discern first those colours which are far apart on the colour scale, eventually making finer and finer distinctions. The same appears to be true of morphology, and, according to some, in lexicon building as well. Differentiation is also an important part of learning to read at an early age. In Mario's case, he responded first to the total graphic stimulus, but as more and more written words were introduced, he learned to differentiate finer and finer aspects of words until eventually he distinguished their components, or individual letters.

But whatever the strategies, most people recognize the child as a problem-solver. And whether he proceeds deductively at times, forming hypotheses and testing these out, or sometimes inducing concepts based on data and evidence, the system he produces is always one which is internally coherent. His knowledge appears to be cumulative to a point and then discontinuous, for as he acquires increased knowledge he periodically revises his system at different stages in accordance with new evidence.

The optimum time to learn has been of concern to many. If the child raised in isolation cannot acquire human language after puberty, it would certainly seem that this is a crucial point in human development. Some biological and neurological studies seem to lend evidence to this viewpoint. On the other hand, others have pointed out that the adult learner often has other compensating factors such as motivation, interest, improved learning techniques and possibly pedagogical assists which may offset the disadvantage of increased age. Yet for native-like control, especially of phonology, many would agree that early learning in childhood is best. However, the question as to whether two or more languages should be introduced from birth, or at age two, or three, remains largely unresolved.

Some would provide considerable support for not waiting beyond two or three. Aside from the question of optimum age, one must consider factors of socialization, degree and amount of exposure, separateness of language use, social need, and the attitudes which affect learning. These are all factors which are as crucial as considerations of age if the languages acquired are to continue active rather than fall into disuse or disrepute.

Many techniques have been employed in the study of child language; some of these were discussed in an earlier chapter. However, one technique which has not been used, with but one exception, is introspection. St. Augustine provides an interesting account of how he analyzed his own acquisition of language through introspection (or more precisely, retrospection). Needless to say, his example has not been followed; and at first glance, it may appear to be a ridiculous approach. Yet it is true that we have all gone through a language learning experience as children. It is not suggested, of course, that we, as adults, reflect on a process of which we probably have no recall, even though some childhood experiences have been tapped in other ways and for other reasons. Some, who have studied aphasics, have reported interesting accounts in which victims of aphasia recovered a language learned in childhood which they had not spoken for many years.

In any case, what is suggested is a *recreated* language learning experience which permits introspection. Quite simply, if we are concerned with focusing it on the "process" of language acquisition, then perhaps one way of doing this might be by engaging in a second language learning experience. It goes without saying that the adult experience is not identical to childhood acquisition, but it is, after all, a learning experience, and, as such, should help to focus on process. Perhaps one might experiment by moving to another linguistic community (say a village on the Bolivian "altiplano") where learning must take place from the start without assistance. Many people, of course, have already had such experiences when abroad. This time, however, we shall take care not to carry along a dictionary, a text, a tape recorder, and certainly no manual on "field linguistics". Only a pencil and paper will be used, but not to record language. Rather the notes we shall make as neophyte linguists and enthnographers will concern *only* what happens. Our diary will record first impressions: when we first begin to discern various characteristics of the language we hear, salient sounds, at what point we begin to associate sounds with specific function, what do the people communicate to us based entirely on what we see, what are the first words we learn, what theories do we form, how many of these turn out to be wrong or disproven by later data, what are the patterns we discern, and so forth. This approach may seem far afield from our current interest in child language, but it is possible that introspection into our own feelings, interpretations, reactions, strategies, etc., may tell us something about process. One thing it surely does is force us to take a hard look at interaction rather than just the lingistic system of a language like Aymara.

Some of the problem areas in the current study which raise further questions deserve mention. For example, what constitutes style and what constitutes code is not clearly defined. Can it not be viewed that style, which entails modification of sets of linguistic signals, forms part of a continuum, such that if sufficient linguistic modifications are made, the result is a complete change of code? In other words, when is a language so modified that it becomes another language? For example, some speakers of Spanish and Portuguese feel their languages are so distinct they cannot possibly understand each other; others, assuming a different attitude, find that the differences are so slight that they can communicate perfectly. To what extent, then, do the attitudes and norms of the speakers determine language, dialect and styles?

In Mario's case, English developed later than Spanish, and it has been seen how Spanish phonology, fairly well set by the onset of English, affected the child's pronunciation of the latter. Borrowing occurred primarily within areas in which Spanish allophonic variations differed from those in English. One wonders what might have occurred if the reverse development had ensued; i.e. English developing before Spanish. How would English allophonic variations have affected his pronunciation of Spanish? A related aspect is the fact that the Spanish phonemic system has fewer phonemes than English (although some like the /r̄/~/rr/ distinction are foreign to English), so that, by and large, the child was required to develop additional phonemes needed for English by making finer and finer distinctions beyond those he already had for Spanish. Had he acquired English first, and Spanish second, would he have had a fairly complete pronunciation of Spanish at its onset?

Since continuing exposure and contact affect language so dramatically at this early age, one also wonders what time span might be required for the child to completely lose one or another of his languages. There was sufficient evidence of his unwillingness to speak English while in Bolivia, and already there were signs of forgetting. But it is difficult to know at what point English might have been completely forgotten. Memory and forgetting seem closely related to use.

There are many areas of bilingual acquisition, or even monolingual acquisition, which require further exploration. Certainly more studies must focus on socialization and the effects of socialization on language acquisition. More studies are needed which view the entire process from a socio-linguistic perspective. And as one introduces sociological aspects, one is forced to view cross-cultural approaches to language learning; i.e. language acquisition as affected by socialization in different cultures. Studies in which language interaction has been treated as a purely linguistic phenomenon must be broadened to take into account social influences. It is clear in Mario's case, at least, how social factors influenced potential linguistic borrowings. Certainly more studies on the acquisition of Spanish are sorely needed to serve as a basis for comparison with the current data.

As one observes a child acquire his native tongue, one cannot help but ask what possible relevance these observations may have to second language learning. At times similarities have been overplayed and the differences minimized; at others, differences have been exaggerated and the similarities ignored. Since it appears that the strategies of first language acquisition are basically strategies of learning, perhaps we have our first parallel. To build a pedagogical method on any single strategy would seem foolhardy; yet many teaching methods are built on psychological theories of learning which often have been too narrow, too exclusive. Perhaps more should be made of differentiation and generalization as aspects of learning. Just how these might form part of teaching is a question to be studied. But we have seen that maximal contrasts within the same system seem to be a keynote: Mario proceeded from indicative to subjunctive at an early age; yet most texts normally leave subjunctive to an "advanced" stage of learning. There may be some implications here, one of which is that perhaps not all markers of a paradigm need to be learned initially but only those of greatest contrast from the viewpoint of the speaker. Other more obvious implications may be the interactional aspects of the communication act, rooted in social situations, which provided primary motivation for acquisition itself.

Another relevant aspect is the recurrent theme regarding the child as linguist-ethnographer. It would appear that this is an important parallel which must be carried to the classroom. It is true that most teachers express concern about both language and culture, but how these are inter-related and how they should be presented still elude many educators. Yet, if language is viewed as only part of communicative competence, we cannot really teach one without the other. Linguistic elements learned in a vacuum are not necessarily valid for communication. Often even fluent learners of a second language experience embarrassing or difficult moments when they have chosen the wrong style for a given situation. The application of socio-linguistic concepts to language teaching would appear to be a productive undertaking. Any approach must insure that the learner acquires not only the linguistic distinctions between "tú" and "usted", for example, but also important rules concerning their usage. Whether this be done through role play, simulation or other techniques is not so crucial as the fact that the importance of usage be recognized. Like the child, the adult learner is also judged both for grammaticality and for appropriateness.

Although we have looked at only one bilingual child in this study, the processes involved in the interplay of socialization and language acquisition, and the processes involved in style shifting, have wide applications since all speakers learn to modify linguistic features of their language in accordance with their social circumstance. Furthermore, although details vary, socialization must be viewed not only in terms of the language input which is provided, but also in terms of how it shapes the total behaviour of people. Studies must be broadened to include the acquisition of communicative competence of which language forms a part.

Finally, it should be clear that the study of child language is also the study of human behaviour in its nascent state. Through the observation of child language we can perform both synchronic and diachronic examinations, gaining insights into all aspects of linguistics, as well as in other areas of human behaviour. No other study can be more fascinating and more rewarding.

Appendix 1:
Phonetic Transcription

The symbols used in this study are those represented in the following charts:

Vowels:

	Front	Central	Back
High	i I		ʊ u
Mid	e ɛ	ʌ	ɔ o
Low	æ	a	

Notes:

1. Symbols on the left side of each column are voiceless; those on the right are voiced.
2. Aspiration is indicated by the superscript (ʰ). This normally applies only to English.
3. Length, which normally applies only to English and Italian, is indicated by (:).

Notes *continued:*

4. The flaps /r/, /r̃/, and /rr/ are placed in the centre of the column since they tend to be partly or wholly voiceless, depending upon their environment.
5. The sounds /t/ and /d/ tend to be dental in Spanish, but alveolar in English, which explains their entry in two columns of the chart. When it is necessary to show that a sound is pronounced more to the front or the back of its usual position, diacritic marks are used. Fronting is indicated by (<), and backing by (>).
6. All phonetic transcriptions are generally placed between slashes (//) since there is no need to distinguish from a phonemic transcription.

Consonants:

	Labial	Labio-dental	Interdental	Dental	Alveolar	Palatal	Velar	Post-Velar
Stops	p b			t d	t d		k g	ʔ
Fricatives	b	f v	θ d		s z	š ž	h g	x
Affricates						č j		
Nasals	m				n	ñ	ŋ	
Liquids and Flaps					l r r̃ rr			
Semivowels	(w)						y	w

Appendix 2: Excerpts from the Speech Diary

Mario's complete diary contains data from more than ten years. These served as the corpus of data on which this study was based. It is obviously impossible to include the entire diary here. However, excerpts were selected to provide a sense of the child's development through this period. The passages selected for inclusion were chosen with the following criteria in mind: (1) to provide samples of the child's speech at various stages; (2) to illustrate aspects of language development and language use which are specifically addressed in this study; and (3) to provide a glimpse of the child's developing awareness of the world about him as recorded through his own statements.

A note of explanation may help in following the diary format. Notes from the first year and the beginning of the second (up to the onset of speech) are primarily observational in nature; actual utterances are sparse. At this point a transcript of the child's utterances and significant maturational notes appear on the left side of the page, accompanied by observational notes to the right. As Mario begins to say words, these are recorded to the left with the standard language version and a translation (wherever needed) to the right; here, only occasional observations are provided. Beginning with the third phase in which Mario increasingly engages in dialogue, interaction as well as utterances are recorded. Consequently contextual notations are interspersed throughout (e.g. persons entering or departing, background sounds). In the fourth section, Mario's speech appears consistently on the left of the page to permit rapid scanning of just his comments; statements by other participants appear on the right, followed by English translations as required. Each speech event is preceded by the age and location, plus a brief synopsis of the setting and participants. Once participants are introduced, they are referred to by first initial only.

For example, Mario (M) speaking to his mother (mamá, hence MA) is represented as M→MA, or to his cousin, Billy (B), as M→B.

Symbols used in the diary include:

//	phonetic/phonemic transcription
XXXX	muttered or garbled speech
(X)	initial, identifying one of several speakers
. . .	pause in the conversation
— — —	an unfinished word (e.g. "la cos— —" = la cosa)
#	entire utterance repeated verbatim (e.g. "No quiero. #, # " = No quiero, no quiero, no quiero.)

Finally, entries in the early part of the diary are in phonetic/phonemic script. As Mario's speech approaches standard language, however, standard orthography replaces phonetic transcription, except where a special point of pronunciation is being made.

Speech Diary of Alvino Mario

The first year

Child's Utterance	Observations
Birth (7/68; Vermont)	
/æ/	At the moment of birth (at which I was present), the
/a:/	child produced his first cries. During the first few weeks, crying was his principal mode of expression; vocalizations ranged from /æ/ to /a:/. The only other sounds on the tapes are those of sucking, burping, hiccuping, and sneezing.
0;1 (9/68)	
cries, pants	In the second month, the child frequently alternated
varied sounds	between cries and pants. His cries seemed to be linked
cooing	with hunger and discomfort. After diaper changes or
smile	feedings, there were distinctly different sounds,
laughter	especially cooing. In the 7th week, Mario began to smile (9/18/68) and laughed aloud for the first time (9/23/68).
0;4 (12/68)	
active	Mario has become quite active and responsive. He can
responsive	be induced to smile, coo, and even laugh aloud, by
smiles	making gestures and motions. He is especially attracted
coos	by the dog and follows it around the room with his eyes.
follows motion	The feel of the dog, its wagging tail, or a lick from its
reacts to dog	tongue, invariably produces coos of delight, or laughter.
gurgles	Mario also makes sundry other sounds now such as
pants	gurgles, panting, sputtering with the lips as well as crying

Child's Utterance	Observations
sputters w/lips pharyngeal stop /kx/ /akxu/ /aɣu/	and laughter. The most common sound produced is with the mouth open and relaxed, emitting a pharyngeal sound occasionally preceded by a stop such as /kx/, also /akxu/ and /aɣu/. (This may explain why infants are imitated in Spanish with the sounds /agu, agu/).

cooing increases w/music
responds to mamá's
  speech w/smiles
  or laughter
	Normally cooing increases in intensity and frequency when music is played. Mario is responsive to his mother's talking; e.g. when she repeats "ría, ría, ría", (laugh), or "a su sillita, vamos a su sillita" (let's go to your highchair), he responds with smiles or laughter.

0;5 (1/69) turns over movements increase babbling	At 5 months and 3 weeks he turned himself over for the first time, and his physical movements have intensified. He kicks his legs vigorously and moves arms with great excitement. Babbling is quite common now, but the sounds are impossible to transcribe.
0;6 (2/69) sits up alone crawling begins moves in walker	Sat up unsupported for the first time during his 6th month, indicating physical strengthening of the spinal column. Toward the end of this time, he began crawling and was able to push himself around the room in his walker.
follows movements laughs spontaneously seeks attention through babbling greater variety of sounds increased vocal activity	Now more responsive to movement and people. He laughs spontaneously and almost calls for attention by babbling and making other noises. Produces a greater variety of non-descript sounds; vocal activity greatly increased.
begins table foods	Although exclusively breastfed up to this time, he now beings to accept (tastes and eats) other foods.
firm grasp; holds rattle reacts if taken independence	Has developed a firm grasp and holds on to a rattle which he plays with for long periods of time. Cries when it is taken from him. Also indications of growing independence.
0;7 (3/69) reaches and grasps	Reaches for objects for the first time, trying to grasp things beyond his reach.
0;9 (5/69) hearty laughter variety of sounds recognizable sounds	Easily provoked to hearty laughter. Continues to produce a great variety of sounds, however, many are easier to identify.
repetition of fixed sounds	Notable aspect of vocalizations is the repetition of certain fixed sounds and their predominance and
/la da da da da/ /da da da da da/ /dæ dæ dæ dæ/ /ta ta ta ta ta/	repetitiveness in long sequences. Most common repetitions are /la/, /da/, /dæ/, and /ta/. (Leopold reports similar utterances in the 9th–10th months, Vol. I, pp. 23–24). Joins C + V.

Child's Utterance	Observations
Vs range /a/–/e/ sound combinations all 　end in V pharyngeal sounds /ombře/; flap /ř/	Vowels usually range from /a/ to /e/, with all sound combinations always ending in a vowel. Other sounds are produced with an open mouth and relaxed tongue, emanating from the pharyngeal area. Both parents distinctly recognized the sound /ombře/ (hombre/man) clearly pronounced but obviously said without intent or meaning. The sound included the flap /ř/.
0;11 (7/12/69) takes first steps walks alone	In his 11th month, Mario stood alone and took two steps unassisted. One week after his first birthday, he began to walk.
evidence of understanding 　"Bimba"	Definite evidence of understanding at this time. Saying "Bimba" (the dog's name) usually caused Mario to look around for the dog. If he was crying, the dog's name was often used to distract him, causing him to cease crying.

The second year

Child's Utterance		Observations
1;0 /m n n n n n n n/ /m m m m m m m m m/ /m ŋ ŋ ŋ ŋ ŋŋ/ /ñ ñ ñ ñ ñ ñ/ /dikʌ dikʌ dikʌ/ /a lí ki lik/ /xa:/ /da: da:/ /ba ba/		Within 2 months after his first birthday, Mario's vocal activity increased greatly. Although the variety of sounds produced was still great, certain vocalizations became temporarily dominant and were repeated with greater frequency, especially nasals and the dental /d/. Distinct and familiar intonational patterns were noted. Other sounds recorded.
/dída/	Bimba	By the end of his 12th month (late August, 1969), Mario pronounced his first word. Seeing his dog enter the room, he exclaimed /dída/ (Bimba); however, the sound was not repeated again until several months later.
1;1 crawls walks, climbs stairs		Now extremely active, crawling, walking, and eventually climbing stairs.
1;4 (12/69, Vermont)		Now pronounced his first series of words. For the next few months, his repertoire consists entirely of these few words, learned at 1;4 and 1;5.

Child's Utterance		Observations
/ba bá/ /pa pá/	papá	a + {b/p}; V/labial C opposition; /p/~/b/ alternation; i.e. vd vs. vl opposition. a + m; V/nasal C opposition (first word differentiation).
/ma má/	mamá	
/dikʌ dikʌ/		

1;5 (1/70, Bolivia)
| /á ta/ | aqua (water) | /p/m/t/; labial/dental opposition. |
| /tí ti/ | diente (tooth) | /a/i/; wide/narrow V contrast. |

1;8 (4/6/70, Vermont)
progress in vocalizations
responds to speech
signs of understanding
imitative period

Made great progress in vocalizations by the end of this month. Responds to speech and shows greater signs of understanding. This is a tremendously imitative period during which he often pretends to talk on the telephone. Once, during a taping session he grabbed the microphone and passed it over his face, imitating the sound of the electric shaver which he observed every day.

reacts to firm and soft voice

Mario also responds significantly to varying vocal expression. He reacts to a stern voice by puckering his lips; and if it continues, he cries. A soft voice calms him; a command usually stops him from touching an object; etc.

/ɖaɖa/
/a: lu/
/atʔ/

Random sounds recorded, which have no conspicuous meaning.

/dʌli dʌli dʌli/

Common sound used to call attention; he also uses it when he wants something; sometimes he makes this sound with strong emotion or desperation.

1;9 (5/70, Vermont)
/bʰíbʰa/

Explosive or aspirated sounds; calls dog, Bimba, excitedly.

/babá/ /papá/	papá	Continues alternation of /b/~/p/; /ɓ/ appears but without any connection to Spanish phonology as yet.
/mamá/	mamá	
/dá dá/		Frequent use of phone /d/.

The onset of speech

Note: Up to this point, Mario's lexicon consists of only a few words; however, by about 1;10, his vocabulary begins to grow rapidly as he also develops increasing phonemic distinctions. Toward the end of this period he begins to develop some two-word utterances.

Child's Utterance	Standard Language	Translation	Observation
1;10			
no	no	no	Monosyllabic words only; first use of phoneme /o/.
va	vaso	glass	First use of /v/, allophone of /b/ in Sp.
ma	más	more	
taw taw	ciao ciao (It.)	bye-bye	Off-glide; first use of /w/; repetition of same syllable, monosyllabic words.
titíu	chi-chíu (Bolivian baby-talk)	sore, hurt	Diphthong.
paw paw	pao-pao (Bolivian baby-talk)	all gone	Off-glide.
bíba	Bimba	Bimba (the dog)	Early biphonemic stage; changes the V or C, but not both.
pío pío	pío-pío (Bolivian baby-talk)	birdie	
dédo	dedo	finger	Develops /e/, making finer V distinctions. Correct use of fricativized /đ/.
mano	mano	hand	Front/back nasal contrast, /m/~/n/. Biphonemic words increase.
ayí	allí	over there	On-glide /y/.
—	ojo	eye	Recognition of body parts;
—	boca	mouth	child responds by pointing
—	cabeza	head	(confirms passive acquisi-
—	nariz	nose	tion of other words).
—	pie	foot	
—	potito (Bolivian baby-talk)	rump, behind	
1;11			
dínti	diente	tooth	Improvement over /titi/ used at age 1;5; vl vs. vd distinction.
gátun	gato	cat	/a/i/u/; V triangle complete; also velar/dental opposition.
áutun	auto	car	Tendency to close off final V with a nasal.
¿on tá?	¿Dónde está?	Where is it?	First question, asked with a rising intonation; still holophrastic.
¡ay tá!	¡Al lí esá!	There it is!	Reply to above; usually an exclamation; also holophrastic.

Child's Utterance	Standard Language	Translation	Observation
ta tʌč!	Don't touch!	Don't touch!	First English phrase, learned from grandmother. Employs /ʌ/, not part of Sp.; also /č/, a late sound according to Jakobson.
2;0			
áǥwa	agua	water	Correct use of /ǥ/; uses this word for *all* liquids.
ƀápo	barco	boat	Use of /ƀ/ for first time.
aƀwelíta	abuelita	grandmother	Correct allophone; /b/>/ƀ/ intervocalically.
lála	leche	milk	First use of /l/.
{ dúsis / dúčis }	dulces	candies	First use of /s/, alternates with /č/.
kóa kóa	Coca Cola	Coca Cola	Appearance of phoneme /k/; dental/velar opposition.
akí	aquí	here	
áš:yas	gracias	thank you	First use of /š/; first courtesy expression.
datór	tractor	tractor	First use of /r/; fails to reappear.
2;1			
gato	gato	cat	Final nasal dropped from these words.
auto	auto	car	
nene	nene	child	Uses to refer to self.
2;2			
bím:a	Bimba	Bimba	Lengthening of /m/, replaces C cluster. Syllable structure thus far is V, VC, CV; diphthongs used, but C clusters do not exist.
avón	avión	aeroplane	
ayá	allá	there	
{ adatáte / atatáte }	chocolate	chocolate	No /č/, suggests unstable phoneme as yet.
mamaméma	Magdalena	Magdalena	Stress correct in long words; C cluster not pronounced.
mamíma	Marina	Marina	Lack of /ř/.
ánana	Angela	Angela	Lack of /x/; stress correct.
lála	leche	milk	No /č/, although it occurs sporadically elsewhere.
bápu	barco	boat	Often exchanges /p/ for /k/.
nóna	nonna (It.)	grandmother	Lacks geminate C, required for Italian.
papé(y)	café	coffee	/p/~/k/.
móko	moto	motorcycle	/k/~/t/.
ménte	puente	bridge	
mamón	camión	truck	/m/~/k/, labial velar.
yiyiyéta	bicicleta	bicycle	/kl/ cluster eliminated.

Child's Utterance	Standard Language	Translation	Observation
káka	caca	dirt, filth	
⎰dáme⎱ ⎱tóma⎰	⎰dáme⎱ ⎱toma⎰	⎰give me⎱ ⎱take⎰	Semantic confusion; uses both words indiscriminately for either action.
čičíu	chi-chíu (Bolivian baby-talk)	sore, hurt	Well developed /č/; seems to be a permanent feature now.
te kéđo	te quiero	I love you	No /r̄/, /r/~/đ/; a frozen expression; words not spontaneously joined.
dayí	—	—	Invented word, often used to call attention.
2;3 póte	Pochi	Pochi (name)	
žíke	Enrique	Enrique	Use of /ž/.
šáka	saca	take out	Use of /š/.
táta tótes	buenas noches	good night	

Emerging phrases

Note: During the next months Mario makes great strides in syntax. By 2;3, he progresses from one-word utterances and begins to combine words. By 2;7, utterances are four words and sometimes longer. This is accompanied by differentiation of parts of speech. Nouns are used in various parts of utterances. Verbs appear. Mario also uses for the first time, an adverb (2;4), an adjective and a demonstrative (2;7). Questions, negations, and commands are formed in addition to declarative statements.

On the morphological level, the first article (1a) appears, followed by the masculine form (el) about 2;7–2;8. There is no noun-modifier agreement nor noun–verb agreement yet in most cases. The predominant verb ending is -a, formed on the 3rd person of -ar verbs. Other sporadic forms appear but only as direct imitations, hence an occasional gerund, and several irregular forms and commands. The past tense marker appears (2;6), the imperfect tense (2;11), and the first person marker to refer to himself (2;11).

English words also appear during this period. Some mixing of languages occurs between 2;6 and 2;8, but ceases beyond this time.

Child's Utterance	Standard Language	Translation
2;3		
Bima ʊn tásal.	Bimba (está) en la casa.	Bimba is in the house.
Vamos al autos.	Vamos al auto.	Let's go to the car.
Yeo Yike, ven tasa.	Tío Enrique, ven (a) casa.	Uncle Enrique, come home.
Nakí.	No (está) aquí.	It's not here.

Child's Utterance	Standard Language	Translation
2;4		
Ven akí, papá.	Ven aquí, papá.	Come here, daddy.
Te yeyo.	Te quiero.	I love you.
2;6		
Mɔr disért.	More dessert.	—
Bili titíto ʌpstés.	Billy "chiquito" (is) upstairs.	—
Máis vino.	Más vino.	More wine.
2;7		
Nel ayón.	En el avión.	On the aeroplane.
No kito.	No (lo) quites.	Don't take it away.
Tis e yoto.	"This" está roto.	This is broken.
En la tasina.	En la cocina.	In the kitchen.
Se kayó.	Se cayó.	He fell down.
Ayá en la kasa.	Allá en la casa.	There in the house.
Oto sútalal.	Más (otro) azúcar.	More sugar.
En la uya.	En la uña.	In the fingernail.
En na árwol.	En el árbol.	In the tree.
En la pákel.	En el parque.	In the park.
Dis is la siya.	"This is" (de) la Zia (Zia = aunt, It.)	This is Zia's.
Dis mas dis, otey?	"This" más "this", o.k.?	This and this, o.k.?
Pío ko la taye.	Pío (pájaro) también en la calle. (ko=an invented word.)	Birdie also in the street.
Xe lesíta.	Here it is.	—
Alélala mamá moto.	Arréglala, mamá (la) moto.	Fix the motorcycle, mamá.
Bili titito n xávits.	Billy chiquito can't have it.	—
Papá na ta akí.	Papá no está aquí.	Papá isn't here.
Ese e la pié.	Ese es el pie.	That's the foot.
2;8		
Tyen pasa akí.	(El) tren pasa aquí.	The train goes by here.
On ta syasyasía?	¿Dónde está la policía?	Where's the police?
El tayó tolo.	El toro se cayó.	The bull fell down.
Ese no tota nene?	¿Ese no toca (el) nene? (nene = yo).	This, the child, can't touch? (child = I).
E peva lo potito?	¿Y (lo) pegas (en) el potito?	And you'll spank (him) on the behind?
Santa dulci tyáe.	Santa trae dulces.	Santa (Claus) brings candy.
L'ayón wela.	El avión vuela.	The aeroplane flies.
Ese la apakó mamá.	Esa la apagó mamá.	Mamá turned it off (TV).
F:wé a la taye, ayá lésos.	Fue a la calle, allá lejos.	He went to the street, far away.
2;10		
Se ayaya fete.	Se agarra fuerte.	You hold on tight.
No pila yoto ese.	Esa pila está rota.	That battery doesn't work.

Child's Utterance	Standard Language	Translation
Also no papel.	No alces el papel.	Don't pick up the paper.
No, el come webo.	No, el comió huevo.	No, he ate egg.
Ese queso veya datón.	Ese queso lleva el ratón.	The mouse takes that cheese.
Ese yusta.	Ese me gusta.	I like that.
N peye, en tene manos.	No puedo, no tengo manos.	I can't, I don't have hands.
No se cái, se ayaya fete.	No se cae, se agarra fuerte.	You don't fall, you hold on tight.
2;11		
Ya yegó mamá.	Ya llegó mamá.	Mamá has arrived.
¿Mamá vino solita?	¿Mamá vino solita?	Mamá came alone?
¿Blanca se quedó?	¿Blanca se quedó?	Did Blanca stay behind?
¿Ya n'ay so:l?	¿Ya no hay sol?	Isn't there any sun now?
¡Dexa, Blanca!	¡Deja, Blanca!	Leave it alone, Blanca!
Oye, se yía mučačas.	Oye, se reían las muchachas.	Hey, the girls were laughing.
Se yompe ilo.	Se rompe (el) hilo.	The string breaks.
¿Dónde están?	¿Dónde están?	Where are they?
Akí estóy.	Aquí estoy.	Here I am.
¿No estava?	¿No estaba?	Wasn't it there?
Oye, la nena tene papel.	Oye, la nena tiene papel.	Listen, the girl has paper.
Oye, ese tene ba:ba akí.	Oye, ese tiene barba aquí (barba = bigotes).	Listen, he has a beard here (meaning moustache).
¿Oye, ke es eso?	¿Oye, qué es eso?	Hey, what's that?

Language mastery and socialization

Note: The period from about 3;0 to 4;0 is marked by a fair degree of language mastery. The phonemic systems of Spanish and English are well set with few exceptions. Vocabulary continues to grow at a rapid pace. The system of articles, of noun gender, and of plurals is almost entirely solved during this phase, and noun-adjective agreement becomes standard. Mario also makes great strides with verb morphology. Not only does he work out the inflectional system according to person, but he also adds markers to distinguish past and imperfect tenses from the present. He develops a construction to express future action also as he begins to understand time conceptually. A subjective mood, essential to Spanish, also appears during this period.

Mario has increased contact with English through his attendance at nursery school. He becomes adept at code switching and sometimes uses English in the home for specialized purposes: to quote English-speaking people, with imaginary friends during role play, and as a general language during play. Contact with Italian increases, especially at meal times.

Mario begins to demonstrate an awareness of his role and relationship with others. He also observes and comments on the behaviour of other children. He begins to observe courtesy requirements. This is also a period in which he asks questions incessantly on a variety of topics. He is interested in everything in his environment. He asks about animals and insects, natural phenomenon, birth and babies, and the supernatural. He uses language to learn about the word in which he lives.

Dialogue	Standard Language	Translation

2;11 (Mexico)
(Mario is on a trip to Cacahuamilpa. He sees a worm crawling on the ground and picks it up, examining it in detail. He then asks a variety of questions about the creature and concludes that it can't talk because it doesn't have a mouth.)

Ese gusanito . . . ¿no pica?	Ese gusanito . . . ¿no pica?	That little worm . . . doesn't it bite?
¿No vuela?	¿No vuela?	Doesn't it fly?
¿No camina?	¿No camina?	Doesn't it walk?
¿No tene eso?	¿No tiene eso?	Doesn't it have that?
¿No avla?	¿No habla?	Doesn't it speak?
Ah . . . no tene boca.	Ah . . . no tiene boca.	Oh . . . it doesn't have a mouth.

3;2 (Texas)
(Mario and his papá (P) are looking at a book together. His father asks Mario a question in English to see the child's reaction).

M: ¿Qué hace ese nenes?	M: ¿Qué hacen esos nenes?	What are those children doing?
P: Están jalando el perro. Alvino Mario, how do you speak with the little boys and girls?		They're pulling the dog.
M: (laughingly, teasingly) Halo, blaka, blaka, blaka, blak. Gu bai!	Hello, blaka, blaka, blaka, blak. Good bye!	

3;2 (Texas)
(Mario is leafing through story books with his father.)

Voy a tyaél ota livlo.	Voy a traer otro libro.	I'm going to bring another book.

(Returns with another book; opens it.)

¿Y dónde va esta chica?	¿Y adónde va esta chica?	And where is this girl going?
¿Y dónde va este?	¿Y adónde va este? (el lobo)	And where is he going? (the wolf)
¿Al boque?	¿Al bosque?	To the woods?
¿Y qué hace este oso, papá?	¿Y qué hace este oso, papá?	And what's this bear doing, papá?
¿Y va suvyendo acá?	¿Y va subiendo acá?	And is he climbing up here?
¿Y qué hace este oso?	¿Y qué hace esta osa (la mamá)?	And what does that mama bear do?
¿Cocina, papá?	¿Cocina, papá?	Is she cooking, papá?

3;2 (Texas)
(In the living room. Mario has just returned from a visit to the doctor. He recounts his visit to his father by showing pictures in a pamphlet.)

Esta femena e nene no toca eso.	Esta enfermera y (el) nene no tocan eso.	This nurse, and the boy don't touch that.

Dialogue	Standard Language	Translation
Yo hice a ponel esto.	Yo hice poner esto (el auscultador).	I had this put on (the stethoscope).
Yo poní esto.	Yo puse esto.	I put it on.
Lo poyó el dotol.	Lo puso el doctor.	That doctor put it on.
Se yiye este dotol.	Se ríe este doctor.	This doctor is laughing.
No tene sangue este nene.	No tiene sangre este nene.	This boy's not bleeding.

3;2 (Texas)
(Driving in the car through the main street of Austin, Mario begins to question about the place he's in to distinguish it from Vermont.)

M: ¿Esto Austin, esto, papá? ¿Stamos, Austin, stamos?	M: ¿Esto (es) Austin, esto, papá? ¿Estamos (en) Austin, estamos?	(Is) this Austin, papá? Are we in Austin? Are we?
P: Sí, Mario, estamos en Austin.		Yes, Mario, we're in Austin.
M: En Bemón hay juguetes en Bemón.	M: En Vermont hay juguetes en Vermont.	In Vermont there are toys in Vermont.
Y hay todo, todo, todo . . .	Y hay todo, todo, todo . . .	And there's everything, everything, everything.
Y hay esquís a Bemón.	Y hay esquís en Vermont.	And there're skiis in Vermont.
P: Yo te voy a llevar allí en avión.		I'm going to take you there by plane.
M: Y hay numes en layón.	M: Y hay nubes en el avión.	And there are clouds on the plane.
Y sale humo atrás.	Y sale humo (por) atrás.	And smoke comes out in the back.
Y hay tyes ayones.	Y hay tres aviones.	And there are three planes.
Se sacan la gyadas y se seya la peta de layón.	Se sacan las gradas y se cierra la puerta del avión.	They take away the steps and the door of the plane closes.
Va muy lejo va layón, papá.	Va muy lejos, va el avión, papá.	It goes very far, the plane goes, papá.

3;2 (Texas)
(Playing alone in his room, speaking to the toys and dolls.)

Sit down, you.	Sit down, you.	
Oh, no, no.	Oh, no, no.	
No do dat!	Don't do that!	
Uh, uh.	Uh, uh.	

3;2 (Texas)
(At night. Going outside he sees a quarter moon.)

Mila la luna, papá.	Mira la luna, papá.	Look at the moon, papá.
¡La luna yota!	¡La luna rota!	The broken moon!
¡La luna está yota!	¡La luna está rota!	The moon is broken!

3;3 (Texas)
(In his room. His mother is dressing him and he contemplates a crucifix on the wall and recalls a church with a similar crucifix from his previous summer in Mexico.)

Dialogue	Standard Language	Translation
M: ¿Po:qué lo pegalon a esta Ayós? ¿Qué hacía?	M: Por qué lo pegaron a este Dios?	Why did they hit God? What was he doing?
MA: Nada, eran señores malos.		Nothing, they were bad men.
M: Lo pegalon con palos . . . ¡paf, paf!	M: Lo pegaron con palos . . . ¡paf, paf!	They hit him with sticks, . . . bang, bang!
Ayós monito.	Dios bonito.	Nice God (says affectionately).
Ayós me /tčajo/ juguetes.	Dios me trajo juguetes.	God brought me toys.
MA: Sí. Y cuando estás dormido en la noche, está contigo.		Yes, and at night, when you're asleep, he stays with you.
M: (Ignoring MA's comments, he continues thinking of Christ's wounds).		
Sí . . . e se hace chichíu . . .	Sí . . . y se hace chichíu (daño).	Yes . . . and he gets hurt.
Así.	Así.	Like this (holding thumb and index finger together to indicate "a little").

3;3 (Texas) (Playing alone. He pretends to take medicine.)
M: /máy médIsIn/ . . .   M: My medicine . . .
/gut, gut/. Rubbing   good, good.
stomach).
P: What's good?
M: /Dis/.   M: This.

3;3 (Texas) (Makes an observation of sexual differences.)

Lo nenes hacen pis palalos.	Los nenes hacen pis parados.	Little boys pee standing up.
Las nenas, no.	Las nenas, no.	Little girls don't.

3;4 (Texas)
(Telling his father about an imaginary witch he chased out of his mother's room.)

M: Una blusa en cato de mamá.	M: Una bruja en el cuarto de mamá.	A witch in mamá's room!
Yo dije "/get áu ta xIr/!"	Yo (le) dije: "Get out of here!"	I said "Get out of here!"
. . . ¡fuela, fuela, fuela!	. . . ¡fuera, fuera, fuera!	. . . out, out, out!
Yo quité la coba.	Yo (le) quité la escoba.	I grabbed her broom!
P: ¿Qué dijo la bruja?		What did the witch say?
M: Se /yiye/ la blusa, /xa, xa/.	M: Se ríe la bruja: ja, ja.	The witch laughed: ha, ha.
Esa blusa no me /justa/.	Esa bruja no me gusta.	I don't like that witch.
P: ¿No te gusta la bruja?		

Dialogue	Standard Language	Translation

3;4 (Texas)
(Returns from nursery and recounts an incident which happened, quoting the attendant in English.)

M: Tičʌ . . . /gum xIr, no   M: (The) teacher (said):   The teacher said: come
    do dæt no mɔr!/   come here, don't do   here, don't do that
                                   that anymore!   anymore!
    Me pegó en la pyéyna.   Me pegó en la pierna.   She hit me on the leg.
    Yo yolé con los nenes   Yo lloré con los nenes   I cried with the boys under
    abajo de la mesa.   abajo de la mesa.   the table.
    Yo tilé una cosa al   Yo tiré una cosa al   I threw something at the
    árwol.   árbol (de Navidad).   (Christmas) tree.
    Y cayó una bola.   Y cayó una bola.   And a ball fell.

3;5 (Philadelphia)
(Mario is in his den with his cousin, Billy (B) and his grandfather (G). He is slightly in competition with his cousin who feels that the grandparents' home is more his own than Mario's.)

B→G: Let's go to the park.

M→B: /A go da Luis ɛ Lái   M→B: I go to Louis and
    . . . no dɛ pak/.   Larry's (house); not
                           (to) the park.

(M picks up a toy and says challengingly)

M→ALL: /mái, mái . . .   M→ALL: It's mine, mine
       no yaws!/   . . . not yours!

(Father enters.)

M→P: (Looking out window and pointing to the woods)
    Ayí stá Bermont?   M→P: ¿Allí está   Is Vermont there?
                     Vermont?

P→M: Sí, papá.   Yes, daddy (meaning
                                "son").

M→P: Ah, dos Bermónts.   M→P: Ah, dos Vermonts.   Ah, two Vermonts!
(Finds a piece of candy, shows it to B, then eats it.)

M→B: I eat one.   M→B: I eat one.
(G trips while getting up from chair.)

M→G: You fall.   M→G: You fall.
(Sees B moving toward sofa to watch TV; M runs over to another chair.)

M→B: I want dis seat.   M→B: I want this seat.
(Announces fact to P.)

M→P: Aquí estoy, papá.   M→P: Aquí estoy, papá.   Here I am, papá.
(Slides off chair, pretending to fall.)

M→ALL: I fall.   M→ALL: I fall.
(P glances over at M.)

M→P: Me cayí del   M→P: Me caí del asiento.   I fell off the seat.
    asiento.
(M and B begin playing with a toy garage and airport; M picks up a battery-propelled car.)

M→G: Mus da car.   M→G: Move the car.
    I go.   I go.

Dialogue	Standard Language	Translation
Go da car da "bi:i:i:p".	The car goes "beep".	

(Father picks up a box of candy.)

| M→P: Dáme uno, papá. Me voy comer todo, todo, todo. | M→P: Dáme uno, papá. Me voy (a) comer todo, todo, todo. | Give me one, papá. I'm going to eat everything, everything, everything. |

(G takes candy box away from M; M says to him, teasingly.)

| M→G: I no like you no more. | M→G: I don't like you anymore. | |

(Turns his attention to a toy helicopter.)

| M→G: E . . . /kókilo/ . . . waz dat? | M→G: Eh, "helicóptero", what's that? | Hey, "helicopter", . . . what's that? |

(M gets in the way of his cousin who continues playing with the garage.)

| B→M: Hey. Get out of the parking lot! I don wantcha get out of the parking lot you guys! | | |

(M finds B's complaint amusing, even though he hadn't understood the precise words. He tries unsuccessfully to imitate his cousin.)

| M: XXXXXXXXXX! | M: XXXXXXXXXX! | |

(M now decides the garage door should be closed.)

| M→B: Close . . . close it! | M→B: Close . . . close it! | |

(G gets up to leave the room.)

M→P: ¿Dónde va grandpa?	M→P: ¿Adónde va grandpa?	Where's grandpop going?
P→M: Va a comprar algo en la tienda.		He is going to the store to buy something.
M→P: ¿Va comprá qué?	M→P: ¿Va (a) comprar qué?	What is he going to buy?
P→M: No sé, chiquito.		I don't know, son.

(M decides to invite himself along, and the others as well.)

| M→ALL: Come on! | M→ALL: Come on! | |

(Everyone decides to go along to the store. All go out and enter the car. M notices some pushbuttons for controlling the car windows. He tries them once or twice.)

| M→B: Billy, do dat. | M→B: Bill, do that. | |

(M then speaks aloud to himself as he fumbles with another button, trying to figure out how it works.)

| M→SELF: ¿Cóme se prenda esto? | M→SELF: ¿Cómo se prende esto? | How does this work? |

(Opens the window and pokes his head out; then he utters some nonsense words.)

| M: E po ke le ke . . . | M: E po ke le ke . . . | |

(Then he shouts to an imaginary person.)

| M: Get auta here. | M: Get out of here! | |

(They drive off; they return in a half hour. As they enter the house, G asks B.)

| G→B: Bill, do you like me? | | |

Dialogue	Standard Language	Translation
B→G: No.		
M→G: I like you too.	M→G: I like you too.	
M→B: You like my /dali/? You like my mommie?	M→B: (Do) you like my daddy? (Do) you like my mommie?	
(No reply.)		

3;5 (Philadelphia)
(Alone in his room, he pretends he is role playing with mamá (MA); the role he has taken is obviously one of the nursery attendants and MA is a little girl.)

M: /ílIt/ . . . dats gut!	M: Eat it . . . that's good!	

(Then he begins singing.)

M: A B C D E F G. Now I say my ABC tell me what you sink of me.	M: A B C D E F G. Now I say my ABC tell me what you think of me.	

(Resumes role play.)

M: Dat's ABC . . . you like ABC? You come on here. You bad boy, you wet your pants. You bad boy. Mario no bad boy. Mario good bad boy.	M: That's ABC . . . (Do) you like ABC? You come on here. You bad boy, you wet your pants. You bad boy. Mario's not (a) bad boy. Mario's (a) good bad boy.	
No, you bad boy, you wet the bed. I don't wet the bed.	No, you bad boy, you wet the bed. I don't wet the bed.	

3;6 (Texas)
(Mario is watching television; he misinterprets an English word as Spanish and is startled by it.)
TV announcer: . . . and on all LOCAL stations.

M: ¿LOCO??? ¡Das no "loco"!	M: "Loco?" That's not "loco".	Loco? That's not "loco" (crazy).

3;7 (Texas)
(Mario shows signs of incorporating courtesy items into his speech; he leaves the dinner table and goes into the other room.)

M→ALL: Buen provecho, gracias, con permiso.	M→ALL: Buen provecho, gracias, con permiso.	Good appetite, thank you, excuse me.

(Leaves a table and goes to other room; looking out the window, he sees a neighbour and calls.)

M→Neighbour: Hey! Hey!	M→Neighbour: Hey! Hey!

(MA yells to him from kitchen not to call in that fashion.)

APPENDIX 2 223

Dialogue	Standard Language	Translation

MA→M: Mario, no digas "hey" al señor Díle "hi".

Don't say "hey" Mario, say "hi" to the man.

M→Neighbour: Hi, hi . . .   M→Neighbour: Hi, hi . . .
(Mario then sneezes, no one pays attention so he says to himself.)

M→SELF: ¡Salut! M→SELF: ¡Salud! God Bless you.

(Papá overhears him say this.)

P→M: Oh, salud, chiquito. Oh, God Bless you, son.

3;7 (Texas)
(Playing in the park, a bug alights on his finger.)

M→Bug: Váyate de mi dedo. M→Bug: Véte de mi dedo. Get off my finger.

(Bug flies off; M then spots some holes in the bark of a tree.)

M: Aquí salen bichos.	M: Aquí salen bichos.	Bugs come out of here.
Mamá, ¿no hay hueco aquí?	Mamá, ¿no hay hueco aquí?	Mamá, there's no hole here.
No stán.	No están.	They're not here.
Está una puerta cerrada . . .	Está (= hay) una puerta cerrada . . .	There's a closed door.
no se sa:ga lo bichos.	(que) no se salgan los bichos.	So the bugs don't come out.

M→MA: Mamá, ¿los bichos tinen llave? M→MA: Mamá, ¿los bichos tienen llave? Mamá, do bugs have keys?

MA→M: Sí. Yes.

M→MA: ¡¡No!! . . . aquí hay una puerta. M→MA: ¡¡No!! . . . aquí hay una puerta. No!! . . . there's a door here.

3;8 (Texas)
(Watching television, Cesare Danova speaks some Italian on The Lucy Show; Mario is surprised by this, thinking it's Spanish.)

M→MA: ¿Hablan español, mamá? M→MA: ¿Hablan español, mamá? Do they speak Spanish, mamá?

MA→M: No, amor, es italiano. No dear, that's Italian.

(Father enters.)

M→P: ¡Hablan español, papá! M→P: ¡Hablan español, papá! They're speaking Spanish, papá!

P→M: No, están hablando italiano, como habla papá. No, they're speaking Italian, like papá speaks.

3;8 (Texas)
(Looking at his parents' wedding picture, he then compares it to a family portrait just beneath it.)

M→MA: Mamá, ¿dónde está el nene acá? M→MA: Mamá ¿dónde está el nene acá? Mamá, where is the little boy here?

Dialogue	Standard Language	Translation
(pointing to the wedding picture) MA→M: En la barriga de mamá.		In mommy's tummy.
M→MA: ¿Cómo salió? ¿Salió por la boca?	M→MA: ¿Cómo salió? ¿Salió por la boca?	How did it come out? Did it come out through the mouth?
MA→M: No, por el potito.		No, from the rear.
M→MA: No, por allí sale "yuk".	M→MA: No, por allí sale "yuk".	No, "yuk" comes out of there.
(Later, mamá makes a fuss over him.)		
MA→M: ¿De dónde saliste tú, tan bonito?		And where did you come from, so cute?
M→MA: De la luna . . . de una /rwakɛts/.	M→MA: De la luna . . . de una "rocket".	From the moon, from a rocket.

3;9 (Texas)

(A few days later; lying in the bed with papá.)

M→P: ¿Papá tú tienes baby aquí? (pointing to his stomach)	M→P: ¿Papá, tú tienes baby aquí?	Papá do you have a baby here?
P→M (Laughing): Sí, yo tengo		Yes, I do.
M→P: ¡Tú no tienes! Sólo las mamás tienen. ¿Cómo entan . . . por la boca o por el potito?	M→P: ¡Tú no tienes! Sólo las mamás tienen. ¿Cómo entran . . . por la boca o por el potito?	No, you don't! mommies have them. How do they get in? Through the mouth or the rear?

3;9 (Texas)

(Going outside he notices a dog which has just had puppies; he comments on her teats.)

| M: ¡Mila! ¡Las tetitas del peyo! Es pala dal lekye a los nenitos peyitos . . . a los peyitos nenitos. | M: ¡Mira! ¡Las tetitas del perro! Es (son) para dar leche a los nenitos perritos . . . a los perritos nenitos. | Loook! The dog's teats! That's so they can give milk to the baby dogs. |

3;10 (Mexico)

(Squatting on the ground, he observes a colony of ants carrying off bits of leaves.)

| M: ¡Mila, como las ho:migas llevan las hojitas! ¿Adónde llevan? ¿A sus casas? ¿A sus jitos? | M: ¡Mira, como las hormigas llevan las hojitas! ¿Adónde llevan? ¿A sus casas? ¿A sus hijitos? | Look how the ants carry the leaves! Where to they take them? To their houses? To their little children? |
| P: Sí. | | Yes. |

Dialogue	Standard Language	Translation

3;11 (Mexico)
(Looking at a magazine, he asks questions about various things.)
M: (First looks at a picture of a fetus.)

¿Qué es? ¿Un baby en la luna?	M: ¿Qué es? ¿Un baby en la luna?	What's this? A baby on the moon?

(Now sees a picture of two lovers.)

M: Mila, estos son dos señoles que se quielen mucho, mucho.	M: Mira, estos son dos señores que se quieren mucho, mucho.	Look, these are two people who love each other very much.

Language refinement and a developing world view

Note: During this period Mario begins to view himself as a young child, no longer as a baby. Linguistically, he makes tremendous strides in all areas of language. Vocabulary continues to grow rapidly; however, in other areas, his activity is primarily one of language "refinement". Mario uses language to ask about language and to learn about his linguistic systems. He questions words he doesn't understand, and he often asks for translations or equivalents. He also applies the correct labels for each language. He develops a judgement about the correctness of speech and the appropriateness of language. He suddenly begins producing the /r̄/~/rr/ distinction of Spanish, now lacking only the /d/~/θ/ phonemes of English. He demonstrates good control of the subjunctive mood in Spanish. By the end of this period (6;0), his language is almost standard with only few deviations.

Mario becomes increasingly rational. He thinks, reasons, questions, and expresses many abstract throughts. He is fascinated with numbers and written script. His discussions cover many aspects of his environment as well as many abstract ideas: Indians, the source of food, food and growth, money, behaviour, the origin of man, and death. Mario's view of the world is clearly evolving, and he uses language to understand what he cannot himself experience directly.

Child's Utterance	Other Speakers	Translation

4;0 (Louisiana)
(In a restaurant.)

	P: We'll have pancakes for the baby.	
M→P: Yo no me llamo "baby",		My name's not "baby".
	P→M: ¿Cómo te llamas?	What's your name?
M→P: Mayo (Mario), nene.		Mario, little boy.

4;2 (Vermont)
(At home, Mario and papá are looking through several books. Papá explains in Italian.)

M→P: ¿Cómo se llama este animal?		What's this animal called?

Child's Utterance	Other Speakers	Translation
M→P: ¿Cómo . . . cómo se llama?	P→M: Si chiama scimmia.	Si chiama scimmia. (Italian) What? . . . What's the name?
	P→M: Scimmia, si chiama scimmia.	Scimmia, si chiama scimmia (Italian).
M→P: Papá, ¡habla como yo!		Papá, speak like me!
	P→M: ¿Cómo?	How?
M→P: Así, como hablabas.		Like that, like you were just speaking!

4;2 (Vermont)
(Mario has just finished helping papá to light the fireplace.)

M→P: ¿Por qu tenemos chiminea?		Why do we have a chimney?
	P→M: Para el fuego.	For the fire.
M→P: ¡No, para que entre Santa Claus!		No, so Santa Claus can come down!
	P→M: Y el lobo también. ¿Te acuerdas de los tres cochinitos?	And the wolf too. Do you remember the "Three Little Pigs"?
M→P: Sí . . . ¿y el lobo qué /tčráe/ (trae)?		Yes, and what does the wolf bring?
	P→M: Nada, chiquito.	Nothing, son.

4;2 (Vermont)
(Mamá and papá are discussing painting the room; Mario confuses the word "capas" with another meaning more relevant to him.)

	P→MA: No, este cuarto necesita dos capas.	No, this room needs two coats ("capes" in Spanish).
M→MA: ¿Capas? ¿Qué son?		Capes? What are they?
	MA→M: Cuando se pinta dos veces.	When you paint over twice.
M→MA: ¿La akwedas (Te acuerdas) las otas (otras) capas??. . .		Do you remember the other capes?
	MA→M: ¡Ah! La capa de Batman.	Ah! Batman's cape.
M→MA: ¡¡Sí!!		Yes!

(Later that evening, in the kitchen, Mario hears another word "capaz" which sounds similar to those above.)

	P→MA: El gato es capaz de saltar allí.	The cat is able to jump up there. (able=capaz, which also sounds like "capas")
M→P: ¿¿Capas?? ¿Qué son?		Capas? What's that?
	MA→M: Cuando el gato "puede" saltar.	When the cat's able to jump.

Child's Utterance	Other Speakers	Translation
M→MA: ¡Ah! ¿Y las capas de Batman?		Oh! And what about Batman's cape?
	MA→M: Ah no, eso es otra cosa.	Oh no. That's something else.

4;3 (Vermont)
(In the bathroom. Brushing his teeth, he recalls his grandmother's ability to remove her teeth.)

M→P: Cuando yo sea grande voy sacal (a sacar) mis dientes como abuelita.		When I grow up I'm going to take out my teeth, like grandmom.
	P→M: ¿Cuál abuelita?	Which grandmom?
M→P: El abuelito . . . la abuelita, que se llama "Mary".		The grandpop . . . grandmom, whose name is Mary.

4;8 (Vermont)
(Reading a comic book he sees a tiger and recalls a tiger rug he saw in a friend's house.)

M→MA: Mamá voy a il (ir) donde hay leones . . . no tigles (tigres).		Mamá, I'm going to go where there are lions, not tigers.
	MA→M: ¿En Africa?	In Africa?
M→MA: Y voy a cazal (casar) un tigle (tigre) como tiene Sheli (Shirley).		And I'm going to catch a tiger like Shirley's.
Y voy a ponel (poner) en el suelo como una alfombra, y no vas a cortal (cortar) la cabeza po:que (porque) así tiene.		And I'm going to put it on the floor, like a carpet, and you don't cut off the head, because that's the way she has it.

4;9 (Vermont)
(Sitting in the kitchen, Mario begins a conversation about skeletons.)

M→MA: Cuando yo sea calavera, mis ojos van a ser neglos (negros).		When I become a skeleton my eyes will be black.
Los gusanos van a comer la carne . . . ¿y dónde voy a ir yo?		The worms will eat my flesh . . . and where will I be?
	MA→M: Es la pregunta que me hago yo.	That's the question I ask myself.

Child's Utterance	Other Speakers	Translation
M→MA: ¿Los gusanos van a comer mis huesos?		The worms will eat my bones?
	MA→M: No, los gusanos van a comer solo la carne.	No, the worms will only eat your flesh.
M→MA: ¿Y Bimba? ¿También van a comer su carne?		And Bimba? They'll eat her flesh too?
	MA→M: Sí, Mario.	Yes, Mario.
M→MA: Mamá, cuando tú sesas calavera, yo voy a ser viejito.		Mamá, when you become a skeleton, I'm going to be an old man.

4;9 (Vermont)
(In car, en route to a museum, Mario asks again about death; this has been on his mind for several days now.)

M→P: Cuando yo sea /mwe:to/ (muerto) voy a tapar mi nariz para que puedo yespirar (pueda respirar).		When I am dead, I'm going to cover my nose so I can (still) breathe.

5;1 (Vermont)
(Mario returns from kindergarten and enters the father's study to tell him about his day at school.)

M→P: Papá, una nena trajo a la escuela un "Indian corn" . . . un maíz de indio.		Papá, a girl brought Indian Corn to school, a corn of the Indians.
	P→M: Ah, yo también te voy a comprar uno para Halloween.	Oh, I'm also going to buy you one for Halloween.
M→P: Ah, pero no se come, solo los indios. Los indios comen eso pero no las gentes.		Oh, but you don't eat it, only the Indians eat that, but people don't.
	P→M: Pero los indios son gente también.	But Indians are people too.
M→P: ¿Pero por qué se visten así?		But why do they dress like they do?
	P→M: Se visten diferente, pero son como tú y yo.	They dress differently but they're like you and me.

5;2 (Vermont)
(Papá is working in the basement; Mario comes down to help. He begins trying to understand who was the first parent.)

Child's Utterance	Other Speakers	Translation
M→P: Cuando mamá estaba en la bayiga (barriga), ¿quién la cuidaba?		When mamá was in the tummy, who took care of her?
	P→M: Su mamá . . . la abuelita.	Her mother . . . grand-mother.
M→P: ¿Y ella?		And her?
	P→M: Su mamá de ella.	Her mother.
M: (puzzled look)	P: (Narrates the story of Adam and Eve).	

5;2 (Vermont)
(En route to the supermarket.)

M→MA: ¿Mamá, cuando se termine la comida del supermercado, de dónde van a traer más comida?		Mamá, when all the food in the supermarket is gone, where will they get more food?
	MA→M: Van a traer de otro lugar en camión.	They will bring it from another place, in a truck.
M→MA: ¡Van a comprar en un super-mercado muy, muy grande! . . . ¿como el mundo?		They will buy it at a very big supermarket . . . like the world?
	MA→M: Sí.	Yes.

5;2 (Vermont)
(Sitting at the dinner table.)

M→MA: Mamá, ¿Cómo crece la gente, si se bota la comida?		Mamá, how do people grow, if they throw away the food?
	MA→M: ¿Cómo que se bota la comida?	What do you mean, they throw away the food?
M→MA: Sí, como se sale la caca.		Yes, like when you go to the bathroom.
	P→M: Sí, pero no se bota todo . . . solo lo que no sirve. Lo bueno no se bota.	Yes, but you don't get rid of everything, only what's not good. You keep the good part.
M→P: ¿Cuál parte es lo bueno?		What's the good part?
	P→M: La parte que contiene las vita-minas. Lo demás sale.	The part that has vitamins. The rest goes out.

5;2 (Vermont)
(Sitting in the parlour, mamá is putting his pyjamas on. She then embraces Mario, kisses him, and talks to him.)

Child's Utterance	Other Speakers	Translation
	MA→M: Ay Alvino Mario, ¡cómo estás creciendo tanto!	Oh, Alvino Mario, you're growing so much!
	Estás creciendo tanto que pronto vas a ser más grande que mamá.	You're growing so much that soon you'll be bigger than mamá.
M→MA: Y después como papá . . .		And then like papá . . .
Y después como Guiomar . . .		And then like Guiomar . . .
	MA→M: Y después como el abuelito.	And then like Grandfather.
M→MA: ¡Ah no! Porque yo no quiero ser viejito, y después que me entierren.		Ah no! Because I don't want to be old and then they'll bury me.

(A few moments pass; Mario keeps thinking about their discussion, then . . .)

M→MA: Mamá ¿por qué yo nací como nene? . . . ¿por qué no nací como Dios?		Mamá, why was I born a little boy? Why wasn't I born like God?
	MA→M:¿Como Dios? ¿Por qué?	Like God? Why?
M→MA: Porque a Dios no lo entierran, porque es muy grande . . .		Because they never bury God, because he is so big . . .
¿O por qué no nací como el sol, como una bola de fuego?		Or why wasn't I born like the sun, like a ball of fire?

5;5 (Bolivia)
(Mario has developed an interest in numbers; from time to time he asks about the relative value of numbers. Speaking with his grandmother (A), he raises the issue again.)

M→A: ¿Abuelita, 145 es mucho?		Grandmom, is 145 a lot?
	A→M: Sí, hijito.	Yes, dear.
M→A: ¿Y 68 es mucho, o es poco?		And 68, is that a lot or a little?
	A→M: Es muchísimo.	Oh, that's a whole lot.
M→A: ¿Cuál número mucho conoces más? (meaning:		Which is the biggest number you know?

Child's Utterance	Other Speakers	Translation
¿Cuál es el número más grande que conoces?) Uno, cero, cero, cero, #.		One, zero, zero . . .
	A→M: Alvino Mario, ven a besarme.	Alvino Mario, come over here and give me a kiss.

5;7 (Texas)
(Young boy knocked at door, selling newspaper subscriptions. Mario observes and then questions the use of "thank you".)

	Other Speakers	Translation
	Boy: Would you like to buy a subscription to the evening paper?	
	MA: No, thank you.	
	Boy: OK, bye.	

(Mario closed the door and turned to mamá.)

Child's Utterance	Other Speakers	Translation
M→MA: ¿Por qué dijiste "no, gracias?"		Why did you say "no, thank you?"
	MA→M: Porque no quería. Cuesta plata y con esa plata puedo comprar otras cosas . . . juguetes . . . zapatos . . .	Because I did not want it. That costs money and with the money I can buy other things . . . toys . . . shoes . . .
M→MA: Pero tú puedes comprar con "Master Charge". Eso no hace gastar plata. Eso hace *mucha* plata.		But you can buy with "Master Charge". With that you don't need money. With that, you get a lot of money.
	MA→M: OK, Mario, voy a hacerlo.	Okay, Mario, I'll do it.

5;7 (Texas)
(Mario comments on the behaviour of his classmates at school.)

Child's Utterance	Other Speakers	Translation
	MA→A: ¿Por qué no pintas más?	Mario, why don't you paint some more?
M→MA: No, los nenes de aquí son traviesos. Están pintando, no se fican (fijan) y ponen sus codos y se cae la pintura.		No, the kids at school are mean. They are painting and don't pay attention and they put their elbows here and spill the paint.

5;7 (Texas)
(Seeing an animal on television, he asks about it.)

Child's Utterance	Other Speakers	Translation
M→MA: Mamá, ¿cómo se llama ese ilimal (animal)?		What's that animal's name?
	MA→M: Armadillo.	Armadillo. (In Spanish "armar" means "build" and "illo" could be interpreted as diminutive.)
M→MA: ¡Ah, son esos que ayudan a armar las casas!		Oh, those are the little ones that help build houses!

5;8 (Texas)
(Returns from school and tells how his teacher tried on his pirate's eye patch.)

M→MA: La "teacher" . . . se . . . punió. (Hesitating, voice slows down; un-sure about verb form.)		The teacher . . . try . . . tried . . . it on.
	MA→M: ¿Se puso?	Tried it on?
M→MA: Sí . . . y Johnny crerería (creía) que era de él. Yo le quité de la cabeza, pero él di jo: "I got one."		Yes, and Johnny thought it was his. I took it away from him and he said: "I got one."

5;8 (Texas)
(Returning from school, Mario tells his mother about his friend whose name is like his great-grandfather's in La Paz.)

M→MA: Hay un nene que está en mi escuela, se llama Domingo . . .		There's a boy at my school, his name is Domingo.
	MA→M: Ah, ¿sabes quién se llamaba Domingo? El esposo de la abuelita que hace tortas. Se llamaba Domingo, y era mi abuelito.	Oh, do you know whose name is Domingo? Grand-mother, who makes cakes, her husband's name was Domingo, and he was my grandfather.
M→MA: Pero este nene no es /domíngo/, es /damíngow/ (Changes the pronunciation to English.)		But this boy is not /domíngo/ (Spanish pronunciation) it's /damíngow/ (English pronunciation).

Child's Utterance	Other Speakers	Translation

5;8 (Texas)

(Returning from school, Mario tells of a "sad" incident in which other children called him names.)

M→MA: Mamá, te tengo que decir una cosa triste.
    Mamá, I have to tell you something sad.

MA→M: ¿Qué amor?
    What dear?

M→MA: Un nene me dijo "you idiot". ¿Es malo eso? También me dijo "copy catter".
    A boy said "you idiot". Is that bad? He also said "copy catter".

MA→M: ¿Copy cat?
    Copy cat?

M→MA: No, "copy catter".
    No, "copy catter".

MA→M: Eso no es malo, amor. Quiere decir que haces lo que hacen los otros nenes. Está bien.
    That's not bad, dear, It means that you do something other kids do. That's okay.

M→MA: Y Philip me dijo "idiot". ¿Por qué mamá?
    And Philip called me "idiot". Why, mamá?

MA→M: No sé, díme, ¿qué hacías? ¿Estabas pegando? ¿No sabías algo?
    I don't know. Tell me, what were you doing? Did you hit him? You didn't know something?

M→MA: No, ellos me empujaron y Philip me dijo "you idiot".
    No, they pushed me and Philip said "you idiot".

MA→M: No hagas caso. Son nenes tontos que no tienen todo lo que tú tienes. No los quieren como yo te quiero.
    Don't pay any attention. They're silly kids. They don't have what you have. They're not loved as much as I love you.

M→MA: Mamá, ¿yo tengo más juguetes que ellos?
    Mamá, do I have more toys than they do?

MA→M: Sí amor. Tú tienes muchos.
    Yes, dear. You have lots.

M→MA: ¿Cuántos . . . uno, cero, cero; o uno, cero, cero, cero . . .?
    How many, . . ., one, zero, zero; or one, zero, zero, zero . . .?

Child's Utterance	Other Speakers	Translation
	MA→M: Tienes DOS cero, cero, cero. Mañana voy a reñir a ese Philip, mi amor, ya vas a ver. Esas cosas no se dicen.	You have *two*, zero, zero, zero. Tomorrow I'll talk to that Philip, dear, you'll see. They are not nice things to say.

5;8 (Texas)
(In a taxi with Papá driving to a Volkswagen Service place):

| | Driver→P: I saw quite an accident today with a VW. It was turned completely on its back. | |
| M→P: (Interrupting) Papá, ¿qué es "on its back?" ¿así? (Mario turns on his back on the seat to illustrate his meaning.) | | Papá, what's "on its back" mean? Like this? |

(Later arriving at the service place, Papá spots his car from a distance.)

	P→Driver: There she is. That's my car.	
M→P: (Interrupting) Papá, ¿por qué dices "she", como señora?		Papá, why do you say "she" like (it's) a woman?
	P→M: No sé. Así se dice.	I don't know. That's what people say.

(Getting out of cab, Papá pays, and says:)

| | P→Driver: Thanks a lot. I'll be seeing you. | |
| M→P: Papá, ¿por qu dices que lo vas a ver? | | Papá, why did you say you're going to see him? |

5;9 (Texas)
(Observing several Blacks in a restaurant:)

| M: Las mamás negras peinan a sus hijitos así (para atrás) como papá. | | Black mothers comb their children's hair like this (to the back), like papá. |
| | MA→M: Sí. | Yes. |

(He then observes the waitress)

| M→P: ¿Por qué todas las señoras que sirven son negras? | | Why are all the women who serve Black? |

Child's Utterance	Other Speakers	Translation
5;10 (Philadelphia)		
M→P: Papá, ¿por qué el sol se prende y se apaga, se prende y se apaga? ¿Es porque un señor arriba sopla y apaga?		Papá, why does the sun go on and off, on and off? Is there a person up there who blows and puts it out?

The child linguist-ethnographer and philosopher

Note: By his fifth year, the child had already become a comfortable and competent speaker of his native languages, and an effective participant in its cultures. The years ahead, to ten, provide continuing experiences in Spanish and English to a fairly balanced degree. The child becomes an increasingly sophisticated linguist, improving control over more advanced linguistic forms and deepening mastery of the fine points of the systems. He significantly expands his vocabulary, permitting greater precision of expression. He becomes sensitive to linguistic alternatives and becomes acutely aware of their appropriate use in differing social circumstances. He makes frequent comments on courtesy and taboo forms, offers critical comments on the correctness or nativeness of another's speech, revealing strongly held attitudes about both language usage and social values. Although bilingual use is second nature to him at this point, he continues to ponder his bilingual ability *vis à vis* other persons who "speak only one".

As ethnographer, Mario expresses thoughts about his own identity, social rules and attitudes which others hold, and reactions to social prejudice. He becomes an increasingly sensitive member of the society in which he spends most of his time, and due to continuing cross-cultural experiences, he reveals awareness and sensitivity to a variety of cultural differences he perceives between Spanish and English-speakers.

The diary notes are also a marvellous reflection of the child's cognitive growth and his development of abstract thought. He wonders often about the meaning of things, raising questions about the origin of people, birth, growth and development, and a rather persistent curiosity in death. Interest in the supernatural and the responses provided through his contact with organized religion, permeates his thoughts throughout this period.

Increased proficiency in two language systems and alternating cross-cultural experiences, provide the child with many opportunities to contrast and compare what other children might take for granted. Moreover, his developing language skills coupled with these insights permit him to engage in abstract thought about the meaning of life. In this sense, the child-boy is not only linguist-ethnographer, but a developing philosopher as well.

Child's Utterance	Other Speakers	Translation
6;1 (Vermont)		

(Mario is outside playing around his tree house. Before attempting to climb up, he

Child's Utterance	Other Speakers	Translation

discusses telling God to protect him. He then is sorry he said this aloud as the devil might hear him. He then reasons with the devil.)

Child's Utterance	Other Speakers	Translation
M→Devil: Sólo tienes magia para *desayudar*, no hacer (mal).		You only have magic (power) to "un-help", not to do (evil).

6;3 (Vermont)

	P→M: Mario, no hagas así, te vas a hacer chichíu.	Don't do that, Mario, you are going to get a "bu-bu".
M→P: No se dice chichíu, se dice "lastimar".		You shouldn't say "bu-bu", you say "get hurt".
	P: Ah, O.K.	

6;9 (Vermont)

(With his mother, he asks questions about when he was a baby.)

M→MA: ¿Cuándo estaba en tu barriga, era muy chiquito?		When I was in your tummy, was I very small?
	MA→M: Sí, Mario, muy chiquito.	Yes, Mario, very small.
M: Muy chiquito, ¿así? (forming circle with his fingers).		Very small, like this?
	MA: Sí.	Yes.
M: Y mamá, ¿cómo salí? ¿Por dónde?		And Mamá, how did I come out? Where from?
M: ¿Pero cómo?	MA: . . . de la barriga.	From my tummy. Yes, but how?
	MA: (Avoids answer) P: (Distracts Mario saying): Mm! Tú eras tan impaciente como siempre, que ni siquiera esperaste al doctor.	You were so impatient as always, you didn't even wait for the doctor.

7;6 (Vermont)

(Mario's boy friend, Dana, comes to visit for the day. Mario continues to speak Spanish with his parents (Ps), switching to English when speaking to Dana. At the table, Mario puzzles whether Dana hears and understands what's going on.)

M→Ps: Cuando una persona está hablando con otra persona "sta hablando . . . y, yo estoy hablando . . . él (Dana) ¿oye?		When a person is talking to another person . . . and the other person is talking like I am (Spanish) can he (Dana) hear?
	P→M: ¿Quieres decir que si él comprende?	You mean if he can understand?
M: No, ¿él, *oye*?		No, can he *hear*?

Child's Utterance	Other Speakers	Translation
	P: Pues sí, pero no entiende lógicamente.	Of course, but naturally he doesn't understand.
	P→D: Dana, do you know any Spanish?	
	D: No, um Mario told me something, but I forgot.	
M→D: I learned both things (languages) at the same time . . . Stephanie (a classmate) says, "uno, dos", (making fun at her pronunciation.)		
	P→D: Do your parents or grandparents speak Spanish or Italian?	
	D: Um . . . I think this . . . My daddy's grandparents. They talk different than I do . . . sometimes they talk real strange . . . right?	
M→Ps: I wish he (Dana) could . . . he could go to your school (to learn Spanish).		
	P→D: How old are you, Dana?	
M→D&P: We're growing up together. I'm seven . . . you're seven . . . You got a hole right there (a missing tooth). I got a hole right here . . . We're growing up together . . . Kent, you and me.		
	P→D: And you're in second grade too!	
M: Holly's not. She's in primary. That's for the kids that don't know a lot.		

Child's Utterance	Other Speakers	Translation
	P→M: Ya, Mario. ¡Come! Termina tu sandwich.	O.K. Mario, Eat! Finish your sandwich.
M→D&P: Yo estoy "allergic". I'm allergic to these seeds (on the bread).		I'm "allergic". I'm allergic to these seeds.
M: I'm not allergic to pumpkin seeds.	P→M: Pero tú comes las semillas del zapallo.	But you eat pumpkin seeds.

7;7 (Vermont)
(Marina, a caretaker, is putting the two children to bed.)

M→Mar: Cuando sea grande, ¿me voy a casar, Marina?		When I grow up, will I get married, Marina?
	Mar: Sí.	Yes.
M: ¿Con quién?		With whom?
	Mar: Con una chica que te guste.	With a girl you like.
M: ¿Pero y si no me gusta? ¿No me puedo casar con mi hermana?		But, what if I don't like her? Can I marry my sister?
	Mar: No, porque son hijos del mismo padre y de la misma madre.	No, because you are both from the same mother and father.
M: ¿Cómo es eso?		What do you mean?
	Mar: Son hermanos y no pueden casarse porque a Dios no le gustaría.	You are brother and sister and you can't marry each other because God wouldn't like it.
M: ¿Por qué no le gustaría?		Why wouldn't He like it?
	Mar: Porque lo vería mal y se enojaría.	Because he would not think it is a good idea and He could get angry.
M: ¿Cómo se enojaría? ¿Qué diría?		How would He get angry? What would He say?

(Mario insisted in knowing what God would say.)

7;8 (Florida)
(On the beach, the children are playing in the surf. Leaving the water, Mario comments to his father.)

M→P: Aquí en Florida hay mucha gente un poco viejita . . . ¿verdad, papá?		Here in Florida, there's a lot of old people, isn't it so papá?
	P: Sí, es cierto, Mario.	Yes, that's right.

Child's Utterance	Other Speakers	Translation
M: ¿Por qué, papá? ¿Porque viven aquí mucho?		Why, papá? Because here they live a long time?

7;9 (Vermont) (Marina lost her ring and asked Mario to pray so it will be found.)

Child's Utterance	Other Speakers	Translation
	Mar: ¡Reza!	Pray!
M: Vos reza porque a mí no me escucha . . . no me entiende.		You pray, because He doesn't listen to me. He doesn't understand me.
	Mar: ¿Cómo sabes que no te entiende?	How do you know He doesn't understand you?
M: Yo hablé con mi boca cerrada pero yo escuché lo que hablaba.		I spoke with my mouth closed, but I could listen to myself speaking.

7;9 (Vermont)
(Talking about a baby who was staying at the home with his mother.)

Child's Utterance	Other Speakers	Translation
	Mar: ¿Te gustó el niño?	Did you like the baby?
M: Sí (not very enthusiastically).		Yes.
	Mar: ¿No quieres que tu mamá te compre uno en el mercado?	Would you like your mother to buy one for you in the market?
M: No . . . si los niños no se compran. No, yo quiero un gato o un perro.		No . . . you can't buy children. I'd rather have a dog or a cat.

(Mario later told the visitor, Lise, the same episode.)

Child's Utterance	Other Speakers	Translation
M: Los niños no se compran, nacen de la mamá . . .		You don't buy children. They are born from the mother.
	Lise: How do you know that?	
M: I saw (it) on television . . . the mother pushes and the baby comes out.		

7;11 (Vermont)
(Driving back to Vermont, after attending his uncle's funeral in Philadelphia.)

Child's Utterance	Other Speakers	Translation
M→MA: ¿Se puede mandar cartas a Dios?		Can I sent letters to God?
	MA: No.	No.
M: Ah! . . . Se escribe en papel y se deja y después se lo lleva.		Oh, you write on paper, then you leave it and then He takes it with Him?
	MA: No, cuando quieres decir algo a Dios, se reza.	No, when you want to say something to God, you pray.
M: Ah, ¿no puede tocar lo de aquí en la tierra?		Oh, because He can't touch things here on earth?

Child's Utterance	Other Speakers	Translation
	MA: No.	No.
M: Solo cuando Jesús lo tocó, ¿no?		Only when Jesus touched it, right?
	MA: Sí.	Yes.
(Later on the same day.) M→MA: ¿Por qué murió el tío?		Why did uncle die?
	MA: Su corazón se paró.	His heart stopped.
M: ¿Por qué?		Why?
	MA: Porque la sangre era muy espesa y no llegó al corazón.	Because his blood became very thick and did not get to his heart.
M: ¿Y por qué no sacaron un poco?		And why didn't they take some blood out?
	MA: Porque no llegó bien al hospital.	Because he was not too well when he went to the hospital.

8;0 (Vermont)
(At the dinner table, his father wants Mario to eat more.)

	P→M: Hoy tienes 8 años (while he serves him).	Today you are 8 years old.
M: (Sí pero) mi estómago todavía tiene siete.		Yes, but my stomach is still seven.

8;0 (Vermont)
(Outside, Marina and Mario see an ant. Mario steps on it, but does not kill it.)

	Mar: Mátala, mátala, ¿no ves que está sufriendo?	Kill it! Kill it! Can't you see it's suffering?
M: (Thinks for a while and then replies) Nostros también sufrimos y ¿cómo alguién no nos mata?		We suffer too, and how come nobody kills us?

8;1 (Vermont)
(Walking down the road to pick raspberries, Mario speaks about school. He tells of when his teacher repirmanded him because his homework was not correct.)

	Mar: Pero tienes que prestar más atención.	But you have to pay more attention.
M: Ah . . . pero es que yo no entendí bien . . . porque yo nací español.		Oh, but I didn't understand too well . . . because I am Spanish.
	P→M: Oh Mario, tú hablas y comprendes inglés tan bien como cualquiera.	Oh Mario, you speak and understand English as well as anyone else.

Child's Utterance	Other Speakers	Translation
	MA: Si prestas atención . . .	If you pay attention . . .
M→Ps: ¡¡¡Sí!!! (Yo la presto)		I do!!!

8;2 (Vermont)
(At breakfast table, Papá is speaking English and Carla hears him.)

| | C→P: No hables en inglés a mamá. | Don't speak English to mamá. |
| M→All: A mamá le gusta hablar en español. | | Mamá likes to speak in Spanish. |

8;4 (Vermont)
(Talking at the dinner table, Mario discusses a book he is reading.)

M→Ps: En mi libro hay muchas palabras malas.		There are a lot of bad words in my book.
	P: ¿Ah sí?	Oh really?
M: ¿Puedo decir?		Can I say (them)?
	P: A ver ¿cuáles?	Let's see, which ones?
M: Yo no las digo. Sólo las miro y las pienso.		I don't say them. I only look at them and think them.
	P: ¿Cómo cuáles, Mario?	Like which ones, Mario?
M: (Spelling the words in Spanish) d-a-m-m-i-t- . . . y h-e-l-l. Papá, ¿es malo decir?		Papá, is it bad to say that?
	P: Pues no es nada bonito que se diga. Es mejor no hablar así.	Well, it is not nice. It's better not to say those words.
M: Y también: G-o-d D-a-m-m-i-t.		

8;11 (Flight from Albuquerque)
(Mario increasingly enjoys telling puns in English or Spanish.)

| M→P: ¿Te acuerdas del chiste de Adán y su costilla? | | Do you remember the joke about Adam and his rib? |
| | P: No. | No. |

(He gets distracted and then asks something else:)

M: Papá, antes de los papás de los papás . . . etc. ¿Cómo era el mundo? . . . ¿Como el espacio?		Papá, before the fathers of the fathers of the fathers . . . etc. How was the world? Like space?
	P: ¿Cómo, como el espacio?	What do you mean, like space?
M: Bueno, ¿de qué color era? ¿Cómo era? No puedo entender nada.		Well, what colour was it? How was it? I can't understand anything.
	P: Bueno, nadie sabe en realidad.	Well, nobody really knows.

Child's Utterance	Other Speakers	Translation
M: ¡Púchica! Los científicos ¿tampoco? Ummm . . . cuando vaya al cielo le voy a preguntar a Dios como empezó . . . Dios sabe todo.		Darn it! Not even the scientists? Humm . . . when I go to Heaven, I'm going to ask God how it all began . . . God knows everything.

(Mario sees his speech diary and becomes interested. He begins to read it and laughs about the way he used to speak. He spends about half an hour reading, sometimes with a roaring laughter.)

Child's Utterance	Other Speakers	Translation
M→Ps: Así hablaba cuando era "baby" ¡Qué chistoso!		I used to speak like this when I was a baby. How funny!

(Carla overhears and interjects)

Child's Utterance	Other Speakers	Translation
	C→MA: Cuando yo era "baby" tomaba leche de tu tetita, cuando yo estaba en tu barriga . . . ¿Y cómo salí?	When I was a "baby" I drank from your breasts while I was in your tummy . . . And how did I come out?
M→C et al: Por un rato duerme y el bebé sale poco a poco.		For a while it sleeps and then the baby comes out slowly.
	P→M: ¿Cómo sabes todo eso?	How do you know that?
M: Porque yo ví en televisión donde Ruthie.		Because I saw it on TV at Ruthie's.

(Carla overhears Mario reading parts of the diary, and she asks)

Child's Utterance	Other Speakers	Translation
	C→All: ¿Así hablaba yo también . . . cuando era baby?	Did I speak like that too, when I was a baby?
M→C: Tú no estabas. ¡Te estabas formando en la barriga de mamá.		You weren't there! You were forming inside mamá's belly.
	C→MA: Sí . . . me estaba formando por tu vida.	Yes, I was getting formed for your life.
M→C: Hay muchos globitos y se juntan y se hacen muchos ojos, y después un bebé.		There are a lot of bubbles and they get together and then the eyes are formed, then the baby.
	MA→M: ¿Dónde viste eso?	Where did you see that?
M: En "My Mom is Having a Baby", el "After School Special".		In "My Mom is Having a Baby", the "After School Special".

Child's Utterance	Other Speakers	Translation

8;11 (Albuquerque)
(Walking to the movie theatre, Mario sees some "peep show" signs across the street.)

M→P: (Reading) "Adult Shows" . . . ¿Papá, por qués "for adults only"?
    "Adult Shows" . . . Papá, why is it "for adults only"?

    P→M: Oh, porque tiene algunas personas desnudas.
    Oh, because they have some naked people.

M: Hay cosas malas que no se puede decir, ¿verdad, papá?
    There are bad things that we can't say, right, papá?

    P: ¿Como qué, Mario?
    Like what, Mario?

M: ¿Puedo . . . ?
    May I?

    P: Sí, díme, ¿qué sabes?
    Yes, tell me, what do you know?

M: Bueno, algunos niños de mi clase dicen . . . "A-S-S" ¿que parte es esa? Y Dana dice: "your dink" . . . y se hace así con tu mano, es malo, verdad?
    Well, some boys in my class say "A-S-S" what part is that? And Dana says "your dink" and does like this with his hand. That's bad, right?

9;3 (Vermont)
(Mario sees a book from Bolivia entitled "Guano Maldito". He comments on the title and use of a "bad" word.)

M: "Maldito", that's a bad word! (Shows his "middle finger" to indicate that without saying.)
    Dammed! That's a bad word.

9;3 (Vermont)
(The child's parents are speaking of his grandfather who is ill. Mario reflects on death.)

M→P: ¿Cómo voy a morir yo?
    How am I going to die?

    P: Uf! . . . nadie sabe, Mario, como va a morir.
    Oh . . . nobody knows how he's going to die.

M: ¿Duele más un "heart attack" o un tiburón?
    Is it more painful to die of a "heart attack" or eaten by a shark?

9;6 (Vermont)
(At home, he is thinking and questioning about how the human race began.)

    P: . . . antes de nacer, ya existe el espíritu en el cielo.
    . . . before we are born, our spirit exists in Heaven.

Child's Utterance	Other Speakers	Translation
M: Pero el cuerpo está en la tierra. Dios coge la tierra y forma el cuerpo, los brazos y las uñas . . . No tiene la cabeza todavía porque va a dar alguien . . . y le da la cara de la mamá, y después nace.		But the body is in the earth. God takes dirt and forms the body, the arms and the nails . . . They don't have heads yet, because it will be given to someone . . . and they give the mother's face and then he's born.
	P: ¡Qué inteligente! ¿Cómo sabes todo eso?	You are so clever! How do you know all that?
M: Porque sí . . . soy astuto.		Because . . . I'm astute.

9;11 (Puebla, México)
(Mario has just said the word "puto" (gay or homosexual) which he heard from another child. When asked about the meaning of the word, he replies):

M: Dijo Eduardo que sí . . . creo que significaba . . . un hombre que besa a otros hombres y los abraza . . . ay . . . ay . . .		Eduardo says so . . . I think it meant . . . a man who kisses another man and they hug, ay, ay . . .
	P: ¿Como tú me besas a mí?	Like you kiss me?
M: No . . . "sexy" . . . come haces con mujeres, pero con hombres.		No . . . "sexy" like you do with women, but with men.

10;5 (Vermont)
(Drawing at the table)

M→MA: Ay . . . estoy perdiendo mi talento.		Ay . . . I'm losing my talent!
	MA: ¿Cuál talento?	Which talent?
M: . . . de pintar.		For painting.
	MA: ¿Por qué?	Why?
M: Porque ya no puedo pensar en *un* monstruo nuevo.		Because I cannot even think of *one* new monster.

10;8 (Bolivia)
(Walking along the main boulevard, El Prado, Mario steps on dog excrement.)

M→P: (whispering) "Shit" on my shoes.		"Shit" on my shoes.
	P: No se dice eso, suena feo.	You don't say that. It doesn't sound nice.
M: Ah, se dice "doggie-do".		Ah, you say "doggie-do".
	P: (Laughing) Pues eso, se puede.	Well, that you can.
M: Papá, ¿cuál es la palabra correcta?		Yes but which is the correct word?

Child's Utterance	Other Speakers	Translation
	P: Bueno, lo científico, lo correcto sería "feces" o "excrement".	Well, the correct word, the scientific word is "feces" or "excrement".
M: Pero cada animal tiene otro nombre: doggie-do horse manure cow plop deer droppings . . .		But every animal has a different name: doggie-do horse manure cow plop deer droppings . . .
	P: Sí, pero el nombre genérico — o sea general — para todos sería excremento.	Well yes, but the generic name — in other words the most general — would be "excrement".

10;9 (La Paz, Bolivia)
(At the table with parents and grandparents)

M→Ab: Abuelita, ¿qué quiere decir "denso"?		Abuelita, what does "dense" mean?
	Ab: Ay, Mario, Muy mala costumbre tienes. He oído que preguntaste a tu abuelito, tu papá, y ahora a mí.	Oh, Mario. You have a very bad habit. I heard you ask your grandfather, your father, and now me.
M→All: Pero no, es que me olvido.		But, it's because I forget.
	Ab: No te olvidas. Siempre estás checando.	You don't forget. You're always doublechecking.
	MA→M: Muy mala costumbre es.	That's a very bad habit.
M: No, mira . . . papá dijo que (una persona *densa*) es tontito . . . abuelito dice que es "espeso" y ahora mi libro dice "población *densa*".		No, look here . . . papá said that (a dense person) is dumb . . . grandfather says that it means "thick" and now my book says "dense population".

10;9 (La Paz, Bolivia)
(Mario is sick in bed. He's thinking about Vermont, and says):

M: Papá, ya no me gusta la nieve. Quiero quedarme aquí.		Papá, I don't like snow anymore. I want to stay here.
	P: ¿Quieres quedarte en Bolivia?	You want to stay in Bolivia?
M: Sí.		Yes.
	P: OK.	OK.

(Later on)

Child's Utterance	Other Speakers	Translation
M→P: Mamá es mal educada porque no se persigna antes de las iglesias.		Mamá is not well mannered because she does not make the sign of the cross when she passes in front of a church.
	P: ¿Quién to dijo eso?	And who told you that?
M: Nadie.		Nobody.
	P: ¿Y como sabes eso? ¿Has visto?	And how do you know that? Have you seen it done?
M: Sí. (Thinking some more)		Yes.
M: Pobre de los pobres que están en las puertas de las iglesias.		I feel sorry about the poor beggars in front of the doors of the church.
	P: ¿Por qué?	Why?
M: Porque tienen que estar así . . . ¡Mira! (making the signal of the cross rapidly and repeatedly)		Because they have to be like this. Look . . .

(Later, playing chess with his sister, she makes a move and then wants to change it.)

M: Soltaste Carlina, ya no puedes.		You let it go, Carla. You can't do it now.
	P→M: (As an aside, tells him) Mario, she is six and you're ten . . . déjala.	Mario, she is six years old and you are ten . . . let her.
M: ¡Qué tramposa!		What a cheater!
M: (Aloud) She's cheating!		

Age 10;9 (La Paz, Bolivia)
(Yesterday was a holiday, but Mario stays at home today also because he is still sick. Papá enters the room eating a candy. Mario complains because he cannot have one.)

| M→MA: Mamá, esta comiendo dulces . . . está anto-jándome. | | Mamá, he's eating candies, and he's "craving" me. |
| | P→M: No "antojándome" . . . "me está haciendo antojar". | Not craving me . . . He's making me crave. |

(Shows no interest in the correction, only in his own message; he turns supplicatingly to his mother)

| M→MA: Mamá. | | Mamá! |

Age 10;9 (La Paz, Bolivia)
(Mario returns from school. He exchanges currency with his father; when he gets to 50, he says):

| M→P: ¡Cabalitos! (A new expression) (Then changing topic) | | Just right! |

Child's Utterance	Other Speakers	Translation
Me dieron con el "Pedro Moreno" (a paddle) hoy.		Today I got the "Pedro Moreno" (the paddle).
	P: ¿Por qué?	Why?
M: Hablé.		I spoke.
	P: ¿Te dolió?	Did it hurt?
M: No mucho . . . ah, y sabes qué? Me olvidé llevar mi cuaderno de dibujo hoy.		Not much, ah, and do you know something? Today I forgot my sketch pad.
	P: ¿Y qué pasó?	And what happened?
M: El profesor estaba revisando (los cuadernos) . . . y yo dije a mi profesor que tenía que ir al baño . . . Me fuí, y esperé hasta que tocó el timbre.		The teacher was checking the pads . . . and so I told my teacher I had to go to the bathroom . . . and I went, and I stayed there until the bell rang.

Age 10;9 (La Paz, Bolivia)
(Mario is doing homework. Suddenly he starts imitating his teacher)

M: (Aloud) . . . a quien hable, yo le doy la tuya (tirada del borrador) ¡y va a venir aquí a repetir todo lo que dijo!		Whoever speaks will receive this (a throw of the board eraser). And he will have to come here to repeat everything he said!

(Later, still working, he stops suddenly and comments):

M: Hay tres clases de "lima": Lima, Perú . . . lima, la fruta . . . y lima para las uñas.		There are three kinds of "lima": Lima, Perú . . . lima (lime) the fruit . . . and lima (file) for the nails.

Age 10;9 (La Paz, Bolivia)
(Listening to the radio program "Kalimàn")

M→P: *Aquicito* está la radio.		The radio is "right here".

(Noticing that his father writes down what he just said, he adds jokingly):

M→P: ¡*Che!* qu no escribas, "*pibe*".		"*Ché*" don't write "*pal*".

(Later, reading a magazine where "New" Orleans appears, he asks):

M→P: Papá ¿qué es *New* Orleans?		Papá, what's *New* Orleans?
	P: ¿Sabes qué significa *new*, en *New* York, *New* Jersey . . . ?	You know what *new* means like in *New* York, *New* Jersey?
M: ¿*New*sweek? (Laughing)		And *New*sweek?
	P: ¡Chistoso! Es que cuando querían nombrar ciudades en	Funny! It's because when they wanted to name cities in America, they put names

Child's Utterance	Other Speakers	Translation
	América con nombres de ciudades de Europa, ponían "new" adelante.	of European cities and added "new" in front.

Age 10;10 (La Paz, Bolivia)
(Mario goes to confession at church. When told to say the prayer "Act of Contrition", Mario gets up because he does not understand what is meant. Moments later):

M→P: ¿Papá, qué es Acto de Contrición?		Papá, what's the "Act of Contrition"?
	P: ¿Acaso no lo dijiste estando en confesión? Tenías que recitar junto con el padre, al final.	You mean you didn't say it while you were in confession. You were supposed to say it together with the priest.
M: ¡Ah! ¿Sabes qué me dijo al final? "¡Vete en paz!" (with a stern voice)		Oh! Do you know what he told me at the end? "Go (away) in peace".
	P: Pues, así se dice.	That's the way you say it.
M: Me parecía mal educado . . . enojado . . . "*vete en paz*" (says with a stern voice and serious face).		It sounded rude . . . angry "go (away) in peace".

10;10 (La Paz, Bolivia)
(Mario returns from school, and tells of an incident that day)

M→Ps: El profesor estaba diciendo: "la tarea para el miércoles". Y yo le dije: "No tenemos clases el miércoles". Me dice: "¿Quién eres tú? . . . El ministro? (de educación)"		The teacher was saying: "the homework for Wednesday". And I said: "We don't have classes on Wednesday". And he told me: "Who are you? The Secretary (of Education)?"
Y yo le dije "no" y el dijo a la clase: "Mario Fantini dice que no tenemos clase el miércoles", ¿es cierto?		And I said "no" and then he told the class: "Mario Fantini says there's no school on Wednesday, is that true?"
Y todos dijeron: "Sí, el Día del Maestro."		And everyone said: "Yes, it's Teacher's Day."
"A la macana" dice el profesor de "mate" (matemáticas) (Mario concludes laughing).		"For Heaven's sake!" said the math teacher.

Child's Utterance	Other Speakers	Translation

(Later, Mario is doing homework at his desk. Suddenly he gets up and shakes his foot, and wets two fingers with saliva and rubs them behind his ears.)

	P→M: ¿Qué estás haciendo?	What are you doing?
M: (Esto) calma lo dormilón del pie.		This calms my foot which went to sleep.

(In the morning, the whole family goes to the Mercado Camacho. Carla wants to buy Chocolate Milk, which is sold in plastic bags. Mario is cautious about this, and whispers to her in English):

M→C: Suppose it's "*cut*"
(from "cortada"
meaning "soured")

Age 10;10 (La Paz, Bolivia)
(Mario begins winter vacation today)

	P→M: ¿Estás seguro que empezaron vaca-ciones hoy?	Are you sure vacation started today?
M→P: Yo sé no hay clases hoy porque el hermano dijo: "les veo después de vacaciones . . ." Y si hubiera clases hoy, nos hubiera dado terea hoy. (Laugh-ing, he adds), El hermano dice "hay clases, pero no labores."		I know there are no classes today, because the Brother said: "I'll see you after vacation . . ." And if we had classes today, he would have given us homework. Brother says: "We have classes but no assign-ments."

Age 10;10 (La Paz, Bolivia)
(At the table with everyone, including grandparents and his aunt and uncle, the conversation is about school report cards and grades):

M→All: Saqué un seis en inglés (laughing) . . . pero es que el maestro no sabe bien.		I got a 6 in English . . . but that's because the teacher doesn't know (English) well.
M→P: ¿Cómo dices man-zana? (to prove a point)		How do you say "apple"?
	P: Apple.	"Apple". (/ǽpɛl/)
M: Ves, . . . el profesor dice /apel/		You see . . . the teacher says /apel/.
	C→M: (In reprimanding tone) Tienes que hablar como él, Mario.	You should say it the way he does, Mario.

250 LANGUAGE ACQUISITION OF A BILINGUAL CHILD

Child's Utterance	Other Speakers	Translation

10;10 (Potosí, Bolivia)
(Mario travels with his father and uncle to Potosí. The night of June 24 is St. John's Day and Mario goes with his father and uncle to Aroifila for a bonfire and fireworks. Mario is intrigued with the small stands selling herbs and other things. He also wants to chew coca leaves. He tries coca and he does not like it. He then buys cinnamon sticks to chew on and to make "cinnamon tea". He returns the next day, buys from a different stand. The vendor jokingly says to the other vendor:

| Vendor: Ah no, este joven tiene que comprar a mí, . . . es mi "casero". | | Ah no! This young man has to buy from me, he's my "casero" (customer). |

(Mario is interested in the people who speak Quechua. He asks the maid to teach him and he promises to teach her English in exchange, even "dirty words" which she has asked for. He writes everything phonetically so she can pronounce it. He also writes Quechua phonetically, experiencing some difficulty with the new sounds. His father teaches him a system from the Quechua book and he grasps it quickly, even the terminology (bilabial, dental, palatal, velar, glotal). He learns to form new sounds, even glotalized ones).

10;11 (La Paz, Bolivia)
(All go to the evening mass. Both the Gospel and Homily are quite long, the priest speaking to the question: "the face of Jesus". Somewhat bored, Mario turns to his father):

| M→P: Tremendo discurso para dar una respuesta. | | Such a long speech to answer one question! |

10;11 (La Paz, Bolivia)
(Mario's parents are talking. Papá quotes something he has read, using the word "dam". Mario comments):

M→P: Ay, papá, you sweared.		Papá! You sweared.
	P: ¿Qué? (Laughing)	What?
M: You sweared!		

(Later on, Papá is correcting Carla's homework, Mario walks in):

M→P: Ah ¿le estás *correct*ando?		Oh, you are "correct-ando" (correcting) her.
	P: ¿Qué dices?	What did you say?
M: ¿Estás *correct*ando su tarea?		You're "correct-ando" her homework.
	P: (Correcting Mario) *Corrigiendo*.	"Cor*rigiendo*" (correcting).

10;11 (La Paz, Bolivia)
(Mario is reading in bed. He is cold and asks to be covered with the alpaca blanket, and used the Bolivian pattern of verb stress)

| M: Tapáme, papá. | | Cover me, papá. |

Child's Utterance	Other Speakers	Translation

Age 10;11 (La Paz, Bolivia)
(An American group arrives in La Paz. Mario enters the living room and greets everyone shaking hands with each individual to their surprise)

10;11 (La Paz, Bolivia)
(Returning from evening mass at El Montículo, Mario comments in English about someone in the street so others won't understand)

	P→M: You've got to be more discreto.	You've got to be more "discreet".
M: ¿Qué quiere decir?		What does it mean?
	P: "Discreet" . . . así "discreto" callado . . . usar juicio.	"Discreet" like "discreto" . . . quiet . . . using your common sense.

10;11 (La Paz, Bolivia)
(An American visitor comes to Mario's grandparents' home for tea. Later at dinner Mario comments on his Spanish):

M→P/MA/Ab: ¡Ay! Ese jefe, ni habla español . . . habla muy mal!		Oh, that leader doesn't even speak Spanish, . . . he speaks very poorly.
	P: No es cierto. (Kidding)	That's not true.
M: Sí, dice /veynte treys/ . . . /xúliow/ . . . etc.		Yes, he says /veynte treys/ (instead of /beyntitres/). /xúliow/ (instead of /xúlio/) . . . etc.

10;11 (Philadelphia)
(His aunt is talking about "coloured" people. Mario is surprised by this expression and comments):

M→Aunt: Whaddya mean "coloured" people? Every-body's coloured! (Speaking seriously)

11;0 (Philadelphia)
(Today is Mario's 11th birthday. At night, he is getting ready for bed):

	P→M: Mario, ¿cómo te sientes ahora que tienes once años?	Mario, how do you feel now that you are eleven?
M: Bien . . . bien nomás . . . Así nomás es.		Well, the same . . . That's the way it is.
	P:Pero ¿cómo te sientes?	But how do you feel?
M: Más grande.		Bigger!
	C: (Laughs).	
M: (Sticks his tongue at his sister).		

Bibliography

ABRAHAMSEN, A. A. 1977, *Child Language: An Interdisciplinary Guide to Theory and Research*. Baltimore, Maryland: University Park Press.

ALATIS, J. E. (ed.) 1970, *Bilingualism and Language Contact*. Monograph Series on Language and Linguistics, 21st Annual Round Table, No. 23, Washington, DC.: Georgetown University Press.

ANDERSSON, T. 1973, Children's Learning of a Second Language: Another View. *Modern Language Journal*, Vol. LVII, Nos. 5–6, September–October. 254–59.

— 1977, *A Guide to Family Reading in Two Languages: The Preschool Years*. Evaluation, Dissemination and Assessment Center, Los Angeles, California.

ANDERSSON, T. & BOYER, M. 1970, *Bilingual Schooling in the United States*. Southwest Educational Development Laboratory, Austin, Texas.

ANDRUS DE LAGUNA, G. 1963, *Speech: Its Function and Development*. Bloomington, Indiana: Indiana University Press.

ANGLIN, J. 1970, *The Growth of Word Meaning*. Cambridge, Massachusetts: MIT Press.

BAETENS BEARDSMORE, H. 1982, *Bilingualism: Basic Principles*. Clevedon, Avon, England: Multilingual Matters Ltd.

BAGLEY, C. & VERMA, G. K. (eds) 1983, *Multicultural Childhood: Education, Ethnicity and Cognitive Styles*. Hampshire, England: Gower Publishing Co.

BAR-ADON, A. & LEOPOLD, W. F. (eds) 1971, *Child Language: A Book of Readings*. Englewood Cliffs, New Jersey: Prentice-Hall.

BATES, E. 1976, *Language and Context: The Acquisition of Pragmatics*. New York: Academic Press.

BERGMAN C. R. 1976, Interference vs. Dependent Development in Infant Bilingualism. In G. D. KELLER *et al.* (eds), *Bilingualism in the Bicentennial and Beyond*. Jamaica, New York: Bilingual Press.

BERKO GLEASON, J. 1961, The Child's Learning of Engligh Morphology. In S. SAPORTA (ed.), *Psycholinguistics: A Book of Readings*. New York: Holt, Rinehart and Winston.

— 1973, Code Switching in Children's Language. In T. E. MOORE (ed.), *Cognitive Development and the Acquisition of Language*. New York: Academic Press. 159–68.

BERNSTEIN, B. 1970, Some Sociological Determinants of Perception. An Inquiry into Sub-Cultural Differences. In J. FISHMAN (ed.), *Readings in the Sociology of Language*. The Hague: Mouton.

BIRDWHISTLE, R. L. 1970, *Kinesics and Context: Essays on Body Motion Communication*. Philadelphia, Pennsylvania: University of Pennsylvania Press.

BLOOM, L. 1970, *Language Development: Form and Function in Emerging Grammars*. Cambridge, Massachusetts: MIT Press.

— 1975, *One Word at a Time*. The Hague: Mouton.

BLOUNT, B. G. (ed.) 1974, *Language, Culture and Society*. Cambridge, Massachusetts: Winthrop Publishers, Inc.

— 1977, Prosodic, paralinguistic, and interactional features in parent-child speech: English and Spanish. *Journal of Child Language*, 1–20.

BRAINE, M. D. S. 1971, On Learning the Grammatical Order of Words. In A. BAR-ADON & W. F. LEOPOLD (eds), *Child Language: A Book of Readings*. Englewood Cliffs, New Jersey: Prentice-Hall. 242–43.

BRIGHT, W. (ed.) 1966, *Sociolinguistics: Proceedings of the UCLA Sociolinguistic Conference, 1964*. The Hague: Mouton.

BRISK, M. E. 1972, *The Spanish Syntax of the Pre-School Spanish American: The Case of New Mexican Five-Year-Old Children*. Ph.D. Dissertation, University of New Mexico, Albuquerque, New Mexico.

— no date, A Preliminary Study of the Syntax of Five-Year-Old Spanish Speakers of New Mexico. *International Journal of the Sociology of Language*, No. 2. The Hague: Mouton. Undated Offprint.

BROWN, R. 1958, *Words and Things*. New York: The Free Press.

— (ed.) 1970, *Psycholinguistics: Selected Papers*. Cambridge, Massachusetts: The Free Press.

— 1973, *A First Language*. Cambridge, Massachusetts: MIT Press.

BROWN, R. & BELLUGI, U. 1964, Three Processes in the Child's Acquisition of Syntax. In E. H. LENNEBERG (ed.) *New Directions in the Study of Language*. Cambridge, Massachusetts: MIT Press.

BROWN, R. & GILMAN, A. 1970, The Pronouns of Power and Solidarity. In J. FISHMAN (ed.), *Readings in the Sociology of Language*. The Hague: Mouton.

BURLING, R. 1971, Language Development of a Garo and English-Speaking Child. In A. BAR-ADON & W. F. LEOPOLD (eds), *Child Language: A Book of Readings*. Englewood Cliffs, New Jersey: Prentice-Hall. 170–84.

CAIRNS, C. & SILVA, D. 1969, *How Children Learn Language*. ERIC Document 038-401, Future School Study Project, Albuquerque Public Schools, September.

CALIFORNIA ACHIEVEMENT TESTS 1977, Monterey, California: McGraw-Hill.

CARROLL, J. B. 1961, Language Development in Children. In S. SAPORTA (ed.), *Psycholinguistics: A Book of Readings*. New York: Holt, Rinehart and Winston.

— 1964, *Language and Thought*. Englewood Cliffs, New Jersey: Prentice-Hall.

CARROW, E. 1971, Auditory Test for Language Comprehension. Austin, Texas.

CAZDEN, C. B. 1973, Language Socialization. In Notes from the 23rd Annual Round Table, R. W. SHUY (ed.), *Monograph Series on Language and Linguistics*. Washington, D.C.: Georgetown University Press. 384–50.

CHAFE, W. L. 1970, *Meaning and Structure of Language*. Chicago, Illinois: University of Chicago Press.

CHAMOT, A. 1972, *English as a Third Language: Its Acquisition by a Child Bilingual in French and Spanish*. Ph.D. Dissertation, University of Texas, Austin, Texas.

CHOMSKY, C. 1969, *The Acquisition of Syntax in Children from Five to Ten*. Cambridge, Massachusetts: MIT Press.
CHOMSKY, N. 1957, *Syntactic Structures*. The Hague: Mouton & Co.
CHRISTIAN, C. 1971, Differential Response to Language Stimuli Before Age 3: A Case Study. In Preprint for the *Conference on Child Language*. Chicago. November 22–24.
CLARK, E. V. 1973, What's in a Word? In T. E. MOORE (ed.), *Cognitive Development and the Acquisition of Language*. New York: Academic Press. 65–110.
CONTRERAS, H. 1961, *The Phonological System of a Bilingual Child*. Ph.D. Dissertation, Indiana University, Bloomington, Indiana.
CORDASCO, E. (ed.) 1978, *Bilingualism and the Bilingual Child*. New York: Arno Press.
CORNEJO, R. J. 1969, Bilingualism: Study of the Lexicon of the Five-Year-Old Spanish-Speaking Children of Texas. Ph.D. Dissertation, University of Texas, Austin, Texas.
— 1973, The acquisition of lexicon in the speech of bilingual children. In P. R. TURNER (ed.), *Bilingualism in the Southwest*. Tucson, Arizona: University of Arizona Press.
CUMMINS, J. 1973, *A Theoretical Perspective on the Relationship between Bilingualism and Thought*. Ontario Institute of Education, Working Paper 1, ERIC, Washington, D.C. November.
CURTISS, S. 1977, *Genie: A Psycholinguistic Study of a Modern-Day "Wild Child"*. New York: Academic Press, Inc.
DALE, P. S. 1972, *Language Development: Structure and Function*. Hinsdale, Illinois: The Dryden Press, Inc.
DATO, D. P. (ed.) 1975, *Developmental Psycholinguistics: Theory and Application*. Georgetown University Round Table on Language and Linguistics, Georgetown University, Washington, D.C.
DEESE, J. 1970, *Psycholinguistics*. Boston, Massachusetts: Allyn & Bacon, Inc.
DI PIETRO, R. J., FRAWLEY, W. & WEDEL, A. (eds) 1983, *The First Delaware Symposium on Language Studies*. Newark, Delaware: University of Delaware Press.
DOMAN, C. 1964, *How to Teach Your Baby to Read: The Gentle Revolution*. New York: Random House.
DUNN, L. M. 1959, Peabody Picture Vocabulary Test. Circle Pines, Minnesota: American Guidance Service, Inc.
ERVIN-TRIPP, S. 1964, Imitation and Structural Change in Children's Language. In E. H. LENNEBERG (ed.), *New Directions in the Study of Language*. Cambridge, Massachusetts: MIT Press.
— 1967, *Sociolinguistics*. Working Paper No. 3, Language Behavior Research Laboratory. November.
— 1970, An Analysis of the Interaction of Language, Topic and Listener. In J. FISHMAN (ed.), *Readings in the Sociology of Language*. The Hague: Mouton & Co. 192–211.
— 1973, *Language Acquisition and Communicative Choice*. Stanford, California: Stanford University Press.
ESCOBEDO, T. H. 1982, *ETS Oral Proficiency Testing Manual*. Princeton, New Jersey: Educational Testing Service.
— (ed.) 1983, *Early Childhood Bilingual Education: A Hispanic Perspective*. New York: Teachers College Press.

FANTINI, A. E. 1974, El nino como lingüista y etnógrafo. *Presencia*. La Paz, Bolivia. December.
— 1976a, *Language Acquisition of a Bilingual Child: A Sociolinguistic Perspective (To Age Five)*. Ph.D. Dissertation, University of Texas, Austin, Texas 1974, subsequently published by The Experiment Press, Brattleboro, Vermont, 1976.
— 1976b, Bilingual Acquisition: The Need for a Sociolinguistic Perspective. *MEXTESOL Journal*, Vol. I, Nos. 3 & 4, Fall and Winter.
— 1978, Bilingual Behavior and Social Cues: Case Studies of Two Bilingual Children. In M. PARADIS (ed.), *Aspects of Bilingualism*. Columbia, South Carolina: Hornbeam Press.
— 1982a, *La adquisición del lenguaje en un niño bilingüe*. Barcelona, Spain: Editorial Herder.
— 1982b, Emerging Styles in Child Speech. *The Bilingual Review*, Vol. V, No. 3, September–December 1978, reprinted in J. FISHMAN & G. D. KELLER (eds), *Bilingual Education for Hispanic Students in the United States*. Columbia University, New York: Teachers College Press.
— 1982c, Social Cues and Language Choice: Case Study of a Bilingual Child. In P. R. TURNER (ed.), *Bilingualism in the Southwest*. Tucson, Arizona: University of Arizona Press.
— 1983, Linguistic Transference in Child Speech: A Sociolinguistic Phenomenon. In R. J. DI PIETRO, W. FRAWLEY & A. WEDEL (eds), *The First Delaware Symposium on Language Studies*. Newark, Delaware: University of Delaware Press.
FASOLD, R. W. & SHUY, R. W. (eds) 1975, *Analyzing Variation in Language*. Washington, D.C.: Georgetown University Press.
FERGUSON, C. A. 1959, Diglossia. *Word*, Vol. 15, No. 2.
FERGUSON, C. A. & SLOBIN, D. I. (eds) 1973, *Studies of Child Language Development*. New York: Holt, Rinehart and Winston, Inc.
FISHMAN, J. 1966, The Implications of Bilingualism for Language Teaching and Language Learning. In A. VALDMAN (ed.), *Trends in Language Teaching*. New York: McGraw-Hill. 121–32.
— 1970, *Readings in the Sociology of Language*. The Hague: Mouton & Co.
— 1971, *Sociolinguistics*. Rowley, Massachusetts: Newbury House Publishers.
— 1972, *The Sociology of Language*. Rowley, Massachusetts: Newbury House Publishers.
FISHMAN, J. A. & KELLER, G. D. (eds) 1982, *Bilingual Education for Hispanic Students in the United States*. Columbia University, New York: The Teachers College Press.
FLORES D'ARCAIS, G. B. & LEVELT, W. I. M. 1970, *Advances in Psycholinguistics*. New York: American Elsevier Publishing Co., Inc.
GATTEGNO, C. 1973, *The Universe of Babies*. New York: Educational Solutions.
GILES, H. & POWESLAND, P. F. (eds) 1975, *Speech Style and Social Evaluation*. London: Academic Press.
GILI GAYA, S. 1972, *Estudios de lenguaje infantil*. Barcelona, Spain: Editorial VOX.
GIGLIOLI, P. P. (ed.) 1972, *Language and Social Context*. Middlesex, England: Penguin Books.
GOFFMAN, I. 1963, *Behavior in Public Places*. Glencoe, Illinois: Free Press.
— 1969, *Strategic Interaction*. Philadelphia, Pennsylvania: University of Pennsylvania Press.
— 1971, *Relations in Public*. New York: Basic Books, Inc.

GONZALEZ, G. 1968, *A Linguistic Profile of the Spanish-Speaking First Graders in Corpus Christi*. M.A. Thesis, University of Texas, Austin, Texas.
— 1970, *The Acquisition of Spanish Grammar by Native Spanish-Speakers*. Ph.D. Dissertation, University of Texas, Austin, Texas.
GOODMAN, M. E. 1970, *The Acquisition of Childhood: Child's-eye view of Society and Culture*. Columbia University, New York: Teachers College Press.
GUMPERZ, J. J. 1970, Types of Linguistic Communities. In J. FISHMAN (ed.), *Readings in the Sociology of Language*. The Hague: Mouton & Co.
— 1971, *Language in Social Groups*. Stanford, California: Stanford University Press.
GUMPERZ, J. J. & HERNANDEZ, E. 1969, *Cognitive Aspects of Bilingual Communication*. Working paper No. 28, Language Behavior Research Laboratory, University of California, Berkeley, California.
GUMPERZ, J, J. & HYMES, D. 1972, *Directions in Sociolinguistics*. New York: Holt, Rinehart and Winston, Inc.
HALL, E. T. 1976, *Beyond Culture*. New York: Anchor Press.
HASSELMO, N. 1969, How Can We Measure the Effects Which One Language May Have on the Other in the Speech of Bilinguals. In L. G. KELLY (ed.), *Description and Measurement of Bilingualism*. University of Toronto Press. 122–41.
HAUGEN, E. 1956, *Bilingualism in the Americas*. American Dialect Society. Alabama: University of Alabama Press. November.
HAYES, J. R. 1970, *Cognition and the Development of Language*. New York, John Wiley & Sons.
HERNANDEZ-CHAVEZ, E. *et al.* 1975, *El lenguaje de los chicanos*. Center for Applied Linguistics. Distributed by Harcourt, Brace & Jovanovich.
HILDUM, D. C. (ed.) 1967, *Language and Thought*. New York: Van Nostrand Rinehold Company.
HILL, A. A. 1958, *Introduction to Linguistic Structures*. New York: Harcourt Brace and World, Inc.
HOPPER, R. & NAREMORE, R. C. 1973, *Children's Speech: A Practical Introduction to Communication Development*. New York: Harper & Row Publishers.
HÖRMANN, H. 1971, *Psycholinguistics: An Introduction to Research and Theory*. Translated by H. H. Stern. New York: Springer-Verlag.
HUEBNER, T. 1983, *The Acquisition of English*. Ann Arbor, Michigan: Karoma Publishers, Inc.
HUXLEY, R. & INGRAM, E. (eds) 1971, *Language Acquisition: Models and Methods*. New York: Academic Press.
HYMES, D. 1971, Competence and Performance in Linguistic Theory. In R. HUXLEY & E. INGRAM (eds), *Language Acquisition: Models and Methods*. New York: Academic Press. 2–23.
— 1974, Sociolinguistics and the Ethnography of Speaking. In B. G. BLOUNT (ed.), *Language, Culture and Society*. Cambridge, Massachusetts: Winthrop Press.
INGRAM, D. 1971, Transitivity in Child Language. *Language*, Journal of the Linguistic Society of America, Baltimore, Maryland. Vol. 47, No. 4. December. 888-910.
INTERNATIONAL CENTER FOR RESEARCH ON BILINGUALISM. 1971, *Preprints on Conference on Child Language*. Chicago, November 22–24, 1971. Quebec: Les Presses de l'Université Laval.
JAKOBOVITS, L. A. 1968, the Physiology and Psychology of Second Language Learning. In E. M. BIRKMAIER (ed.), *Britannica Review of Foreign Language Education*. Vol. I. Chicago, Illinois: Encyclopedia Britannica, Inc. 182–227.

— 1970, *Foreign Language Learning: A Psycholinguistic Analysis of the Issues*. Rowley, Massachusetts: Newbury House Publishers.

JAKOBSON, R. 1968, *Child Language: Aphasia and Phonological Universals*. The Hague: Mouton & Co.

— 1971a, *Studies on Child Language and Aphasia*. The Hague: Mouton & Co.

— 1971b, Why 'Mama' and 'Papa'? In A. BAR-ADON & W. F. LEOPOLD (eds), *Child Language: A Book of Readings*. Englewood Cliffs, New Jersey: Prentice-Hall. 212–17.

JONES, R. M. 1969, How and When Do Persons Become Bilingual? In L. G. KELLY (ed.), *Description and Measurement of Bilingualism*. Toronto, Canada: University of Toronto Press. 12–25.

JOOS, M. 1961, *The Five Clocks*. New York: Harcourt, Brace and World, Inc.

KELLER, G. D. 1976, Acquisition of the English and Spanish passive voices among bilingual children. In G. D. KELLER, R. V. TESCHNER & S. VIERA (eds), *Bilingualism in the Bicentennial and Beyond*. New York: Bilingual Press/Editorial Bilingüe, 161–68.

KELLER, G. D., TESCHNER, R. V. & VIERA, S. (eds), 1976, *Bilingualism in the Bicentennial and Beyond*. New York: Bilingual Press.

KELLY, L. G. (ed.) 1969, *Description and Measurement of Bilingualism*. Toronto, Canada: University of Toronto Press.

KENISTON, H. 1938, *Spanish Idiom List*. New York.

KERNAN, K. & BLOUNT, B. G. 1966, The Acquisition of English Grammar by Mexican Children. *Anthropological Linguistics*. Vol. 8, No. 9. University of California, Berkeley, California. December.

KESSLER, C. 1971, *The Acquisition of Syntax in Bilingual Children*. Washington, D.C.: Georgetown University Press.

KHUBCHANDANI, L. M. 1976, Language acquisition in pluralistic societies. In W. VON RAFFLER-ENGEL (ed.). *Child Language — 1975*. (Special issue of *Word*, Vol. 27, Nos. 1–3).

KUO, E. C.-Y. 1972, *Bilingual Socialization of Preschool Chinese Children in the Twin Cities Area*. Ph.D. Dissertation, University of Minnesota, Minneapolis-St. Paul, Minnesota.

— 1974, The family and bilingual socialization: A sociolinguistic study of a sample of Chinese children in the United States. *The Journal of Social Psychology*, 92, 181–91.

LABOV, W. A. 1966, *The Social Stratification of English in New York City*. Washington, D.C.: Center for Applied Linguistics.

— 1969, *The Study of Nonstandard English*. Washington, D.C.: Center for Applied Linguistics.

— 1972, *Language in the Inner City: Studies in the Black English Vernacular*. Philadelphia, Pennsylvania: University of Pennsylvania Press.

LAMBERT, W. E. & KLINEBERG, O. 1967, *Children's Views of Foreign Peoples*. New York: Appleton-Century-Crofts.

LANE, H. 1976, *The Wild Boy of Aveyron*. Cambridge: Massachusetts: Harvard University Press.

LANGE, S. & LARSSON, K. 1973, *Syntactical Development of a Swedish Girl Embla, Between 20 and 42 Months of Age*. (Part I, Age 2–25 Mos.), Report No. 1, Stockholms Universitet: Institutionen för Nordiska Språk.

LENNEBERG, E. H. 1964, *New Directions in the Study of Language*. Cambridge, Massachusetts: MIT Press.

— 1967, *Biological Foundations of Language*. New York: John Wiley & Sons, Inc.

LEOPOLD, W. F. 1939–1949, *Speech Development of a Bilingual Child*, 4 Vols. Northwestern University Studies, Humanities Series, Nos. 6, 11, 18 and 19. Evanston, Illinois: Northwestern University Press. Reprinted 1970. New York: AMS Press, Inc.

— 1971, The Study of Child Language and Infant Bilingualism. In A. BAR-ADON & W. F. LEOPOLD (eds), *Child Language: A Book of Readings*. Englewood Cliffs, New Jersey: Prentice-Hall.

LIDZ, T. 1968, *The Person, His Development Throughout the Life Cycle*. New York: Basic Books Publishers.

LYONS, J. & WALES, R. J. (eds) 1966, *Psycholinguistics Papers: Proceedings of the Edinburgh Conference*. England: Edinburgh University Press.

MACKEY, W. F. 1965a, *Bilingualism as a World Problem*. Montreal, Quebec Province, Canada: Harvest House.

— 1965b, *Language Teaching Analysis*. Bloomington, Indiana: Indiana University Press.

— 1970, The Description of Bilingualism. In J. FISHMAN (ed.), *Readings in the Sociology of Language*. The Hague: Mouton & Co.

MACKEY, W. F. & ANDERSSON, T. (eds) 1977, *Bilingualism in Early Childhood*. Rowley, Massachusetts: Newbury House Publishers.

MACNAMARA, J. (ed.) 1967, *The Journal of Social Issues*. Vol. XXIII, No 2. Problems on Bilingualism, The Society for the Psychological Study of Social Issues, Worcester, Massachusetts, April.

— 1973, Nurseries, Streets and Classrooms: Some Comparisons and Deductions. *The Modern Language Journal*, Vol. LVII, Nos. 5–6, September–October. 250–54.

MAZEIKA, E. J. 1971, *A Descriptive Analysis of the Language of a Bilingual Child*. Ph.D. Dissertation, University of Rochester, Rochester, New York.

— 1973, A comparison of the grammar of a monolingual and a bilingual (Spanish-English) child. Paper presented at the Biennial Meeting of the Society for Research in Child Development, Philadelphia, Pa.

MCCARTHY, D. 1954, Language Development in Children. In L. CARMICHAEL (ed.), *Manual of Child Psychology*. New York: John Wiley & Sons. (Second Edition). 492–630.

MCNEILL, D. 1970, *The Acquisition of Language: The Study of Developmental Psycholinguistics*. New York: Harper and Row.

MENYUK, P. 1969, *Sentences Children Use*. Cambridge, Massachusetts: MIT Press.

— 1977, *Language and Maturation*. Cambridge, Massachusetts: MIT Press.

MESA-VIDAL, L. *et al.* 1973, *Lenguaje y expresión de los niños*. Lima, Peru: Ediciones Retablo de Papel.

MILLER, G. A. 1951, *Language and Communication*. New York: McGraw-Hill Book Co., Inc.

THE MODERN LANGUAGE JOURNAL 1965, Reprints on the Symposium on Bilingualism and the Bilingual Child. Vol. XLIX, Nos. 3 & 4. March and April.

MOORE, T. E. (ed.) 1973, *Cognitive Development and the Acquisition of Language*. New York: Academic Press.

MOSCOWITZ, A. I. 1970, The Two Year-Old-Stage in the Acquisition of Phonology. *Language*, Vol. 46, No. 42 (Part I). 426–41.

MOSKOVICI, S. 1972, *The Psychosociology of Language*. Chicago, Illinois: Markham Publishing Co.

Moss, M. H. 1970, Tests of Basic Experiences (Language). California.
OLDFIELD, R. C. & MARSHALL, J. C. (eds) 1968, *Language*. Middlesex, England: Penguin Books.
OLLER, JR, J. W. 1971, *Coding Information in Natural Languages*. The Hague: Mouton & Co.
OLMSTEAD, D. L. 1971, *Out of the Mouth of Babes*. The Hague: Mouton & Co.
ORNSTEIN, J., VALDES-FALLIS, G. & DUBOIS, B. L. 1976, Bilingual child language acquisition along the U.S.-Mexican border. The El Paso-Ciudad Juárez-Las Cruces Triangle. In W. VON RAFFLER-ENGEL (ed.) *Child Language — 1975*. (Special issue of *Word*, Vol. 27, Nos. 1–3).
OSGOOD, C. E. & SEBEOK, T. A. 1969. *Psycholinguistics: A Survey of Theory and Research Problems*. Bloomington, Indiana: Indiana University Press.
OSTWALD, P. F. & PELTZMAN, P. 1974, The Cry of the Human Infant. *Scientific American*. March. 84–90.
PADILLA, A. M. 1978, The Acquisition of Fourteen English Grammatical Morphemes in the Speech of Bilingual Children. *The Bilingual Review*, Vol. I, No. 3. New York: Bilingual Press. September–December.
PADILLA, A. M. & LINDHOLM, K. J. 1976a, Development of Interrogative, Negative and Possessive Forms in the Speech of Young Spanish/English Bilinguals. *The Bilingual Review*, Vol. III, No. 2, May–August.
— 1976b, Acquisition of Bilingualism. In G. D. KELLER *et al.* (eds), *Bilingualism in the Bicentennial and Beyond*. New York: Bilingual Press.
PADILLA, R. 1977, Language Intercalation. Paper read at the National Association of Bilingual Education. New Orleans, Louisiana.
PARADIS, M. (ed.) 1978a, *The Fourth LACUS Forum*. South Carolina: Hornbeam Press.
— (ed.) 1978b, *Aspects of Bilingualism*. South Carolina: Hornbeam Press.
PAVLOVITCH, M. 1920, *Le langage enfantin*. Paris.
PENFIELD, W. & ROBERTS, L. 1959, *Speech and Brain-Mechanisms*. Princeton, New Jersey: Princeton University Press.
PENN, J. M. 1972, *Linguistic Relativity versus Innate Ideas*. The Hague: Mouton.
PIAGET, J. 1954, *The Construction of Reality in the Child*. New York: Basic Books.
— 1963, *The Origins of Intelligence in Children*. New York: Norton Press.
— 1971, *The Language and Thought of the Child*. Cleveland, Ohio: World Publishing Co.
POPOVA, M. J., ZAKHAROVA, A. V. & BOGOYAVLENSKIY, B. N. 1973, Articles reprinted in C. A. FERGUSON & D. I. SLOBIN (eds), *Studies of Child Language Development*. New York: Holt, Rinehart and Winston. 269–94.
REDLINGER, W. E. 1976, A Description of Transference and Code-Switching in Mexican-American English and Spanish. In G. D. KELLER *et al.* (eds), *Bilingualism in the Bicentennial and Beyond*. New York: Bilingual Press.
— 1979, Early Developmental Bilingualism: A Review of the Literature. *The Bilingual Review*, Vol. VI, No. 1. January–April. East Michigan University.
RICHELLE, M. 1975, *La adquisición del lenguaje*. Barcelona: Editorial Herder.
RICHTER, F. 1927, *Die Entwicklung der psychologischen Kindersprachforschung*. Munich: Munsterverlag.
RONJAT, J. 1913, *Le développement du langage observé chez un enfant bilingue*. Paris.
ROUCHDY, A. 1970, *A Case of Bilingualism: An Investigation in the Area of Lexical and Syntactical Interference*. Ph.D. Dissertation. University of Texas, Austin, Texas.

RUBIN, J. 1970, Bilingual Usage in Paraguay. In J. FISHMAN (ed.), *Readings in the Sociology of Language*. The Hague: Mouton & Co.

SAPORTA, S. (ed.) 1961, *Psycholinguistics: A Book of Readings*. New York: Holt, Rinehart and Winston.

SAUNDERS, G. 1983, *Bilingual Children: Guidance for the Family*. Clevedon, Avon, England: Multilingual Matters Ltd.

SCHMIDT-MACKEY, I. 1979, Language strategies of the bilingual family. In W. MACKEY & T. ANDERSSON (eds), *Bilingualism in Early Childhood*. Rowley, Mass: Newbury House, 132–46.

SELINKER, L. 1972, Interlanguage. *IRAL*, Vol. 10. 209–31.

SHERZER, J. & DARNELL, R. 1972, Outline Guide for the Ethnographic Study of Speech Use. In J. J. GUMPERZ & D. HYMES (eds), *Directions in Sociolinguistics*. New York: Holt, Rinehart and Winston. 548–54.

SHUY, R. W. (ed.) 1972, *Sociolinguistics*. Monograph Series on Language and Linguistics, 23rd Annual Round Table, No. 25. Washington, D.C.: Georgetown University Press.

SINCLAIR-DE-ZWART, A. 1969, *Developmental Psycholinguistics: Studies in Cognitive Development*. New York: Oxford University Press.

SINGH, J. A. L. & ZINGG, R. M. 1966, *Wolf-Children and Feral Man*. Denver, Colorado: Archon Books.

SKOCZYLAS, R. V. 1971, Bilingual Tests and Measures: English and Spanish. Gilroy, California.

SLOBIN, D. I. 1966, The Acquisition of Russian as a Native Language. In F. SMITH & G. A. MILLER (eds), *The Genesis of Language*. Cambridge, Massachusetts: MIT Press. 129–52.

— (ed.) 1967, *A Field Manual for the Cross-Cultural Study of the Acquisition of Communicative Competence*. Berkeley, California: University of California Press.

— 1971a, *Psycholinguistics*. Glenview, Illinois: Scott, Foresman and Co.

— (ed.) 1971b, *The Ontogenesis of Grammar*. New York: Academic Press.

— (ed.) 1972, *Leopold's Bibliography on Child Language*. Bloomington, Indiana: Indiana University Press.

— 1973, Cognitive Prerequisites for the Development of Grammar. In C. A. FERGUSON & D. I. SLOBIN (eds), *Studies of Child Language Development*. New York: Holt, Rinehart and Winston. 175–208.

SMITH, F. & MILLER, G. A. (eds) 1966, *The Genesis of Language*. Cambridge, Massachusetts: MIT Press.

SMITH, N. V. 1973, *The Acquisition of Phonology: A Case Study*. Cambridge, Massachusetts: MIT Press.

SNOW, C. E. & FERGUSON, C. A. (eds) 1977, *Talking to Children: Language Input and Acquisition*. Cambridge, Massachusetts: Cambridge University Press.

SODERBERGH, R. 1973, *Project Child Language Syntax and Project Early Reading*. Report No. 2. Stockholms Universitet: Institutionen för Nordiska Språk.

— 1971, *Reading in Early Childhood*. Stockholm, Sweden: Almqvist & Wiksell.

STERN, C. & STERN, W. 1907, *Die Kindersprache*. Leipzig.

STEWART, A. A. 1974, *The Relative Oral Spanish Proficiency (Lexical) of Second Generation Mexican American Kindergarden Children in Tucson, Arizona*. Ph.D. Dissertation, University of Arizona, Tucson, Arizona.

STOCKWELL, R. P. & BOWEN, J. D. 1965, *The Sounds of English and Spanish*. Chicago, Illinois: University of Chicago Press.

STOCKWELL, R. P., BOWEN, J. D. & MARTIN, J. V. 1965, *The Grammatical Structures of English and Spanish*. Chicago, Illinois: University of Chicago Press.

SUDNOW, D. (ed.) 1972, *Studies in Social Interaction*. New York: The Free Press.

SWAIN, M. K. 1971, Bilingualism, Monolingualism and Code Acquisition. Paper delivered at the Conference on Child Language, Chicago, Illinois.

— 1972, *Bilingualism as a First Language*. Ph.D. Dissertation, University of California, Irvine, California.

SZASZ, S. 1978, *The Unspoken Language of Children*. New York: W. W. Norton & Co.

TAYLOR, M. 1974, *Speculations on Bilingualism and the Cognitive Network*. Working papers in Bilingualism, No. 2. Ontario Institute for Studies in Education, Toronto, ERIC, Washington, D.C.

THONIS, E. 1977, *The Dual Language Process in Young Children*. National Dissemination and Assessment Center, California State University, Los Angeles, California.

THORNDIKE, E. L. 1921, *The Teacher's Word Book*. New York.

TITS, D. 1948, *Le mécanisme de l'acquisition d'un langue se substituant à la langue maternelle chez une enfant espagnole âgée de six ans*. Brussels, Belgium: Imprimerie Veldman.

TREMAINE, R. V. 1975, *Syntax and Piagetian Operational Thought: A Developmental Study of Bilingual Children*. Washington, D.C.: Georgetown University Press.

TURNER, P. R. (ed.) 1982, *Bilingualism in the Southwest*. Tucson, Arizona: The University of Arizona.

VALDES-FALLIS, G. 1976, Social Interaction and Code Switching Patterns. In G. D. KELLER *et al.* (eds), *Bilingualism in the Bicentennial and Beyond*. New York: Bilingual Press.

VALDMAN, A. 1966, *Trends in Language Teaching*. New York: McGraw-Hill.

VAN DER GEEST, T. 1974, *Evaluation of Theories on Child Language*. The Hague: Mouton.

VAN DER GEEST, T. *et al.* 1973, *The Child's Communicative Competence*. The Hague: Mouton.

VILDOMEC, V. 1963, *Multilingualism*. The Hague: A. W. Sythoff-Leyden.

VON RAFFLER-ENGEL, W. (ed.) 1971, *Word*. Journal of the International Linguistic Association, Vol. 27, Nos. 1, 2, 3, April–August–December.

VYGOTSKY, L. 1962, *Thought and Language*. Rowley, Massachusetts: Newbury House Publishers.

WEEKS, T. E. 1979, *Born to Talk*. Rowley, Massachusetts: Newbury House Publishers.

WEINREICH, U. 1968, *Languages in Contact*. The Hague: Mouton & Co.

WEIR, R. H. 1962, *Language in the Crib*. The Hague: Mouton & Co.

WEPMAN, J. 1968, *Auditory Discrimination Test*. Preliminary Edition. Chicago, Illinois.

WOOD, B. S. 1976, *Children and Communication: Verbal and Nonverbal Language Development*. Englewood Cliffs, New Jersey: Prentice-Hall.

Index